FRAUD

Cultural Memory
 in
 the
 Present

Mieke Bal and Hent de Vries, Editors

FRAUD

The World of Ona'ah

Henri Atlan

Translated by Nils F. Schott

STANFORD UNIVERSITY PRESS
STANFORD, CALIFORNIA

Stanford University Press
Stanford, California

English translation © 2013 by the Board of Trustees of the Leland Stanford Junior University. All rights reserved.

Fraud: The World of Ona'ah was originally published in French under the title *De la fraude: Le monde de l'*ona'a © Éditions du Seuil, 2010. Collection *La Librairie du XXIe siècle*, sous la direction de Maurice Olender.

Cet ouvrage a bénéficié du soutien des Programmes d'aide à la publication de l'Institut français/ministère français des affaires étrangères et européennes. This work, published as part of a program of aid for publication, received support from the Institut Français and the French Ministry of Foreign Affairs.

No part of this book may be reproduced or transmitted in any form or by any means, electronic or mechanical, including photocopying and recording, or in any information storage or retrieval system without the prior written permission of Stanford University Press.

Printed in the United States of America on acid-free, archival-quality paper

Library of Congress Cataloging-in-Publication Data

Atlan, Henri, author.
  [De la fraude. English]
  Fraud : the world of ona'ah / Henri Atlan ; translated by Nils F. Schott.
      pages cm. -- (Cultural memory in the present)
  "Originally published in French under the title De la fraude: Le monde de l'onaa, Éditions du Seuil, 2010."
  Includes bibliographical references and index.
  ISBN 978-0-8047-7709-4 (cloth : alk. paper) --
  ISBN 978-0-8047-7710-0 (pbk. : alk. paper)
  1. Jewish ethics. 2. Fraud (Jewish law) 3. Interpersonal relations--Religious aspects--Judaism. I. Title. II. Series: Cultural memory in the present.
  BJ1285.2.A8513 2013
  296.3'673--dc23   2013011215

Typeset by Bruce Lundquist in 11/13.5 Adobe Garamond

To Béla Kohn-Atlan and the blessings of her words

"All things are requital for fire, and fire for all things, as goods for gold and gold for goods."
—HERACLITUS

"Just as there is fraud in buying and selling so there is fraud in spoken words."
—*Babylonian Talmud*, BABA MEZI'A, 58B.

Table of Contents

Acknowledgments — xv

Introduction
The Truth of Exchanges: The World of *Ona'ah* — 1

1. The Circle of Value — 6
   A false paradox — 10
   The circle of value — 10
   The true good and the supreme good — 11
   The philosopher's truth — 14
   The powers of speech — 22

2. Suffering and Doing Evil — 25
   On evil and its banality — 25
   Fraudulent words: Verbal fraud and injury — 33

3. Language and Money — 43
   The words to express it — 43
   Cancellation of debts, loans without interest — 45
   Dematerialized circulation — 53
   Without limits? — 57
   The sacred — 59
   The "Thucydidean moment" of verbal fraud — 62
   Under different skies — 65
   A guilty conscience and shame — 66

4. Technical Objects — 69
   Objects of exchange, objects of desire — 69
   Open machines: The information age — 71
   The autonomy and the repose of technical objects — 80
   Use value and intrinsic value — 82

Contents

5. The Strange Story of an Oven ... 85
   The snake oven ... 85
   Verbal injuries: Words, of life and of death ... 93
6. More or Less than One-Sixth ... 98
   A threshold ... 98
   Why a threshold? And why one-sixth?
   One-eighteenth of being ... 106
   Circumcision, of the heart and of the flesh ... 109
   Measures and values ... 114
7. The Crystallized Sacred ... 121
   The nature, function, and genealogy of experiences of the sacred ... 121
   Between two extremes ... 126
   Athens and Jerusalem
   The world of oracles and prophecy
   Plutarch and the Pythia ... 136
   Prosaic truths and monetary metaphors of desacralized language
   Rabbi Eliezer ... 144
   Eliezer, Christianizing?
   Magic and cucurbit plants
   Holy or sacred?
8. Dissolution ... 157
   Propaganda: Half-truths and total falsehood ... 159
   International public opinion:
      Systemic falsehood in current affairs ... 175
   Contaminated science ... 185
   The complexity of the real and the underdetermination of scientific theory
   Big science: Scientific information and public relations
   Lobbying in biomedicine
   Political ecology and the uncertainties of scientific ecology

Conclusion ... 203

List of Abbreviations in Notes	209
Notes	211
Name Index	235
Subject Index	239

Acknowledgments

My thanks go to Jean-Michel Bloch, Laurent Bove, Julien Darmon, Jean-Pierre Dupuy, and François Rachline for our exchanges and for the orientation they provided for my bibliographical research; to Isabelle Stroweis for her help in the preparation of the manuscript; and, as always, to Maurice Olender for his encouragement and his keen assistance from the moment this work was started to its completion.

FRAUD

Introduction

The Truth of Exchanges: The World of Ona'ah

"Don't take my words at face value!" "Silence is golden." "Don't try to put anything over on me!" What is more banal than lying? Who can truthfully claim never to have lied—even if it was for a good cause, out of compassion, tactfulness, or politeness, not to mention less noble motives? We exchange objects for money. We exchange words, and we write words about those words. This, after all, is what distinguishes us from other animal species and their societies. It is also the place where a specifically human evil can show itself, an evil whose standard-bearer is fraud. The Hebrew word *ona'ah* designates a tort or damages produced by a fraud and suffered by an individual or community. Yet curiously, the Talmud tells us that there is an *ona'ah* of words as well.[1] This refers to damages and misdeeds that are the result of fraud against sincerity and the truth of words, just as there is fraud against the truth of prices—in other words, there are all sorts of fraud in the exchanges among human beings. Indeed, language already bears the traces of this complicity between commerce in the strict sense and verbal exchanges, expressing the complicity in its monetary etymologies and metaphors.

But we shall see that *ona'ah* is a fraud at the very edge of what is lawful, differing in this respect from counterfeit money; by the same token, *ona'ah*, as a verbal injury, is different from lying in general, even if some lies can cause *ona'ah*. What we have here is an intermediate area between absolute truth (of the marketplace or of speech) and total disintegration into systemic fraud and lying. In fact, talmudic legislation institutes the idea of a threshold below which the harm or damage suffered is "forgiven." Above that threshold, the injury is unacceptable; it is then identified as theft and the transaction is canceled, even though it may leave behind something irreversible in the form of the injury undergone by the person who was initially injured, an injury to the person's very being.

Talmudic *ona'ah*, then, generally designates harm, injury, damages caused by any kind of fraud or deception. It may affect what one has but also what one is. It may concern a commercial action but it may also, like the Latin *injuria*, be purely verbal: an *ona'ah* of words, or in words, or by means of words (or speech)—which are all interchangeable ways of translating the talmudic expression *ona'at dvarim*, which establishes this kind of *ona'ah*. It may be a matter of leading someone—voluntarily or involuntarily—into error, but also of causing a moral wrong by means of humiliating words, even if these express a certain reality. In the most general way, it has to do with a particular kind of harm that human beings, as members of society, can do to one another in the very area that is, above all others, supposed to ensure social cohesion: namely, in *exchanges* of objects and words.

The world of *ona'ah*—in which we confront a kind of intrusion that is fraudulent, hurtful, and sometimes "forgiven," simply because it is necessary—is situated in a space in which absolute purity leads to catastrophe, and impurity that goes beyond certain hard-to-specify limits is equally catastrophic. This holds true for everything involving exchanges between human beings: words, which raise the question of absolute truth and of lies that must be tolerated; money and necessary, allowable divergences from fair prices; technical devices and the allowable distance of the artificial from the (human) natural that produces them. Some talmudic laws covering financial fraud and verbal injuries, and some legends that have sprung up around these laws, dramatically highlight what is being played out in this space: forgiveness.

The injunction to "love your neighbor as yourself" and its negative formulation—not to do to others what we would not like to have done to us—are often considered to be the golden rule of a universal ethics that goes far beyond the cultures that are heirs to the Bible and Confucius. But this unanimous assent is deceptive. Here we already have "deceptive labeling." What is at stake here is not a feeling, like loving one's neighbor (and who is this neighbor or these others, anyway, that we are called upon to love?). Nor is it a kind of negative balance in our self-restraint when faced with what we believe to be a common perception of evil, as if what everyone else does not want to have done to them were identical with what I do not want to have done to me. Thus, for example, I would certainly not want to be recruited to become a "martyr," the agent of a suicide bombing, whereas it appears that for many people that is their greatest wish. For such people, the application of the rule would surely not imply an obligation to dissuade or keep someone else from committing a suicide bombing.

Here, behind the passion of this unconditional universal love and the subjective equilibrium of terror, we find the following question about the nature of the social bond: what makes up the positive and negative exchanges and interactions that ensure the existence of human societies? The study of animal societies allows us to observe that many of the characteristics and behaviors considered to be specifically human (including the altruistic components of these and therefore also their moral components) are already present as conditions for the adaptive survival of these animal societies within their particular environments—at least that is what we understand through the filter of our Darwinian interpretational framework.[2] These observations lead us to accept a biological basis, rooted in the animal nature of Homo sapiens, for the development of moral law, or a demand for ethics, or a set of values—whose existence is in fact universal even if its contents are not—as a condition for the adaptive survival of the human species across all the societies that make up the species. But this interpretation, which is difficult to reject in any research concerning the "genealogy of ethics,"[3] reaches its limits at the point at which Homo sapiens appears, with specific characteristics that are not developed to this extent in any other species, particularly because of Homo sapiens's brain, with its capacity for memory, imagination, and abstraction, expressed in its reflective and artistic languages. This in no way disrupts the substantial unity of nature, which includes the unity of the animal world, in which Homo sapiens, like every other species, has a place. But like any other species, humanity had to evolve by developing its own particular properties, properties that are thus literally "specific" to it but which, while being as natural as its other properties, of course, also differentiate humanity, however incrementally, from other species. These properties differentiate human societies from animal societies in that they have rendered the nature of the social bond more complex: the complexity of the exchanges between human beings corresponds to the complexity of the human brain.

New problems arise from this escalating complexity, problems that cannot be solved by simply applying neo-Darwinian adaptive schemas to discover and understand the nature of the social bond.

We must therefore strive to focus our analyses on that which is specifically human in exchanges between individuals, that is, the fact that these exchanges are not observed on such a large scale in animal societies. There is an evolutionary continuity that roots the human being in nature and which makes it impossible, following Spinoza's devastating analyses, to consider humanity as an "empire within an empire" because of such alleged supernatural properties as free will; nevertheless, this continuity must not prevent us from analyzing what it is that, due to this very continuity, constitutes humanity's particular power to exist—its "virtue" and its "perfection"—just as flying is what is particular to birds and other flying animals or as running is the "perfection" of the horse, to use Spinozist terminology.

What is particular to humans is expressed in social exchanges through a series of specific practices that we will analyze from the point of view that they all share, although they appear at first to be very different from one another, belonging as they do to a variety of areas of activity and regulated as they are by different institutions. These include linguistic exchanges, which bring up the issue of the truth of propositions and the possibility of lies and errors; economic exchanges, involving the institution of money and its successive manifestations; and the production of and exchanges of artificial, technical objects, related to the objects that allow us to share the pleasures of culinary conviviality and sexual knowledge, where the discovery of others in fact takes place—as may also be the case with animals, but in this case with all the connotations of the aforementioned exchanges which serve to differentiate the human from other animals. Running through these exchanges of money, of words, and of technical objects are individual desires, amplifying and competing with each other: desires to possess and to dominate, to create and to consume.

In this context, we will try to explore a particular field in which the issues at stake in the uses and abuses of money, language, and technical objects intertwine with each other in complex ways.

What we are talking about, then, is fraud, or deceptive advertising or labeling of goods or merchandise, in both the literal and the figurative senses. This covers a much wider field than one might at first think, if we do not limit it to commercial exchanges and if we allow the figurative sense all the importance that it deserves. A mendacious, fraudulent, mistaken, instrusive, or humiliating exchange of words on any topic can constitute such a deception, in which the topic of the exchange, whatever it is, takes the place of the "merchandise" or "goods" about which one can deceive others or be deceived oneself. Deceptive or dishonest labeling or advertising, if we understand it this way, is the subject of long debates in the treatise of the Talmud where it is designated as *ona'ah*, in which all of these meanings, as well as the damages to one's possessions or one's being that may result for the injured person, are concentrated. "Just as there is fraud in buying and selling so there is fraud in spoken words."[4]

This switching back and forth between exchanges of goods and exchanges of words provides the opportunity for subtle analyses of their commonalities but also of their differences, analyses that bring to light the world of *ona'ah*, in which a very particular phenomenology of the experience of others and of the social bond unfolds. The effects of *ona'ah* are rather similar to those of counterfeit money, which can be thought of literally or figuratively, but they differ noticeably in that counterfeit money clearly and obviously belongs to the category of theft and lying. In the hierarchy of transgressions and ruptures of the social bond, *ona'ah* is situated a little below counterfeit money. Sometimes *ona'ah* appears to be somewhat inevitable, and agreement may be reached on a threshold of tolerance. But how can *ona'ah* be accounted for, such that it can be regulated and controlled as far as possible, when it is not measurable—in fact beyond measure—and such a threshold can therefore not be quantified? We encounter the same kind of difficulty when we deal with the effects of virtual exchanges. For a long time now, theater and games of all sorts have accustomed us to these effects, which rest on illusion and on the fiction of a staged reality that is at least partly imaginary. But the digital transmission of information amplifies such effects beyond all proportion.

The French phrase *fausse monnaie* (for "counterfeit money") can also be used to talk about falsified, inauthentic, deceitful, and mendacious speech. The Latin *injuria* reminds us that injurious words can inflict injuries, and indeed the English derivative, *injury*, covers both bodily damages and damages to personal honor and dignity. As we shall see, damages to goods due to intentional or unintentional deception in commercial transactions can be included in a whole set of injuries in which commercial fraud and deceptive words are two different aspects of damage to personal integrity. Paradoxically, the most serious, even fatal, bodily injuries are excluded from this category, which is sometimes presented as comprising the worst of crimes. But this only appears to be a paradox: bodily injuries inflicted on others or by others are not specifically human. They are the actions of animals and often constitute a central element of animals' lives—unlike false advertising and violations of someone's dignity. Here we encounter the same apparent paradox as in the modern notion of crimes against humanity: the majority of murders and assassinations are not considered crimes against humanity, whereas slavery and other degrading behaviors are. This is because what is at stake there is precisely the "humanity" in the individual, which is denied by affronts to dignity and the humiliation that results from them. In fact, the two notions of crimes against humanity and affronts to dignity, both of them difficult to define clearly, are interlinked, with each referring to the other: dignity can thus be negatively defined as that which is attacked in crimes against humanity.[5] And humanity, whose opposite is the inhuman rather than the nonhuman, is that which is specifically attacked by degrading behaviors, whether or not (like the Roman *injuriae*) they are accompanied by bodily injuries.

Let us nonetheless note that humanity is also made up of solidarity, love, generosity, and disinterested knowledge, virtues that may, like their opposites, be inherited from humanity's distant animal ancestors and amplified. But it is easier to perceive humanity's misdeeds against itself and its environment. And yet we do know that exchanges are occasions for material good deeds, gifts of money and other gifts, as well as for verbal good deeds, although we will only be able to deal with those indirectly here.

1

The Circle of Value

A false paradox

If we focus on what is specifically human in the hierarchy of faults and crimes, we end up with a paradox in which it would appear that we underestimate the gravity of crimes involving behaviors that we share with other animal species, even if they are particularly odious. Looked at this way, crimes that express the animal nature of human behaviors would be less serious than crimes in which it is a specifically human behavior that is behind the injury. But in fact, this is not the case and the apparent paradox is no paradox at all. The potential legal consequences make it clear where matters stand, since a physical attack will always be considered to be more serious—and punished accordingly—than an annoyance caused by humiliating words or false advertising. However, this same paradox resurfaces among philosophers who are fixated on condemning the gravity of *telling lies* as a cardinal error that must be forbidden *under all circumstances.*

We may already see a trace of this in the condemnation, in the Psalms, of language that has been corrupted by a loss of trust:

They utter lies to each other; with flattering lips and a double heart they speak . . . the tongue that makes great boasts, those who say, "With our tongues we will prevail; our lips are our own—who is our master?"

In contrast to this, divine speech is already characterized using the metaphor of refined silver, "promises that are pure, silver refined in a furnace on the ground, purified seven times."[1]

We see an extreme version of this condemnation in the prophet Isaiah, for whom the perversions of "the mouth" and "the tongue" are furthermore part of a "seed of lies"[2] (which evokes its opposite, the seminal reason, or logos, of the ancient Stoic philosophers).

This absolute condemnation of lying, with no exceptions, seems disproportionate given the banality of lies and their usual classification as a relatively minor fault. And in fact, among the behaviors condemned by morality, lies do in fact have a special status: they constitute both a relatively trivial sin that may at times be justified and in certain situations even be recommended and at the same time, at least for certain philosophers, an extremely serious attack on the very foundation of moral life. Let us look at Baruch Spinoza and Immanuel Kant, two such philosophers.

For Spinoza, saving oneself from mortal danger thanks to "treachery" is not the deed of a "free" man who uses his reason to distinguish good from evil. Such an action is the effect of the passions instead, especially of the effort to preserve one's being, an effort common to all passions.[3]

For Kant, the principle of telling the truth is a first principle that will brook no exception whatsoever: "To be *truthful* (honest) in all declarations is therefore a sacred command of reason prescribing unconditionally, one not to be restricted by any conveniences."[4] This principle, discussed in several places across his work, is presented here in the context of an extreme case, in defense of the idea that "it would be a crime to lie to a murderer who asked us whether a friend of ours whom he is pursuing has taken refuge in our house."[5] Although the possible consequences of lying in this case are discussed in detail—the murder is not a certainty if the truth is told; the lie itself may accidentally cause harm despite the good intentions that motivate it—the core of the argument consists in the fact that the maxim cannot be universalized: "Truthfulness in statements that one cannot avoid is a human being's duty to everyone, however great the disadvantage to him or to another that may result from it," because a lie would lead me to "do wrong in the most essential part of duty *in general* by such falsification, which can therefore be called a lie (though not in a jurist's sense); that is, I bring it about, as far as I can, that statements (declarations) in general are not believed, and so too that all rights which are based on contracts come to nothing and lose their force; and this is a wrong inflicted upon humanity generally."[6] For Kant, "[i]t is noteworthy that the Bible dates the first crime, through which evil entered the world, not from *fratricide* (Cain's) but from the first lie (for even nature rises up against fratricide), and calls the author of all evil a liar from the beginning and the father of lies."[7]

Why and how, then, is truthful speech considered by these philosophers to be the greatest virtue and lying to be a fault, or even a crime, that cannot be justified by any circumstance or good intention? We have here one of the areas in which the discrepancy between the law and morality seems the greatest, because none of these philosophers pushes this "purism," as Vladimir Jankélévitch calls it, so far as to imagine the law punishing the telling of falsehoods, under all circumstances, with a penalty commensurate with the gravity they attribute to it. Moreover, there is reason to doubt that in their own practice they never violated this rule and that they never lied, under any circumstances. We will return to this.

Others, however, and not just Niccolò Machiavelli, consider lying to be a necessary element of government because, like Plato, they think that "our rulers will have to make considerable use of falsehood and deception for the benefit of those they rule."[8] These lies serve the public good in the same way that a physician serves the good of a patient by administering a remedy. But we can see how slippery is this slope when we recall the context in which Plato claims to justify this lie for the public good: a radical eugenics that aims at improving the quality of the "human herd" by organizing marriages such that "the best men must have sex with the best women as frequently as possible, while the opposite is true of the most inferior men and women." But this can only be done without the knowledge of the parties most concerned. "Then there'll have to be some sophisticated lotteries introduced, so that at each marriage the inferior people we mentioned will blame luck rather than the rulers when they aren't chosen." The rulers, therefore, will show their concern for the public good not only by watching out for the "quality of the herd," that is to say of society from the point of view of breeding, but also by preventing, as far as possible, the trouble that would break out if these goings-on were known by the governed.[9]

Is there a supreme good, public or private, that could trump the duty to tell the truth? If so, how can we determine that? And if not, on what can the absolute value of truth be based if not on the recognition of a highest good that would be immediately abolished by any lie? This is Kant's argument, put in different terms: for Kant, this supreme good is human *dignity*, the humanity of all in each of us, which would be negated in this scenario, for the simple reason that lying cannot be universalized; like counterfeit money, which destroys the economy, the universalization of lying would destroy every possibility of human commerce, both literally and figuratively. For Kant, then, this possibility of commerce is the supreme value.

In Spinoza, this supreme value is freedom, conceived of as behavior ruled by reason. The problem, for Spinoza, is that relations between human beings are naturally determined by the passions and that this freedom is nothing but an approximation of virtue, not a basic command directed at a moral will that is presumed to be preexisting, informed, and efficient. Let us recall that for Spinoza, reason by itself has no force in the economy of the emotions that govern us and that learning freedom consists, among other things, in transforming reason into affect, through the experience of the joy that comes from understanding.

The circle of value

How can we overlook the fact that the question of lying, of fraud, of deception is caught up in a circle of value, a circle, both vicious and virtuous, of the truth of values and of the value of truth? This circularity, this circulation, is part of a double relativism: a moral relativism of values and an epistemological relativism of truth. At the same time, the circularity is flattened in the well-known logical paradox of the undecidable truth or lie of the proposition "I am a liar."

What is a "value"? Something that has a price, that is worth our sacrificing something—namely, the price one is prepared to pay—for it. But certain things are "priceless" and have, for this very reason, even greater value. For the moralists, this is what distinguishes human beings from other living creatures and from things: they are endowed with priceless values, such as dignity or honor. The life of a human being is often identified with these priceless values. But here, there is a welcome distinction between ethics and the law: that which is priceless in ethics is nonetheless evaluated by the law —and assigned a price—whenever it becomes something to be traded, as in slavery, or something to be compensated for, as when damages such as dishonor, humiliation, bodily injury, or homicide arise from the violation of these values.

In all such cases, the question arises of the fair price, of the evaluation of value: according to what criterion can it be determined? It is assumed that the market will determine the fair price of commercial objects, resulting in the establishment of a certain balance between supply and demand, though we know that that is not always the case. But what about that which cannot be bought or sold, that which is priceless? Within any given society, at least, there is a certain common agreement on the truth of value itself. False values are interlopers, playing a role like that of counterfeit money in these exchanges between persons that do not involve objects. In this context, truth appears as a supreme value, endowing values with their value! But then what gives truth this status as a value? There is a circle here that is broken only by the assertion of the primacy of truth. The truth guarantees and serves as a foundation for values, but only because we have assigned truth a value in the first place, as an absolute beginning, an absolute criterion.

Yet consciousness of the true only appears along with consciousness of the false, of lies or error. This is why, as we have seen, lies—and sometimes errors, too, considered as unintentional lies—have this very particular position in moral philosophy, which seems disproportionate when lies are compared with other offenses or crimes that are usually seen as much more serious. In fact, the mistake made about truth, as it were, consists in seeing it as a given, well-identified and framed once and for all. The question of truth is of course that straightforward in the case of simple lies about factual events that leave little room for interpretation, such as events that are the objects of police investigations. This is no longer the case, however, when an affirmation or negation can be interpreted in different ways depending on the context, which leads us to find categories other than "lying," such as "mistakes" or simply different "perspectives" on a truth that may take many forms.

In the case of the circle of value, this fixation on truth in general as a foundation, as if the truth or falsehood of a value could be easily evaluated, is even more problematic.

The true good and the supreme good

Spinoza, as is his wont, resolves the problem of this circularity by dissolving it into a single experience—and a sole definition—of what the "true good" would be: not something established in advance, once and for all, as constitutive of human nature, but the object of a progressive liberation, instead, constructed from what is initially an alienated human nature.

Breaking with the tradition, dating back to Plato, of searching for a definition for the highest good, Spinoza takes as the object of his philosophical itinerary, both practical and theoretical, an investigation into whether there exists, in opposition to the false goods that human beings usually pursue, a genuine good and a way to attain it.[10] A false good can be recognized as such by its effects: riches, sexual gratification, and honors produce pleasure, but it is a transitory pleasure, the pursuit of which eventually leads to disappointment. A true good would result in unalloyed joy and could potentially be connected with the aforementioned false goods in that those false goods would no longer be the only ones that are unreservedly pursued. And this true good is the joy that comes from the act of understanding and the *experience* of the true that ensues: the search for and the discovery of truths, even limited truths, have value by virtue of the joy—the good—they produce. The value of truth, then, becomes self-evident through the experience of truth, and can at the same time serve as a foundation for other values.

This is how, for Spinoza, the logical circularity of and circulation between the value of truth and the truth of values is broken, a break he explicitly achieves by showing that the certainty of the true in a "true idea" is itself given.[11] Yet the task remains to make the value of truth and the truth of values coexist in practice, in the practice of our individual and collective existences, where they continue to be in conflict: conflicts between values and conflicts between people.[12]

Yet it is difficult to develop a theory of this coexistence. The moral philosopher Vladimir Jankélévitch tries to do it by distinguishing between two perspectives, or two moments, within sincerity in order to refute what he calls the "infernal aporia," the alternative between two impostures: the imposture of bad faith, which accepts the principle of lying because some form of hypocrisy is unavoidable, and the purist imposture of an angelism that "flies off toward the truth" without taking the necessary intermediate steps or being willing to recognize them in retrospect as the lesser evils, as necessary means within a continuous progress. The first lies more than is strictly necessary. The second does not want to see this necessary minimum that is encountered along the way as an essential means.

Yet all of this happens in a person's innermost self of intention and good faith, as an internal sincerity, a rejection of lying to oneself, in the two moments of a dialectic of all-encompassing goodwill magnificently described by Jankélévitch:

> Pious lies to spare the miserable, sacred lies to deny nonexistence, to kill what would kill, to kill evil, to kill death—these are the two dispensations which the sincere allow themselves when they want not oratorical, formal, or notional truth but effective truth. Both perspectives . . . apply to sincerity as well as to intention: beforehand, the sincere want nothing but the true, and they want it absolutely . . . : "in their soul and conscience" and in the innermost forum of their free consent, the sincere do not accept or acknowledge the principle of lying; and up to this point, the *Metaphysics of Morals* is true. But that being said, the sincere *will do what they can*, granted that in this world of misery and limitations we cannot do everything that we want to do and that, furthermore, we must speak the truth *as much as possible*. . . . And as a result, that serious and passionate goodwill which a priori never even glances at these impure means and necessary evils will a posteriori make use of these evils and these means if it really wills with all its soul. In other words, those who do not admit the principle of lying do in fact admit the fact of lying, for the good reason that creatures only do what is possible. The prior and platonic will that theoretically wants the truth, the truth-and-nothing-but-the-truth: that will, in an ataxic and painful world, becomes a will that consistently wills necessary lies, necessary for the manifestation of a more profound and more general truth.[13]

But it is clear that the concrete achievement of this dialectic necessarily goes through a casuistry of judgments on the minimum of evil necessary in each situation. Even that which has seemed obvious under all circumstances, the recourse to "pious lies to spare the miserable," as in the case of the compassionate lie that a doctor tells a patient, is largely called into question today and adapted to each new case in discussions of medical ethics on the duty to tell the truth, since truth, for some, brooks no exception. The "golden rule" held to be "universal"—to do unto others as we would have them do unto us—comes up against one of its boundaries here.

For his part, Jankélévitch establishes the elements of such a casuistry by suggesting a classification of ten kinds of good and bad faith based on combinations of three parameters, each of these indexed as positive or negative: the intention of the speech (helpful or harmful), the objective reality that corresponds to what is said, and the relation between the speaker's conviction and what is said (a kind of index of the consciousness of lying).[14] (Jean-Paul Sartre, in *Les Chemins de la liberté* [*The Roads to Freedom*], also tried his hand at a kind of phenomenology of bad faith, using literature as his starting point.)

Later, we will see how, in the development of a biblically inspired law but in a postbiblical world, without prophets and without prophecy, two conceptions of truth can oppose each other head-on, with sometimes dramatic consequences. On the one hand there is revealed Truth, fallen from the heavens onto the inspired prophet, passed on by tradition, or conveyed in transcendental philosophies by a priori ideas of Reason; and on the other hand, set against this, there are truths that are constructed locally, empirically, and case by case but which are nevertheless not arbitrary, like plants that are quite alive that grow up from the soil as long as they are well watered. This is what makes the difference between the *pretension* to *possess* Truth and the *concern* for seeking out its aspects, as in a police investigation, without any guarantee and sometimes taking shortcuts or detours, ruses inspired by cunning in order to foil other ruses, lies, and illusions. A talmudic legend recounts how the utopia of a city that is nothing but pure Truth necessarily implies death because certain lies, especially lies arising out of a sense of decency, are indispensable in order to preserve that part of truth that must be veiled so that it will not be disfigured. Hence one of the characteristics of those concerned with the truth and dedicated to seeking it out, the "students of the Sages," the Hebrew equivalents of the Greek "philosophers": they alone, in principle, can claim the right to know when it is appropriate to lie, on the condition that the only use they make of that right is a disinterested one in the service, precisely, of the search for truth.[15]

According to another legend,[16] the angels of the "family on high" protested the creation of human beings, among other reasons because humans damage the Truth by introducing lies into the world. The Creator's reaction is to throw Truth out of heaven and assign it the destiny of "sprouting from the earth," following the biblical saying, "Truth will sprout from earth."[17]

The philosopher's truth

After centuries in which philosophy was dominated by the contemplation of Ideas, through which Being revealed itself in its exclusive Truth—handed down, despite the marginalized efforts of Sophists, cynics, and other skeptics, by the theology of the unique Word of the One

God—*doubt* has progressively taken hold, doubt that is even more radical than that of the so-called philosophers of doubt—Nietzsche, Marx, and Freud—in that now the doubt is about the very attempt to have Truth speak through Philosophy or even Science. The twentieth century tried that, with its totalitarian barbarisms, its massacres in the name of ideologies calling themselves metaphysical, historical, and scientific Truth. The philosophical tyranny of Being, which Plato, from the heights of his contemplation of Ideas, had planned in his *Republic*, was manifested there in all its physical and theoretical force, accumulated through the religious and secular, idealist and materialist expressions of two thousand five hundred years of Greco-Roman philosophy. Given this, it is not surprising that there are contemporary philosophers who try to draw the appropriate conclusions from this state of affairs and to tear down this she-devil goddess "Truth" who had seemed to reign in the heaven of Essences.

Some of these, post-analytical philosophers in the United States or post-Heideggerians in Europe,[18] just dismiss Truth and the search for it as an agenda for philosophy, purely and simply. In so doing, they renew the romantic attitude of the late nineteenth-century philosophers of Life, albeit in the current context of a science of life that has turned into physicochemical and mechanical biology. Those nineteenth-century philosophers of Life were reacting against the positivist excesses of the Enlightenment and of the ideologies of uninterrupted Progress that were the underpinnings of industrialization. Now the issue is the genocides and other crimes that were perpetrated in the twentieth century in the name of Truth by scientistic ideologies, chasing the same phantasmagorias that took over where the revealed truths of earlier centuries left off.

The question of relativism comes up again here, in its various aspects: moral relativism, in which all rules of behavior and criteria of good and evil are equivalent to all others (as in Pascal's saying "truth on this side of the Pyrenees, error on the other"), but also epistemological relativism about the truth value of our knowledge, considering all beliefs—sciences, religious dogmas, superstitions, Reason and Faith—to be equivalent: no discourse, then, can lay claim to the privilege of expressing, better than any other, the truth about the things of the world such as they are "in reality."

Wishing to avoid the trap of a dogmatic relativism that would destroy itself by making its own discourse absolute, I have argued for a "relative relativism" that is as epistemological[19] as it is moral.[20] There are local norms and criteria of good and evil, proper to each culture, but with some possibility of dialogue and agreement or compromise, which are all the more necessary because we live in multicultural societies. And there exist local truths as well, which appear as such by distinguishing themselves from lies, errors, illusions, and fictions.

To put it another way, it is important to distinguish the aspiration and claim to a theoretical Truth of Everything, unique and all-encompassing, from experiences of the truthfulness of first-person testimonies, which are complementary to experiences of errors and lies. Or to put it yet another way, behind these rejections of theoretical Truth as a supreme value and ultimate objective, which philosophy and science claimed for themselves, there is an experience of the true, as well as of integrity, that produces an aspiration to a kind of "meta-truth," although the term "meta" is not exactly right and should not lead us astray. For the issue here is not an overflow from above but rather the effect of the underground work done by experiences of error, lies, and dishonesty. It is remarkable that the very same Plato for whom only the world of essences was real elsewhere suggests systematic falsehood as a means of governing, as we have seen.

This brings us back to the standpoint of the American pragmatists, from Charles Peirce and William James in the nineteenth century to contemporaries of ours such as Hilary Putnam and Richard Rorty. These latter do not agree on everything, as we shall see, but they were both raised on analytic philosophy and then disillusioned about the possibility of finding any criteria in that philosophy that would allow, on the model of the logical empirical method of the natural sciences, for the attribution of any objective truth value to philosophical statements. Rorty is probably the one who pushes the consequences of this disillusionment the farthest. In a now-classic book,[21] he says farewell to the "philosophy of representation," renouncing the idea that language has the power to produce representations of reality. In so doing, he abandons such traditional philosophical debates as appearance versus reality and realism versus antirealism, in the form in which they are taken up by analytic philosophy, which have become sterile and outdated, in his eyes, like a form of new scholasticism. He distances himself from his Anglo-American colleagues, with a few exceptions (such as Donald Davidson, Robert Brandom, and Saul Kripke) and even goes so far as to identify—at least to some extent—with "continental" hermeneutics and Derrida's "deconstruction." In this, he draws conclusions, which some find extreme, from the repeated failures of philosophical schools in their attempts to give an account of what Truth is in a general and absolute manner and thus to base any discourse whatsoever on truth. For Rorty, the conclusion to be drawn is that no discourse is entitled to any privilege from the point of view of truth, not even the discourses of the sciences, despite the predictive properties some of these possess. For Rorty, the *philosophical* question of truth simply has nothing to do with how the world really works.

In a rather testy exchange with Pascal Engel, a French philosopher who has gone in the opposite direction, Rorty responds by appropriating a formula of William James's according to which if a debate has no practical consequences, then it should not have any philosophical consequences either.[22] This is how he positions the field of the theoretical, epistemological, and ontological discussions—"philosophy seminar" discussions—that he criticizes. He considers the traditional distinctions, between discourses of truth that are said to adhere to the reality of the world and other discourses that do not have this property, to have no social use or practical consequences, and he prefers a pragmatic distinction between different kinds of discourse that are differently *justified* in different contexts. This pragmatic view of philosophy is difficult to refute because it relies on distancing itself from the very history of philosophy and rejects, not one particular position or another, but the philosophical interest in the traditional distinctions between the different positions.

Nonetheless, if it is understood that "[t]he philosophical distinction between justification and truth seems not to have practical consequences,"[23] this rejection of the privileging of certain theoretical discourses said to be truer than others does not imply that lies or illusions are therefore valued. In the same way, the fact of affirming that the proposition "torture is an evil" is neither true nor false does not imply that no value is attributed to the proposition. This means that in rejecting a relativist ethics, a value is accorded to certain moral virtues said to be "virtues of truth," such as truthfulness, accuracy, sincerity, and trust, as well as to practices that are opposed to them, such as lies, deception, and cheating. These virtues are different from Truth as a virtue. But the fact that they presuppose experiences of truthfulness, which are in fact experiences of local truths, does not—attempts such as those of Bernard Williams[24] notwithstanding—make it possible to salvage a form of reductionist scientistic realism. It is this realism, quite characteristic of an analytic philosophy that seeks the model and norm for all philosophical discourse in the discourse of the physical sciences, that leads Williams to try to found an "absolute conception of the world."[25]

Rorty, having declared his pragmatism, as we have seen, nonetheless vigorously defends himself against accusations of relativism:

> I think it's important for pragmatists to say that the fact that there aren't any absolutes of the kind Plato and Kant and orthodox theism have dreamed doesn't mean that every view is as good as every other. It doesn't mean that everything now is arbitrary, or a matter of the will to power, or something like that. That, I think, has to be said over and over again.[26]

It is obviously even less a question of skepticism, which as we know opens the door to all kinds of obscurantism; it is only a question of stepping back from ontology and metaphysics as disciplines that aim to know the essence of things, underneath their appearance, and which are said to give to scientific and philosophical discourses their foundation in truth. As Rorty jokingly says at the outset of his debate with Pascal Engel, after believing that analytic philosophy was the future, he now thinks "that it has run out of gas."[27]

But the search for essences is not limited to the circles of professional philosophers. And it may in fact have practical consequences that are not always desirable. The concern with defining what the essence of things *is* is often present, even if it is not always formulated as such, in current public debates about the ethics of science and technology. What is the essence of Life, the essence of the Human, the essence of technology, the essence of an embryo? In a form of spontaneous philosophy diffused into the public at large, answers to these questions seem to be the prerequisites for correctly analyzing the ethical problems posed by new technologies and for then justifying, or prohibiting, one practice or another. Although science and technology do not in themselves provide solutions to the ethical problems they pose, we have been able to observe the extent to which they have been able to undo traditional essentialist definitions that had seemed well established and had become common sense; under these conditions, the debate about ethics can only benefit from abandoning such definitions and replacing them with evolutionary or gradualist definitions.[28]

Contrary to what is still far too often asserted, genes are not the essence of Life, and consciousness is not the essence of Humankind; that which is not alive can become alive, that which is not human can become human (and possibly inhuman), the tree is not contained in the acorn, the future human being is not contained in an initial cell that could, under certain conditions, become an embryo, and so on.

Pragmatism, in this context, results in a casuistic approach to problems, an approach which has, by the way, become of necessity widely established as the norm in the discussions and recommendations of ethics panels, to greater and lesser degrees of explicitness and according to the cultural and legal traditions of different societies.

But the message remains difficult to hear because it requires us to become aware of the tricks played on the thinking of each and every one of us by the different uses of the word *being* or *to be*, the noun and the verb, and the traps for philosophy that have followed from that. Since Parmenides and Plato,[29] philosophy has often fallen into such traps, often even jumped into them with a certain joy, thus entering the infinite regress of the problem of *truly* knowing what reality is *really* about. The fact that the verb *to be* is not used in the present tense in the Hebrew language, often considered a philosophical weakness for that language, can thus also yield some advantages.

Be that as it may, we can see that society has a stake in these debates about the vocation of philosophy. What these debates show, far from a skepticism or a relativism in which everything is equivalent, is instead a concern with lucidity and integrity in our relation to words and sentences.

A flamboyant version of this search for integrity can be observed in Nietzsche, who is often considered the forerunner of the modern and postmodern philosophers who are disappointed by the pretensions of Truth, which have so often served as alibis for violence, oppression, and the machinery of death. With Nietzsche, we come full circle.

Like Spinoza before him, who recognized that reason is only compelling to us when accompanied by the strength of emotion, Nietzsche found that truth emerges "only very late . . . as the weakest form of knowledge,"[30] because "the *strength* of knowledge does not lie in its degree of truth, but in its age, its embeddedness, its character as a condition of life."[31] And yet the "will to truth," to "truth at any price," has established itself even though life is made for "semblance, i.e. error, deception, simulation, blinding, self-blinding. . . . 'Will to truth'—that could be a hidden will to death."[32] It appeared with the Eleatics and culminated in the conviction that science is necessary. But where does this conviction come from? "This unconditional will to truth—what is it?" if not that which means "I will not deceive, not even myself.... Thus the question 'Why science?' leads back to the moral problem."[33]

Thus, in his own way, Nietzsche rejects the idea of some neutral version of science, one that separates facts from values, what is from what we want it to be. He also affirms that "we immediately construct" everything we see for the first time "with the help of all the old experiences we have had *depending on the degree* of our honesty and justice. There are no experiences other than moral ones, not even in the realm of sense perception."[34] What we find here, of course, is our circle of value. But as one might suspect, the future author of the *Genealogy of Morality* does not stop here, as we can see with a look at the end of paragraph 344 of *The Gay Science*, on the belief in science, which comes right before the paragraph on "Morality as a problem":

Thus the question "Why science?" leads back to the moral problem: *Why morality at all*, if life, nature, and history are "immoral"? No doubt, those who are truthful in that audacious and ultimate sense which faith in science presupposes *thereby affirm another world* than that of life, nature and history; and insofar as they affirm that "other world," must they not by the same token deny its counterpart, this world, *our* world? ... But you will have gathered what I am getting at, namely, that it is still a *metaphysical faith* upon which our faith in science rests— that even we knowers of today, we godless anti-metaphysicians, still take *our* fire, too, from the flame lit by the thousand-year-old faith, the Christian faith that was also Plato's faith, that God is truth; that truth is divine.... But what if this were to become more and more difficult to believe, if nothing more were to turn out to be divine except error, blindness, the lie—if God himself were to turn out to be our longest lie?[35]

Yet Nietzsche is neither a nihilist nor a skeptic. He wants to "believe in life," all the more so as the end of his illness causes him to perceive the problematic character of life. One need only read the first paragraph of *The Gay Science*, with its allusion to "laughter allied with wisdom"; and not just any laughter, since "[t]o laugh at oneself as one would have to laugh in order to laugh *from the whole truth*—for that, not even the best have had enough sense of truth, and the most gifted have had far too little genius!"[36] And in the preface to the second edition, he seeks to enlighten the reader by evoking his own experience of the *intoxication* of recovery, which opens the doors for him to an artist's knowledge, a savoir vivre, "superficial for its depth," just as he characterizes Greek art, in a seemingly paradoxical fashion, by celebrating the virtues of *modesty* or *decency*[37] and of the veil that covers the truth:

> We no longer believe that *truth remains truth when one pulls off the veil; we have lived too much to believe this*. Today we consider it a matter of decency not to wish to see everything naked, to be present everywhere, to understand and "know" everything. "Is it true that God is everywhere?" a little girl asked her mother; "I find that indecent!"—a hint for philosophers! One should have more respect for the *decency* with which nature has hidden behind riddles and iridescent uncertainties. Perhaps truth is a woman who has grounds for not showing grounds? Perhaps her name is—to speak Greek—*Baubo*?[38]

This does not contradict Nietzsche's previously cited affirmations. We always come back to the necessity of distinguishing between the absolute Truth of the ideologue and of certain scholars and philosophers, on the one hand, and the pragmatic truth of everyday language on the other.

This is what Hilary Putnam, more soberly, reminds us of in describing the evolution of his own philosophical attitude, an evolution that caused him to abandon the physicalist reductionism of his first writings of the 1950s and the scientistic metaphysics that went along with it. After he, too, experiences the failures of analytic philosophy in his attempts to base an absolute conception of the world on a model of absolute truth suggested by the sciences, he nonetheless refuses to "throw out the baby with the bathwater," as he says, by letting himself get carried away in relativism and deconstructionism.

Taking Wittgenstein's last writings and John Dewey's political philosophy as his model, Putnam follows a philosophical path that allows him to "see our various forms of life differently without being either scientistic or irresponsibly metaphysical."[39] For, after all,

> [t]he collapse of a large number of alternative philosophical accounts of truth is a very different thing from the collapse of the notion of truth itself, just as the collapse of a large number of different philosophical accounts of certainty is a very different thing from the collapse of the ordinary notion of certainty, as Wittgenstein tried to tell us in his last work.[40]

And indeed, one cannot help but be struck by the incessant use, in the very same philosophical discourses that contest the reality of any cognitive objective truth, of the expression "it is true that . . ." and its opposite.

This is the meta- (or infra-) truth of usage that Wittgenstein also describes when he writes about certainty:

> One might say: "'I know' expresses *comfortable certitude* [*beruhigte Sicherheit*], not the certainty [*Gewißheit*] that is still struggling." Now I would like to regard this certainty, not as something akin to hastiness or superficiality, but as (a) form of life. (That is very badly expressed and probably badly thought as well.) But that means I want to conceive it as something that lies beyond being justified or unjustified; as it were, as something animal.[41]

The powers of speech

In an earlier work on "education and truth,"[42] I discerned "three powers of speech" and the necessity of their being separate and critically independent. These three powers are political power, scientific power, and the power of the media, which I called "poetic" in a tribute to the role accorded by Protagoras to the epic poem, namely to "teach virtue," in contrast with Socrates, who relies for that on the science of the True. (Economic power was considered to be distributed among the three powers just named.) In a discussion of the debates on the ethics of science that were going on at the time, I recognized Protagoras's victory over Plato, the rehabilitation of the role played by images and stagings, aptly named *figures* of rhetoric, which had been unjustly discredited. At the same time, Plato appears as a hidden Sophist, even craftier than Protagoras because he hides the tricks of his rhetoric, claiming to *possess* the unique and straight Truth by virtue of a pure philosophy no longer tied to cunning.

In the present work, the scope of the exchanges circumscribed by the world of *ona'ah* will also allow for a different kind of approach than one that begins with the definition of a formal, theoretical Truth as opposed to lies and errors. Here, the lies and deceptions that are to be prevented or compensated for are instead defined pragmatically, starting with the arena of human relationships, which brings together language, money, and technical objects. Money, like language, is a sign. It is a sign of the value of the objects that are exchanged. Language is the shared sign of the reality of the objects that surround us. And here, too, the question of truth or, to use the language of linguists, of the fidelity of the signifier to the signified, arises. What is the nature of the relation of language to the reality of what it designates, by way of our mind's representations or otherwise? What is this capacity for adaptation that allows us to name, that is to say to form common names, proper names, and phrases that designate and describe, objects, beings, and the state of the things that surround us, and not only that but also, similarly, allows us the possibility of both making and naming those particular objects that have never existed in nature, namely technical objects? This question, called the question of reference, is among those which have troubled generations of philosophers of language.

In response to a young correspondent who had recently converted to Catholicism following a revelation and wanted to convince Spinoza of the truth of his new religion, and who challenged Spinoza to show him how he knew that his "philosophy is the best of all those that have ever been taught in this world, are now being taught, or will ever be taught in the future," Spinoza wrote:

> But surely I have far better a right to put that question to you. For I do not presume that I have found the best philosophy, but know that what I understand is the true one. If you ask me how I know this, I reply that I know it in the same way that you know that the three angles of a triangle are equal to two right angles. That this suffices no one will deny who has a sound brain and does not dream of unclean spirits who inspire us with false ideas as if they were true. For truth reveals both itself and the false.[43]

This is an application of the method Spinoza established at the beginning of his philosophical career in the *Treatise on the Improvement of the Understanding*. Starting with a given "true idea," a step-by-step production process for truths is put in place, like the process for the fabrication of tools that make it possible to produce other tools. This method is very different from the establishment of knowledge based on something other than itself.

In his own way, Wittgenstein also seems to be expressing this same intuition. He too breaks the circle of value as it relates to truth: "If the true is what is grounded, then the ground is not *true*, nor yet false"[44] because, contrary to the idea that a blank slate is necessary to begin with, "[t]he reasonable man does *not have* certain doubts;"[45] and "[d]oesn't one need grounds for doubt?"[46] The circle is broken: it is doubt that needs to be grounded, not the true. A belief accepted by "every reasonable being," primitive evidence of the true sign of itself experienced by every person endowed with "a healthy brain" (as Spinoza writes to his correspondent), precedes doubt.[47]

Finally, the circle of value can also be broken when we view speech and discourse not from the point of view of their truth but instead from the point of view of their effects, especially of the injuries they convey (in the sense of the Latin *injuriae*, wounds, which is also to be found in the English word *injury*). Words, money, and objects of exchange, too, can be viewed from this perspective. This is what the geography of the world of *ona'ah* is about.

Fortunately, we experience other, more positive effects of speech as well: songs, praises, lamentations, and consolations are all words, or speech, of *blessing*, in which the abundance of good that is received is in proportion to the good that is said. To continue the parallel with money and objects of exchange, the economy of this speech is the economy of the gift. But that is not a task we can undertake here, except very indirectly.

We will see, however, in discussing the effects of *ona'ah*, that verbal injuries can, to a certain extent, be identified with the injuries produced by frauds in that they violate a kind of truth: the truth of exchange, that is to say of good commerce, both literal and figurative, between human beings. But we will also see that the effects of verbal injuries are not simply confined to the effects of injuries of truth, because of the humiliations that they can inflict and, in general, because of the evil they can do, even, sometimes, when they are words of truth.

We must begin, then, by discussing the status of evil in relations between human beings and the status of ethics as an attempt to avoid that evil.

2

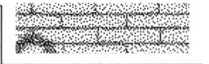

Suffering and Doing Evil

On evil and its banality

Openness to others, the search for justice, generosity, love for our neighbors, and compassion: these are what religions and philosophy have taught us, for millennia, as the ways with which to fight evil and make good triumph. It cannot be said that they have really met with success. Condensed to their essentials, these virtues converge toward what is often considered to be the "golden rule" of a universal ethics: not to do unto others what we do not want to have done unto us. The kernel of this minimum kernel comes down to avoiding making someone else suffer. And we need to recognize that even reduced to this absolute minimum, morality, whether secular or religious, has not, after countless centuries of trying, succeeded in eradicating evil. This should tell us that we are not going about it appropriately. Our conception of evil, even stripped down to suffering and misfortune, in a world from which evil cannot be completely removed, leads us to two basic types of attitudes which have been shaped to varying degrees by the different doctrines that are dogged by this problem. Either the suffering of human beings (like that of animals) is produced by the same blind and indifferent nature that causes births and deaths, earthquakes, volcanic eruptions, and tempests . . . in which case the evil inflicted by human beings on their fellows, on themselves, and on the rest of nature is but one particular aspect of this activity of the very nature that shapes them and that runs through them; or else the evil done by human beings seems different to us, like a specific moral evil added on to the pain that (sometimes but not always) accompanies it. It is in relation to this latter attitude that the failure of our attempts to understand the origin of evil is most problematic: if this specific evil of the misdeeds of human beings goes on indefinitely, in spite of the human activities, driven by a desire for and an aspiration toward good and aiming at eliminating evil, that exist right alongside it, its persistence would seem to be the effect of a kind of essence of evil. And it is this idea of an essence of evil that inspires pessimistic philosophies and the religious doctrines of the fall or of original sin. This essence of evil, then, would be what is expressed, for example, in individuals' criminal drives, but also in the great collective catastrophes for which human beings are responsible, starting with "banal" wars but most of all in large-scale massacres and genocides. These last seem to have reached new heights in the last century and are all the more human for being accompanied by doctrines, systems of thought, and narratives; in short, by ideologies that serve to justify them. Predatory animals, which of course make their prey, sometimes even of their own species, suffer, obviously never justify what they do with any ideology whatsoever. The phenomenon of the "banality of evil," on which Hannah Arendt famously remarked during the Eichmann trial, is also a paradoxical effect of this idea of an essence of evil, which one would expect to find on display to an extraordinary degree in an author, planner, and executor, such as Eichmann, of the Nazi "final solution" that exterminated Jews, Gypsies and other minorities judged to be subhuman. We are not, however, astonished by the banality of natural catastrophes, in spite of the fact that they, too, often take on extraordinary dimensions; or, if we are astonished by them after all, it is an astonishment that often leads to a magical search for hidden human causes of these natural outbreaks: in other words, they are seen as divine punishment for the evil conduct of human beings.

It seems, therefore, that we cannot escape this alternative: human crimes are either catastrophes that are just as "natural" as other catastrophes, or else they are the effects of an essence of evil that is characteristic of the human species in its confrontation with the moral problem.

We will see, however, that it is possible to extricate ourselves from this dichotomy by resituating human evil within the framework of nature's activities without at the same time denying its human specificity, which is connected to those properties of the species which cannot be observed in any other species. Among these properties, articulated and reflexive language and the kinds of economic, intellectual, and affective exchanges that it conveys are what most obviously set apart the human species, and for this reason they have made it possible for us to believe that humanity is called on to be anti-natural, supernatural, or extra-natural.

This radical division between an evil that is just part of nature and a moral evil, whose essence is unique to human beings, is in fact just another form of the dualist conceptions of human nature as material in its body and spiritual in its soul or spirit; in these conceptions, moral good or evil cannot be anything other than attributes of the spirit (potentially corrupted through its union with the body), by way of which the Human Being, thus idealized, in some way goes beyond its natural existence. Before philosophy, religions had taken control of these experiences by attributing them to the effects of gods or good spirits on the one hand and of demons on the other, and later to effects of the various forms taken by God and the Devil.

We will try here to develop an approach that is not "humanist"—since "humanism" has turned into the road paved with good intentions that dead-ended in hell—but rather both naturalist *and* human. This approach will make it clear that the virtues of speech are at the very foundation of the relationships between human beings and that which makes up their nature, for better or for worse.

To avoid evil in relations between human beings, the supposed "golden rule" is often, and much too easily, invoked: "You shall love your neighbor like yourself." This "rule" is supposed to be common to all cultures, to be found in Confucius as well as in the Bible, something on which everyone can agree as the foundation of a universal ethics. The fact that it not only appears in Leviticus (19:18) but is then taken up again in the Gospels (Matthew 5:43)[1] no doubt explains its wide distribution in the West beyond its original Hebrew context. And yet, is it even really a "rule" with a relatively simple application to all, or at least almost all, circumstances? In fact, the "rule" is not free of ambiguity, since it would seem to imply assumptions, less obvious than they appear, about the content of this "love" and the nature of this "as" or "like," that is to say assumptions about the nature of the relation between the "neighbor" and yourself. It would seem obvious that you love yourself and that that is the way in which you must love someone, namely your neighbor, who is also defined—through another meaning of "as" or "like"—by his or her similarity to you. Your neighbor is as you are yourself, and you must love him or her as you love yourself. Understood this way, which is after all, on the face of it, the simplest and most "universal" way to understand it, it is easy to see that this prescription is not as altruistic as one might believe. It is in fact yourself whom you will love in the other; concretely, the content of this love will be the content of your love for yourself: you will inflict on the other person what you would like to have inflicted on yourself, naturally supposing that he or she appreciates and desires what you yourself appreciate and desire. This love of one's neighbor, which seems to go without saying but which in fact encloses the beloved in the more or less egotistical and unconscious self-interest of the one who is doing the loving, is infamous for its sometimes catastrophic consequences, the unhappiness inflicted on another in good faith, always intended for her happiness or "for his own good."

We can improve the situation a little by taking the prescription as more of a negative one than a positive one. It is in fact easier to agree on an evil to be avoided than it is to agree on the content of a happiness to be pursued. Hence the reversal of the formula: "Do not do to others what you do not want to have done to yourself." As we will see, this is not enough—far from it—to remove all misunderstanding and to avoid doing evil to others. But the positive formula, "You shall love your neighbor . . . ," in a literal reading of the original Hebrew, in fact itself already expresses a doubled negation that opens up an abyss of quid pro quos in the relation between oneself and one's neighbor, for the neighbor is not as close to us as all that. Two different words from different biblical contexts are both translated, wrongly, as "your neighbor." One of them is *'amit*, from the same root as *'am*, "people" or "community," and the root *'im*, "with," which does in fact express this proximity of the neighbor. We will come back to this word later. But this is not the word used in the prescription we find in Leviticus. The word used there is *rea'*, which means "friend" instead and derives from the same root as *re'ut*, "friendship," but is also very close to *ra'*, "evil," "bad," both in the moral sense of "that which does evil" and in the affective sense of "unhappiness, misery and pain suffered." Our formula thus offers a quite different meaning: "You shall love what is your evil, as yourself (you are its evil)." This obviously implies that an encounter with another is first of all lived, at least potentially, as an encounter with evil, with a source of pain, with aggression, just as that person's encounter with myself is also, for him or her, an encounter with evil. Is this not what we are alerted to already in Genesis, in the first book of the Bible, "since the imagery of man's heart is evil [*ra*] from its youth" (Genesis 8:21)? The prescription we find in Leviticus is a dramatic call for us to overcome this condition with the entirely relative optimism that can be drawn from this last statement, which only talks about "youth," which leaves an opening for some hope for maturity.

Be that as it may, in this call to "love as yourself," the person who resembles us must be characterized as "distant" rather than "close" or our "neighbor."

The relationship between men and women does not escape this ambiguity. Quite the contrary: it is amplified in their ambivalent designation as husband and wife. The most general name for "wife" is simply *isha*, the generic name for "woman." But a more colloquial name is *re'ah* or *ra'yah*, "companion," "friend," "beloved," where we find the same root as in *ra'* and *rea'*, the evil and the distant neighbor that we have already seen in the original phrase. As for the husband and his wife, while the Bible is content to name them "man" (*ish*) and "woman" (*isha*), the talmudic institution of marriage names the man who takes a wife "husband," *ba'al isha*, that is to say, "master of *isha*." This designation obviously implies a superiority in the hierarchy of power and possession, but it also implies an inferiority in being, given that, in general as well as in the specific dialectic of master and slave, the *ba'al* of someone or something is *defined* by that which gives him this status (as for example the *ba'al bait*, the "master of the house," *ba'al mum*, the "master [in the sense of 'bearer'] of a fault," *ba'al isha*, "husband," etc.). Here, too, we thus find the ambivalence of meanings, amplified in the case of men and women in the naming of their relation. But the biblical simplicity of the *ish–isha* relation remains a goal, or a hope, or a promise like that of the prophet Hosea who follows the metaphor of the feminine–masculine couple and projects it onto the troubled relations between the community of Israel and its God. Announcing the future reconciliation of the suffering couple, he uses these doubled designations in prophesying that she "will no longer call him *ba'ali*, 'my husband,' but *ishi*, 'my man,'" and adds an allusion to the future disappearance of the idolatrous worship of the *ba'al*s (Hosea 2:18–19).

During the Vietnam War, in the sixties, hippie protesters shouted: "Make love, not war!" As if the one excluded the other! In fact, the injuries of love are just added to the injuries of war, with reunion and peace the promises or hopes that go along with them. And the love for our neighbor lies at the end of the road, not the beginning. Where things begin is with fear or worried questions, or even an injury. What we are given is the love of self, of people and things that are close to us, of the familiar, and the fear of others, what is far away, foreign people and things: this is the material we start with, to be transformed over a long process.

This is how we may understand Hillel the Elder's famous response when he was asked to sum up all of Torah while standing on one leg: "What is hateful to you, do not to your neighbor [*'haver*]: that is the whole Torah, while the rest is the commentary thereof; go and learn it."[2] The prescription we find in Leviticus is replaced here with its negative form, which already makes things clearer, as we have seen. But that is not enough. We still have to understand what makes up "what is hateful to you," what these wrongs, damages, and injuries that we spontaneously inflict on one another consist of, and how we can learn to prevent them or potentially make reparations for them.

Among the wrongs that human beings can suffer because of natural actors, human and nonhuman, the analysis of which fills several treatises of the Talmud, there is one kind that occupies a particular place and that we have already mentioned: a set of wrongs resulting from fraud or deception, in business transactions or in speech, voluntary or involuntary, by which someone "harms" someone else, all of which are united in the one word, *ona'ah*. The "harm" or damage suffered is an "injury" in the etymological sense of *injuria*, encompassing injuries and harmful speech.

Remarkably, in the biblical injunctions on the possible misdeeds of speech, the one that directly concerns lying, "You shall not steal, you shall not deny falsely, and you shall not lie one man to his fellow" (Leviticus 19:11), is separate from this set and connected, instead, with perjury and the possible use of the divine name in a false oath. And indeed we also find numerous admonitions and warnings about other misuses of language, such as false testimony, defamation, words of cunning (or "sinister wisdom," pretexts that weave "intrigues"[3]) as well as wishes and promises of all kinds. Wishes and promises create the danger of not keeping one's word, and one's word becomes sacred when it makes claims on the future.

The ambivalent nature of language is underscored and emphasized as strongly as possible in the status of the "vow" (*neder*) and of the "oath" (*shevuah*). It is the subject of an entire treatise of the Talmud, *Nedarim* ("Vows"). In this treatise, the vow's creative role as promise comes to the fore, as something that voluntarily makes claims on the future without being the object of a legal obligation. Its future execution will be a plus, a bonus, as compared to the simple unfolding of time, regulated simply by the application of the obligations of the Law: it will be a kind of creation ex nihilo (even though in an absolute sense, obviously, it is not, since the promise is itself the effect of the decisions of the moment in which it is pronounced). This creative role endows the vow with a sacred character. When it fails to be carried out, then, that failure appears as a very serious transgression, hence the warning not to heedlessly place oneself in danger by making a vow that one may not be able to fulfill. But this ambivalence of language turns back on itself when the day comes, when the future has become the present. The promise made in the past that had sealed the future can have become a confinement. A means of liberation must then be found, in canceling the vows, but that can only be done by a formal legal decision. Therefore, once a year, Yom Kippur, the Day of Atonement, is chosen for a solemn ritual in which vows are collectively annulled. This ritual, which in fact begins this Day of Atonement, is known under the name *Kol Nidre* . . . ("All Vows . . ."), the first words of the liturgy with which all vows and other oaths are annulled by the assembled community, which thus plays the role of a supreme tribunal. We shall see how this theme of pardon is also applied, in a way that we might not expect, to the field of *ona'ah* as a whole, in its commercial applications as well as in speech acts: as if the realm of one's being, which is at stake in verbal exchanges, were being extended to the realm of one's possessions, the realm of commercial exchanges.

Because it presents a paradox, the *Kol Nidre* ritual has been the subject of many different interrogations and interpretations. The paradox is that although the breaking of promises remains a serious transgression, the ritual solemnly annuls all vows, all oaths that make claims on the future. Since its establishment in the Middle Ages, the ceremony has served as an opportunity for anti-Semitic interpretations that accuse the Jews of easily letting themselves out of agreements into which they have entered. A short essay by the psychoanalyst Michel Steiner,[4] which differs from the best-known psychoanalytic interpretations (by Theodor Reik, Karl Abraham, Jean-Pierre Winter, and others), accounts for this paradox and gets to the crux of the problem. For Steiner, *Kol Nidre* articulates biblical and, even more, talmudic reservations about the simple fact of making a claim on the future with an oath, whether or not that promise is then kept. For oaths present us with something like a desacralization, a taking possession of the future time that should normally be reserved for the god of time to whom the future belongs. And yet, this hoarding of and attempt to master time is to some degree essential, given the reality of social relationships, which are always opaque and imperfect in comparison with an ideal in which exchanges between human beings are characterized by purity and transparency. In fact, this closing of the future also affects our relationships with the divine world itself, at least according to a cabalistic interpretation connected with the text of the ritual. In that reading, the annulment of vows applies to divine promises themselves, loaded as they are with threats of misfortune to come, such as the unending prolongation of exile. It is as if the seal of the pact Israel and its god have entered into had confined the god and obligated him in such a way that a legal, collective annulment of vows, oaths, and promises was necessary to set him free.

The Bible's absolute prohibition of lending at interest presents us, again, with the same issue of the mastery of time (and of its desacralization). Lending at interest, providing credit, is also a claim on the future that belongs to no one but God, and postbiblical economic activity would be impossible without it. Credit thus must be permitted (and regulated, particularly through the institution of thresholds) in Jewish, Muslim, and Christian jurisprudence, all of which are confronted with this prohibition.[5]

We continue to encounter, as in the world of *ona'ah*, the search for a balance, in social relationships, between absolute timeless purity and the chaos of a history of war, of each against all, that manifests itself in systemic deception and lying.

But the world of *ona'ah* proper is introduced by specific biblical injunctions that have in common the explicit use of the verb *lo townu*, "you shall not hurt . . ." or *al townu*, "do not hurt . . ." (or "do not defraud . . ." or "do not offend . . ."), from which derive the nouns *hona'ah*, for the active form (fraud or offense *committed* by the offender), and *ona'ah*, for the passive form (fraud or injury *suffered* by the victim). The following verses from Exodus and Leviticus, which in the Talmud serve as starting points for long explanations of *ona'ah*, will occupy us here:

You shall not hurt [*lo towneh*] or oppress a stranger, for you were strangers in the land of Egypt. (Exodus 22:20)

When a stranger dwells among you in your land, do not hurt [*lo townu*] him. The stranger who dwells with you shall be like a native among you, and you shall love [him by going towards him—*HA*] like yourself, for you were strangers in the land of Egypt—I [am-is] YHVH, your God. (Leviticus 19:33–34)

When you make a sale to your neighbor or make a purchase from the hand of your neighbor, do not hurt [*al townu*] one another. (Leviticus 25:14)

Each of you shall not hurt [*lo townu*] his neighbor, and you shall fear your God; for I [am-is] YHVH, your God. (Leviticus 25:17)

Here, the neighbor in question is the *'amit*, your fellow, the "one who is close," the "brother" even, not the *rea'*, the "one who is far," whom, according to Leviticus 19:18, we are to "love" generally. Nonetheless, talmudic interpretation includes "the stranger who resides with you" in the definition of your fellow, *'amit*.

The biblical text speaks explicitly of commercial exchanges, "sale and purchase." Yet talmudic interpretation sees in the repetition and the apparently redundant form of the text an implicit extension to the field of speech.

Fraudulent words: Verbal fraud and injury

Following its usual method,[6] the Talmud analyzes the ways in which biblical commandments should be applied by setting up particular situations. Its goal is not to find a single preexisting meaning that would be regarded as the only true meaning of the text.

Sellers harm buyers by selling to them above market price. Buyers harm sellers by buying below market price. The difference between the price paid and the market price constitutes the *fraud* (*hona'ah*) *committed* by the seller or buyer and measures, at the same time, the *harm* (*ona'ah*) *suffered* by the other partner in the transaction.

But we also learn that "just as there is commercial fraud [in buying and selling], so too is there fraud in speech [*ona'at dvarim*]" that hurts the one to whom it is addressed. This is followed by the first three examples:

One must not ask another, "What is the price of this article?" if one has no intention of buying. If a man was a repentant sinner, one must not say to him, "Remember your former deeds." If he was the son of proselytes one must not taunt him, "Remember the deeds of your ancestors," because it is written, "You shall not harm or oppress a stranger, for you were strangers in the land of Egypt." (Exodus 22:20)[7]

The same Hebrew word, *ona'ah*, is thus used to designate both injuries caused by words and deceptions about the fair price of things in commercial exchanges. This mixture of genres in a single word, this strange union of the concrete and the abstract, renders the word practically untranslatable. Yet for this very reason the word is also evocative of a whole new field, which it opens up for exploration.[8] But isn't this also the case for terms such as "economy" and "trade" between human beings, commercial exchanges, but extended to include all sorts of exchanges? In the next chapter, we will see the breadth, permanence, and richness of the semantic field shared by language and money; we will also see the underground work carried out by that semantic field through the oldest forms of the sacred.

Advertising falsely, deceiving about goods. Damaging one's partner in a transaction. Humiliating the victim. Injuries, harm done, possibly vengeful, sometimes fatal, literally and figuratively, for the victim as well as for the deceiver. Lies, too, are false advertising, deceptions about goods; are they also injuries to those who are caught in them? And is not mistaken speech like an involuntary lie, like not speaking the truth without knowing it? And what are we to do with the words of the learned or the wise when they are rejected by their peers who, wrongly perhaps, prefer false science or false wisdom? And what about works of art that are ignored in favor of literal and figurative artistic counterfeits? These are all kinds of language, venues for exchanges in one's possessions and one's being and therefore venues for deception, intrusions, fraud and burglaries, insults and injuries that are sometimes irreparable and that can possibly end up being fatal.

But how do we get from transactional or financial fraud to the injury to one's being of humiliating speech? What can the first teach us about the second, possibly for the sake of redress but in any case for the sake of prevention? Can we *measure* the magnitude of the fraud, the intensity of the injury? Can reparations be made? It is these improbable-seeming questions to which the chapter of the Talmud from which we quoted at the beginning responds.

Formally, the *ona'ah* of speech is introduced by emphasizing the differences in formulation between the two verses from Leviticus we cited with regards to *lo townu*, "you shall not hurt," and *al townu*, "do not hurt." While the one is explicit about the commercial context of the harm done, "sale and purchase," the other says nothing on this point but adds, "you shall fear your God." This verse, then, which does not specify the context in which the harm is done, is interpreted as referring to something other than sale and purchase. And the reference to "the fear of your God" suggests, as we shall see, a more intimate context than that of exchanges of goods: namely, the context of the effects on the interiority of a person's being, such as the effects produced by exchanges of words.

The three examples put forward in our *mishnah*—and there will be others as the talmudic commentary progresses—vividly capture both the semantic continuity and the discontinuities between the different kinds of injurious frauds or harm inflicted on one's neighbor, depending on whether they result from deception in the exchange of goods or of injurious words, whatever those might be.

— The first example puts forward the injury of a potential seller, even though there is no transaction, because of the false hope that the deception of the (false) buyer has kindled in him. This is where we leave the realm of real financial damages produced by commercial deception, fraud over goods, in buying and selling, which are analyzed at length in the passages that precede this *mishnah*, to enter the realm of the other kind of injurious fraud, the *ona'ah* of speech.

— The second example shows us words that are humiliating although they are factually correct: the former offender did indeed do what he is now reminded of, yet these words are as humiliating as if they were false and slanderous, because they concern a past gone by. And such a reminder of a past that has ceased to exist, that repentance has transformed from transgression into liberation, is indeed a humiliating dishonesty.

— The third example does not even concern the past of someone who has become someone else but, rather, only the reminder of such a person's origin when that origin is "foreign," that is to say, different from the origin that defines the collective identity of a given society, with its particular behaviors and rules of belonging. As a foreigner who has been "integrated" for more than a generation, the person is nonetheless recalled to this origin, which for him or her is now prehistory. Such a reminder amounts to exclusion, both humiliation and material damage, an injury in the social being of the foreigner among us, of the "stranger in Egypt" who from the beginning and for all eternity we have all been and still are.

Thus the question arises of the relations of similarity and difference implied by this application of the same warning, *al townu*, "do not hurt," to situations as different as commercial interactions and exchanges of words. The first, obvious, difference is that the first case is about goods and the second about people. All of the other differences will derive from this. But unexpected similarities that lie beneath these differences are sometimes of interest: they concern the "measure" of the harm which is known in advance to be immeasurable.

While financial damages are calculated by the divergence from the fair price, damages to someone's person are made up of the affects of sadness that cause tears to well up, such as sorrow, shame, humiliation and, generally, what we would today call a violation of dignity, with dignity being understood as self-esteem.

The notion of dignity is difficult to define, even though it is omnipresent in the discourses of ethics and of human rights. "All human beings are born free and equal in dignity and rights," says the Universal Declaration of Human Rights. As Mireille Delmas Marty remarks, the term "dignity" is never defined in law "other than by the articulation of the prohibitions it underlies."[9] It establishes a relation, both symmetrical and asymmetrical, between rights and their "reverse," that is to say the prohibitions necessary to enforce the respect of those rights. "As the reverse of the right to life and the right to property, the code punishes homicide or theft; in the same way, as the reverse of the right to human dignity, it is said to punish crimes against humanity."[10] This is expressed in the fact that legal prohibitions that articulate the right to dignity (in other words such prohibitions as the prohibition of torture, of inhuman and degrading treatment, and of slavery), even though this right is not explicitly named as such, seem to be placed above the prohibition of killing. Indeed, the prohibition of killing, unlike the legal prohibitions having to do with the right to dignity, is subject to exceptions, such as killing one's enemy in war, legitimate self-defense, or, in countries that have not (yet?) abolished it, the death penalty.[11] There is a seemingly paradoxical inverse hierarchy here: the right to dignity seems to be placed above the right to life. We will find the same inversion in the case of humiliations by means of verbal injuries.

Following Pico della Mirandola,[12] I have previously tried to define human dignity by way of related concepts such as glory, honor, modesty, and their negatives, such as shame and humiliation. In particular, inspired by the contrasting ways in which Spinoza illuminates the concept of "glory,"[13] I have suggested that human dignity be defined as a certain basic degree of glory, that is to say a basic minimum of self-esteem as well as of recognition and praise from others, without which the condition of a human being would be inhuman. If we start with the Hebrew word *kavod*, for "glory," "honor," which refers back to the word *kaved*, "heavy," what is at issue is what makes a human being "weigh" some irreducible amount, a minimum "weight" granted to a human existence without which it would become inhuman.[14] As with crimes against humanity, we see that the inhumanity in question must not be confused with not belonging to the human species. It is a qualification that refers us to particular affects that only human beings can experience, through their bodies, their spirits, and the relations, verbal and otherwise, that incorporate them into human societies. Only human beings can be inhuman.

When someone's dignity is violated, it is as if his or her personhood has been canceled or nullified, as if he or she has been transformed into an object of manipulation, a manipulation of the person's goods or of their image.

This is why, on this topic, I want to recall a set of formulas that would seem to be even further from commercial fraud. Their scope is more general: they indicate the degree to which humiliating someone, especially in public, is more serious than the weightiest faults. "[H]e who publicly puts his neighbor to shame has no portion in the world to come," and "Since the destruction of the Temple, the gates of prayer are locked. . . . Yet though the gates of prayer are locked, the gates of tears are not," are among the talmudic phrases to which I refer.

The talmudic text insists on the protection of foreigners or strangers, among them former idolaters, as being particularly exposed to humiliation, as well as the protection of women, or more exactly certain women in certain situations, who are linked with foreigners, because their inferior legal status makes them more susceptible to being humiliated.[15]

While every deception produces a humiliation, not all humiliations are produced by "fraudulent speech." Fraudulent speech has at least one particular characteristic that makes it like commercial fraud: it is not necessarily intentional. Indeed, no one can know whether the harm or damage was caused voluntarily or not. In the case of buying or selling, however, the reality of the harm done, as well as its magnitude, can be objectively evaluated and there can be procedures for redress. In commercial fraud, therefore, the voluntary or involuntary nature of the fraud moves into the background. In the case of injurious speech, on the other hand, it is intention that determines moral guilt because the effects of such speech are practically irreparable. But that intention remains buried within the interiority of the person who has committed the injury, which is why such a person cannot be subjected to an objective judgment. Any potential punishment can only come from that person's god. This is also what underlies the talmudic interpretation that differentiates between the two verses that involve "do not hurt" and that formally introduces, as we have seen, the notion of "harm in speech." The reference to "fear of your god," in the verse that does not speak of buying or selling and is thus referring to something else, suggests that what is at issue is a realm that is not accessible to human objective judgment: the realm, precisely, of the *ona'ah* of speech. The god implied here is the god of each and every person's interior alchemy, where good and bad faith develop and to which no one has access.

As an example of someone who causes harm with speech, the medieval commentator Rashi brings up a bad adviser who induces his or her neighbor to err but without it being possible to know whether this was intentional or not, in other words whether the advice was given in good faith or not. And Rashi emphasizes the conclusion of the verse (a conclusion that is not present in the verse that explicitly mentions the objective reality of commercial exchanges): "Anything given over to the heart, which no one can recognize except the one in whose heart the thought is, of it is it said 'You shall fear your god.'"[16]

But the answer to this is not even always clear to the subject himself or herself, the person who caused the damage—to the extent to which we recognize the possibility of showing bad faith with one's own self. This is also what is described in Lurianic Kabbalah as the stakes of the moral life, seen as a struggle between two elementary forces, good and evil, that compete, in the form of urges, for the mastery of the individual that they inhabit and regulate. In the model proposed by Hayyim Vital in his book *'Etz Hayyim* (*Tree of Life*), these two elements cover the soul like a piece of clothing (at the place where the soul is connected with the body). They inhabit the human being whose *tselem* ("form") they constitute, but they are neither its body nor its soul, like "angels that are in the human being itself without being the human being itself."[17] When a subject inflicts a verbal injury on someone and there is no way either to evaluate whether the injury is intentional or to measure the harm suffered, it is the objectively—and legally—irreparable nature of the injury that sends us back to a "divine" measure, that is to say, a measure hidden in the interior of subjectivities. Only the effects of this speech—not only on its addressee and its speaker but also on their environment—can, after the fact, by their magnitude, give some idea of its measure.

In all such cases, the conditions under which verbal injuries can be inflicted become ever more delicate and cause ever more misunderstandings the further one moves away from the realm of measurements and possible redress, potentially regulated by law.

What we have here is an unexpected hierarchy within the seriousness of the different kinds of injuries that human beings can inflict on one another. Verbal offenses and injuries show up at the top of the hierarchy, surpassing in gravity not only material damages to goods but even bodily injuries. One would have expected these last to be the most serious. The paradox in this progression, which one would have expected to be the other way around, with bodily harm as the most serious kind of harm, arises because the focus here is on the specifically human character of these damages. Bodily injuries, even fatal ones, are not exclusive to the human species. Cruelty can be seen just as much in the animal kingdom, even if it is not expressed in the same way. But while theft and robbery can be seen in animals as well, commercial exchanges and their regulation are exclusive to human societies and purely verbal exchanges even more so. But furthermore, it is the question of the measure of the damage that propels verbal injuries to the top of the scale. For it is not only harm to goods, but also injuries to the body, that can be measured by the *lex talionis*, transformed into financial reparation for damages. Verbal injury, on the other hand, is not measurable, in fact it is literally immeasurable, and irreparable except, perhaps, under the specific conditions of certain pardons. In this case, we cannot help but be reduced to the mystery of a good or bad faith that is impossible to establish and to the mystery of an interior injury that is impossible to measure. It is thus, from this point of view, that verbal injury appears as the most serious.

And yet it is as though, through words of blame or praise and the mobilization of "fear of your God," the effort to measure and redress the assumed effects of injurious speech were not being renounced after all, because what words can destroy would be prevented or redressed by other words, warnings, and moral condemnations, possibly followed by forgiveness.

The famous story of the Oven of Akhnai illustrates this almost infinite effect of verbal injuries.[18] It is a story full of reversals, pitting Eliezer ben Hyrcanus, one of the greatest masters of the academy, against the rest of the masters. Rabbi Eliezer, nicknamed "the Great," is placed in the minority in this story even though it seems that he is right and everyone else is wrong, in any case from the point of view of an absolute standard of truth that it would seem they would all have to share. Rabbi Eliezer invokes divine authority to show that he has the truth and that the others are wrong and, to this end, he brings about some miracles. But this does not convince his interlocutors, who rule by majority vote in favor of their thesis, recalling that "the Torah is not in heaven." The story is best known in a form that ends with this conclusion, instituting the authority of the sages "on earth" as higher than the authority of those sages, possibly greater than they are, who make "heaven" speak.

Yet matters do not end here, for the story is in fact one of successive humiliations, and it is often forgotten that the story is brought up, in this talmudic passage, as a particularly cogent illustration of the notion of *ona'at dvarim*, "fraud or harm in speech" in various and multiple forms. In fact, it marks the conclusion of the chapter, following an enumeration of different examples of such speech and its destructive effects on those who hear it and those who pronounce it. The stakes of the story are most certainly the highest ones possible, namely the search for truthful speech in the teaching of the law—that is to say the search for what is truly "divine speech" on earth and not in heaven. But with all its reversals, it nonetheless ends with the death of a man in tragic conditions following Rabbi Eliezer's painful expulsion. In chapter 5, we will return at length to several aspects of this story, which is even more abundantly instructive when it is not separated from its context in these pages of the Talmud dedicated to the *ona'ah* of speech.

But we will have to look in greater detail at how the question of measure, which we have already mentioned, is dealt with in the context of commercial *ona'ah* in its narrow sense, the *ona'ah* "of buying and selling." To this end, we need to go further back in the talmudic text, because this question is the subject of long discussions in the pages that precede the innovation introduced by the notion of an *ona'ah* of speech. For beyond its formal aspect, this innovation with respect to the biblical text constitutes a feat that is rather characteristic of the transition from biblical Hebraism to talmudic Judaism: namely, to take an experience that starts out as a social and objective experience and interiorize and subjectivize it, in spite of obvious differences between the situations in which these experiences are pertinent. For our purposes here, one major difference is striking: when one partner to a transaction is harmed, the damage he or she suffers (which is also the other partner's gain) can be measured in relation to a fair price, which can be evaluated. When the damage is inflicted by injurious speech, on the other hand, its extent is impossible to measure. Furthermore, it is irreversible and never completely reparable (even if forgiveness is possible), unlike with fraudulent transactions, which can always be canceled or compensated for. Finally, as we have seen concerning injurious speech in general, the fault committed cannot be evaluated, either, unless it is "in the heart" of the person who committed it: no one can know whether the words were spoken voluntarily, with the intention of injury, or involuntarily, except of course for the person who spoke them.

And yet, the paradigm of commercial fraud is the paradigm that will be used to extend to all kinds of fraud in speech. And in this paradigm, the question of *measure* occupies a central place, all the more important for being the object of another innovation, also quite unexpected, with respect to the biblical text. The question is, at what level can one begin to speak of fraud (*ona'ah*)? While nothing in the biblical text suggests the possibility of an acceptable threshold, talmudic law establishes that a small divergence from the fair price is not yet a true fraud and that it is "forgiven," in the sense that the transaction remains valid; a threshold of loss is instituted, and only above that threshold is fraud established and the transaction annulled. The use of the notion of "forgiveness" is instructive in this context: it is a transposition from the domain of offenses and subjectivity to the domain of objective damage, whereas the metaphor that is introduced later, in the institution of the *ona'ah* of speech, seems to move in the opposition direction.

The question then becomes, as of what amount (and what percentage) of loss does one speak of damage (*ona'ah*) inflicted on the buyer or the seller? From the outset, a definition is posited which will subsequently be abundantly commented on: if one-sixth too much or too little of the value of an object is paid, this constitutes *ona'ah*: fraud committed and damage suffered.[19] The teaching is enigmatic in that it is presented as a principle without either explanation or justification: why a threshold at all, and why specifically one-sixth? In chapter 6, we will analyze a number of rather technical elaborations of this principle, for it is only in their wake that, as we have seen, the equally new notion of an *ona'ah* of speech is introduced.

While the Talmud does not address it directly, we cannot help but ask: what about a possible transposition of the one-sixth rule to the case of verbal injuries? We have seen how the intention to harm and good or bad faith appear as criteria of the fault committed by the person who inflicts this type of injuries. We have also seen how bad advice is cited as an example that brings up the question of the adviser's good or bad faith, which can obviously not be objectively evaluated. But in other cases, the "injury" is unavoidable because of stakes that go beyond the protagonists, as we will see in the story of the Oven of Akhnai. In such cases, then, the task would be to reduce the injury to a minimum, to "less than one-sixth." But what does that mean when it no longer concerns a fair price that is more or less dictated by the market?

To address this question, we will have to go through the cabalistic commentary of the Talmud to find elements of an answer in which this arithmetic of *ona'ah* is taken up in a very different context: the context of an economy of desire, in one's being and one's possessions, and the sources and satisfactions of that desire.

But first, let us make an excursion into a sphere that is shared by language, money, and technical objects; this excursion will teach us to appreciate some of the stakes involved in this bringing together of commercial fraud and verbal injuries, which is not as strange as it may seem at first.

3

Language and Money

The words to express it

Money and language have often been linked as the bases for exchanges in the establishment of human societies. The linkage between the two is expressed in etymology and also in the work of numerous philosophers who begin their treatments of the functions of language with monetary imagery, used more or less metaphorically. In a "poetic encyclopedia" on the origins of language, Maurice Olender has conducted an astonishing inquiry into the semantic fields shared by language and money, ranging from Aristotle to Foucault and Derrida via, among others, Augustine, Humboldt, and Saussure; Olender also provides a rich bibliography.[1] We learn, among other things, what role shared *value* plays in a human society as a foundational property that is common to language and money as places of (truthful) exchange that create the social bond. This is a new and, in this case, operational aspect of the circle of value and truth. The analogy also works in the other direction, going from language to money, in the work of certain older economists such as Anne-Robert-Jacques Turgot in the eighteenth century or the amazing Nicole Oresme, a fourteenth-century bishop, mathematician, physicist, and commentator on Aristotle and the author of a *Treatise on Currencies*, to which Olender introduces us.

Let us first note one obvious difference between language and money that jumps out right away. A commercial exchange obviously implies a change of owner: the former owner of the merchandise being sold or the money being paid no longer has it in his or her possession. The information carried by language, on the other hand, can be indefinitely duplicated. A person who provides or sells information does not lose the information. And yet this seemingly irreducible difference has been diminished by the multiplication of forms of credit as the predominant vehicles of commercial exchange. The borrower receives and uses a certain sum, yet the lender, for all that, has nonetheless not lost it: something connected with it does in a certain way remain in his or her possession, in the form of securities as signs of the loan.

In fact, the history of currencies—which have become more and more dematerialized as silver and gold have given way to bills, letters of credit, and the various kinds of electronic currency that are now being developed—only reinforces these associations and analogies, to the point that we recognize today a truly shared identity between language and money in their capacity as vehicles of information: the symbolic function that the word and the coin have in common has completely invaded the realm of exchanges, where it is now the value of information that constitutes the main resource of modern and postmodern, postindustrial societies. It is as though the social and economic realities being established in the twenty-first century had appropriated the sometimes unexpected semantic fields that etymology unveils. Olender recalls the origins of the French *monnaie* [and the English *money*] in the Latin *moneta*, from *monet* ("advises against and warns of" a fraud; cf. *admonet*, "admonishes"), as well as the origins of *nomisma*, borrowed from the Greek, from *nemein*, "to share," and *nomos*, "law," but also from *nomizein*, which indicates usage, custom, common law; hence the word *nomisma* for coins. Coins "bear the signature of the name and the effigy of the prince,"[2] and at the same time, from the time of the constitution of a human community with the *agora*, the "market," coins are, in themselves, a "*symbolon*, a conventional 'sign' for the sake of exchange."[3] We may add to this list the etymology of "fiduciary," from *fiducia*, "confidence," opening up the supplementary dimension of time, the importance of which becomes clear as credit develops in all its forms. But what may be the richest presentation of this metaphor—or, rather, this analogy of functions—comes from another of the authors introduced to us by Olender, namely Lorenzo da Brindisi, a Capuchin monk in the 1580s. In a commentary on Adam's naming of the animals in Genesis, Lorenzo follows up on Aristotle's remark on the specificity of the human being, the only animal capable of transforming voice into speech and thus of *naming*: "The voice is the material of meaning as silver is the material of the coin, or the vessel."[4]

We will come back to this human function of meaning, or signification, shared by speech, money, and manufactured objects (the "vessels"), which currency throughout history has increasingly reduced to neutral information, which carries less and less meaning in itself, as the currency is increasingly dematerialized and distanced from the goods and the artifacts that are the objects of exchange.

Let us also add to our list the *interpres*, which is brought up by Jean Starobinski in an "exchange" with Olender.[5] This is of course the interpreter, the intermediary vehicle of speech, but before that the *interpres* was "the intermediary in a negotiation, the broker,"[6] which is perhaps linked to the *pretium* (hence "interpreter"), the "price."

Furthermore, etymology also directs us toward two other realms—the sacred and the inner life, as constitutive elements of the social bond—to which we will return in other contexts.

Moneta also happens to be the name of a goddess. The Roman goddess Moneta, who was quickly identified with Juno, wife of Jupiter, brought together under her tutelage and in her temple on the Capitol not only money but also prophetic speech, recalling the past and warning—admonishing—about the future. According to legend, the saving warning cries of the Capitol's geese came from her temple.[7]

Cancellation of debts, loans without interest

Yet these connections, semantic and otherwise, are not limited to the Greco-Roman world. And it is not just money and language that are linked in this manner. In this locus of exchange in which money and language articulate themselves, we find a knot of many strands, including different forms of the sacred as well as the hidden aspects of the inner life (what Olender calls the "intimate") and the wounding intrusions into it.

In fact, from the moment it was invented, money was invested with a sacred character that to some degree guaranteed its legitimacy and value. A particular kind of shell, the cowrie shell, known since at least 3500 BCE, was used in China, Oceania, Africa, and Europe both for protective amulets and as currency until the nineteenth century, serving both commerce and the art of divination.

Magical powers were long attributed to precious stones and to the gold of the treasuries. When coins were minted, representations of the gods, and later of the prince or king invested by the deity, testified to the coins' value, while it was priests who administered the coins in the temples before banks and bankers were invented.[8] The desacralization of money seems to have coincided with its dematerialization, which began when paper money came into general use and continues before our eyes in the various forms of electronic currency, though the groundwork was laid for it even earlier, as soon as it was recognized that money was not just a medium for exchanging goods and manufactured objects but also a generative source of new wealth that allows debts to be drawn on the future through loans and investments. As soon as it was discovered that loans could be made at interest, the practice was immediately and widely banned as a sort of act against nature and as sacrilegious oppression, as evidenced in Aristotle, the Bible and the Gospels, the Qur'an, and other texts.[9]

For Aristotle, money should only serve as an equivalent, allowing goods to be exchanged, and never in any way as a self-contained means of enrichment, reproducing itself on its own as if it were producing offspring.

For money was intended to be used in exchange, but not to increase at interest. And this term interest [*tokos*, i.e. "interest" and "offspring"—HA], which means the birth of money from money, is applied to the breeding of money because the offspring resembles the parent. Wherefore of all modes of getting wealth this is the most unnatural.[10]

As for the Bible, its legislation establishes a very particular economic system; we may well wonder whether it has ever been put into practice. Not only is lending to a "brother" in difficulties an obligation that is immediately accompanied by an absolute ban on any interest, but in addition, the institution of the sabbatical year implies the cancellation, pure and simple, of all debts.[11] The sabbatical year is the biblical obligation to let all lands lie fallow every seventh year, counting on a double harvest the sixth year. But it is also to be accompanied by a reset to address the most egregious inequalities, canceling all debts contracted in the meantime. And evidently, the simple math that increasingly discouraged the rich from lending to the poor as the seventh year approached was condemned, as an expression of the selfishness of the well-off who "do not fear their god."

We can see how laws such as these could only have been conceived in the context of an agricultural society that we may characterize as pre-economic, a society in which the very idea of autonomy for a currency, allowing the currency to create wealth on its own, through loans, was a sacrilege.

That is why, in this area as well as others, the transition from ancient biblical Hebraism to post-prophetic talmudic Judaism is reflected in the rupture of a desacralization. Elsewhere,[12] I have examined the progress of this desacralization, which transformed the oracular randomness of ancient rituals into a randomness of indifference, guaranteeing equal chances in the absence of any knowledge of a possible cause or reason that would favor one event over others. In the same way, currency and speech, especially written speech, passed from the sphere of the sacred into the economic sphere, from guaranteeing exchanges to themselves being the objects of those exchanges.

Promises, assurances *given*, oaths, alliances, sometimes but not always sealed in writing, all had the sacred character of that which escapes time, both a memory of the past and a projection onto the future. From this derives the very notion of sacred Scripture, of *hieroglyphs* in the etymological sense of the word, by which the Greeks designated Egyptian writing. In the same way, money was initially a quantity or weight of matter that would allow for the measurement of a value while being as impervious as possible to the wear and tear of time. This matter was for this reason considered *precious*, because it was both rare and not subject to depreciation over time: such was the wealth accumulated in royal treasuries and in temples, ostentatious wealth, signaling the stability and majesty of power in the gilding of palaces and temples. But the monetary economy that followed this desacralization completely changed the status of money. Money began to move, and increasingly, its circulation appeared as a source of growing wealth in itself. As a result, it lost its hieratic character as the symbol of an established and unchangeable value and became the vehicle of a fluidity in which what is exchanged is no longer just merchandise but money itself. Modern economy begins with that use of money in which loans at interest and returns on investment actually play a central role. The theory that follows from this practice expresses it perfectly:

Money of account, namely that in which debts and prices and general purchasing power are *expressed*, is the primary concept of a theory of money. A money of account comes into existence along with debts, which are contracts for deferred payment.[13]

Since the beginning of this economy, a social bond founded on "pure" solidarity—interest-free loans and the cancellation of debts every seven years—has been purely and simply inconceivable.

From the very beginning of the post-biblical era, the talmudic masters realized that the systematic cancellation of all debts every seventh year was impractical for their time. And this cancellation was abolished for all practical purposes by a famous decision of Hillel the Elder's at the beginning of the first century of the Christian era. This decision, called "Hillel's prosbul,"[14] instituted a procedure for recovering debts that provided for the intervention of a court, as an intermediary, well after the sabbatical year. The formal justification rested on the fact that the biblical obligation to cancel the debt had to do with the interpersonal relation between lender and borrower, between "you and your brother," and not the social regulation of the economy, for which the court was responsible. Beyond the formal aspect, the obvious concern was with avoiding a situation in which those in need became increasingly unable to borrow as the seventh year approached. But as we shall also see in the case of the legislation on *ona'ah*, the Talmud continues to be concerned with reconciling the ideal of interpersonal relationships of "pure" solidarity, coming as close as possible to a system of sharing and giving, with the necessities of an economic organization of society.

As for loans with interest, talmudic legislation set about legalizing them a few centuries later. And there, too, the goal was to reconcile, as far as possible, the biblical ideal of the "purity" of interpersonal relationships, according to which the charging of interest was banned (even when the borrower voluntarily agreed to it), with the new collective necessity of circulating money. At first, in fact, the Talmud extended the prohibition on any loans with interest at all (not only on usury in the modern sense of unreasonable or inflated interest) to all forms of indirect derivative profits, large and small, perhaps even in kind, in which a lender could have benefited from the borrower. The trend only began to reverse itself a few centuries later, after the destruction of the Temple in Jerusalem, in the work of the third-century masters of the Babylonian Talmud dealing with the necessities of an economy of communities in exile that have little left in common with the economy of their ancestors' agricultural society in Palestine. The entire fifth chapter of the *Mishnah Baba Mezi'a*, which follows the chapter on the problems of *ona'ah*, is dedicated to this question, which is then discussed in the *Gemara* of the Babylonian Talmud.[15] The discussions in the *Gemara* increasingly weaken or roll back the extensions of the biblical prohibition reported in the *Mishnah*. In the centuries that followed, and up through the modern era, successive legal decisions by post-talmudic masters have found ways to reconcile the rabbinical legal tradition (the *halakha*) with the kind of lending and credit practices that have become indissolubly linked with a market economy.

This reconciliation is expressed by way of regulatory procedures in which the loan is only one element of a more general transaction that cannot be reduced to mere financial speculation. Finally, a procedure was established based on a "business authorization" (*hetere 'iska*) that associates lender and borrower. The borrower invests the borrowed money in a company or project, and the lender receives potential profits (but also shares in potential losses), sometimes with a minimum profit that is guaranteed provided the lender pays the borrower a salary, even a nominal one, for the borrower's labor in managing the enterprise. Over time, contracts establishing this kind of association have become more and more of a formality, to the point that they are almost implied in all transactions involving non-usurious credit in compliance with the laws of the country in which they take place. Interest-free loans, meanwhile, have regained their original status as a brotherly, friendly, or charitable gift.

Islam, too, had to legislate on the conditions under which the Qur'an's prohibition could nonetheless allow the economic machine that was now running on credit to continue unstopped. Islamic law (*sharia*) therefore established procedures for bank loans that are compatible with the spirit of the Qur'an's prohibition. Just as the Bible does in the case of *ona'ah*, the Qur'an highlights the *harm* inflicted by the charging of interest:

You who believe, beware of God: give up any outstanding dues from usury, if you are true believers. If you do not, then be warned of war from God and His Messenger. You shall have your capital if you repent, and without suffering loss or causing others to suffer loss.[16]

If it is a matter of helping those in need, interest-free loans—or, even better, alms—are the rule.[17]

But *sharia* has instituted procedures that make it possible to charge interest on a loan by associating the lender (an individual or a bank), in a variety of ways, with an investment that is likely to produce a profit. The lender can thus be associated with the profits of the project, as well as with the losses. To this day, Islamic banks function by the use of several procedures that tend to connect loans more closely with the production of goods, for example purchasing goods at a higher price at a later date. The loan is thus more "rooted" or "grounded" in relation to what we may consider economic "reality,"[18] and thus these rules, in principle, prohibit speculative loans. One could argue that the banking and financial crisis of 2008 could have been avoided if all banks had worked this way. And yet, if the evaluation of the risks shared by the lender and the borrower turns out to have been too optimistic, the lender's sharing in the risk does not necessarily preclude the possibility of "bubbles" and of crises of a new kind.

Finally, the history of the Catholic Church's complex relations with usury is particularly interesting to study because in the end, a Christian environment was the context in which modern capitalism developed, following a long evolution in which lending at interest, a practice initially consigned to hell and eternal damnation, was transformed into bank loans as the *sine qua non* of economic development. At numerous church councils and in the words of countless theologians and preachers, the Church often reaffirmed the total ban on what the Church called "usury" (*usuria*).[19] Taking up the biblical and evangelical prohibition, especially as found in Deuteronomy 23:20 and Luke 6:35, the Church understood by usury all forms of charging interest on a loan, not only on loans of money but also on in-kind loans, for example in returning a certain quantity of borrowed wheat with a certain amount added to what was borrowed, whatever that amount might be. But the first outlines of a capitalist economy based on the circulation of money began to take shape in the twelfth and thirteenth centuries, and the Church had to face the temptation to enrich itself, which only grew stronger as the merchant bourgeoisie blossomed; this explains the twelfth-century excommunication of usurers and the development of mendicant orders that tried to promote a return to the poverty preached by the primitive Church. Usury was condemned as a mortal sin, as "*shameful* profit," as against nature, as a "thief of time" and as blasphemous because "the usurer sells his debtor nothing that belongs to him, but only time, which belongs to God alone."[20] Thomas Aquinas, like Aristotle, characterizes usury as a procreation against nature, a begetting of money by money itself. Unlike labor, and even unlike market exchanges for which an interest rate corresponding to the market price is legitimate, usury is also a fundamental injustice. In fact, it implies an intolerable divergence from what a *fair price* ought to have been, which in the case of a loan is zero because the loan as such involves no true commercial transaction. Jews (to whom canon law did not apply), controlled by princes and the Church, were the "solution" for a while. Of course, the Bible prohibited the children of Israel from lending money with interest not just to their "brother who has fallen into poverty" but also to the "resident foreigner" (*ger toshav* in Hebrew) (Leviticus 25:35–37). But it did permit loaning with interest to the *nokh'khi*, the stranger from outside, so to speak (Deuteronomy 23:21). In the Christian societies of the Middle Ages, it was obviously this last situation that was the relevant one now that the Jews, having lost all national territorial sovereignty, lived scattered among strangers or foreigners themselves. Furthermore, they had little choice, since they were prohibited from engaging in almost all activities that were seen as "noble" because they were "productive" activities. The division of labor in these societies implied a hierarchy of activities in which certain professions, including butchers, barbers, and surgeons, were despicable and despised, though indispensable. But at the very bottom of the hierarchy were those destined for the demons of hell and unworthy of being buried in a Christian cemetery: prostitutes, "jugglers" and other actors, and above all usurers. Since the Jews were impure and damned anyway, the linkage between "Jew" and "usurer" was only normal, and it also reinforced the general contempt and anti-Judaism of the day, which were fueled even more by the competition with Christian usurers.

We should note that for a time, another kind of profit was identified with usury as a "theft of what belongs to God," namely the payment received by the new university lecturers who taught outside the framework of the monasteries and churches. In accepting payment from their city students, they were nothing but "vendors, merchants of words."[21] Just as the usurers were selling time, these teachers were selling the words of science that belonged to no one but God: another disgraceful encounter, this time the meeting of money and language in the shadow of the sacred.

But it was not long before it was recognized that this intellectual activity, too, had the dignity of *labor*. At the same time, incidentally, usury itself, under the pressure of the changes that had arisen in commercial trade practices in the thirteenth century, began to see its social and religious status change, as it became the "common good" that played the role of a precursor to what the economy required. More and more often, usury could be seen as a means to gain wealth and even, under certain conditions, as a means of upward social mobility. The notion of usury rates that were "inflated" compared to an interest rate that was "legitimate," because moderate, which already existed as a concept as applied to the usury permitted to the Jews, was now extended to Christian merchants. Furthermore, until then, the only way for a usurer to escape eternal damnation had been through contrition and the restitution of the profits from usury, but now, the invention of Purgatory meant that, after a wait that might be short or very long but was in any case finite, contrition and restitution could be accompanied by hope for Paradise. From that point on, as Jacques Le Goff points out, Christian usurers could hope to have it both ways, to gain "their money *and* their life," money here on earth and eternal life in the beyond.

As was the case for rabbinical Judaism and for Islam as expressed in *sharia* law, the goal was then in all cases to integrate lending into exchanges of real, material, or energy-based goods and to prevent it from being a somewhat disembodied source of wealth in and of itself.

In this way, the demonic[22] character of lending at interest, seen as being against nature, was gradually replaced by an acknowledgment of its virtues as a way of creating wealth, for the borrower as much as for the lender, especially through the institution of *banks*, which themselves are both borrowers and lenders. It appears to have been in the fourteenth century that a money market, in which merchant bankers distinguished between usury and acceptable interest, was first instituted: a legitimate interest at the *market rate* is thus distinguished from usury, by which a dishonest creditor crushes a lender under the weight of exorbitant interest payments. And finally, the Reformation allowed the Christian West to enter completely and without reserve into this "spirit of capitalism" which it had, according to Max Weber, helped to bring about. Calvin had also distinguished between loans invested in production, for which interest is a remuneration justified by the loan's economic function, and loans for the simple purpose of consumption, for which all interest must remain strictly forbidden.[23]

But this process was accompanied by a dematerialization of money. The value of money depended less and less on the quantity of gold or other precious matter that had been accumulated and more and more on money's *circulation*. Increasingly sophisticated means naturally developed to facilitate this circulation: the first bankers' letters of exchange, paper money, and now, today, credit cards and electronic exchanges that make it possible for cash to flow between banks and stock exchanges at the speed of light, exchanges that for this reason are said to take place "in real time."

Above all, this wealth-creating dematerialization reached new, previously unthinkable heights with the institution of modern or, rather, postmodern banking at the end of the twentieth century.

Dematerialized circulation

The economist François Rachline's summary of the mechanisms of dematerialized circulation is enlightening:

When a bank grants a loan that is pure credit, not based on any prior deposit, it credits the amount to the beneficiary's account. This account figures as a liability for the bank since it corresponds to the position of a client to whom the bank owes this amount. Because the bank is granting a loan, the beneficiary will have to repay it. The bank thus acquires a claim on the beneficiary that it registers as an asset while registering the same amount as a liability. And the miracle happens. A sum of *money* has spontaneously been created. From nothing. . . . [This sum] can be doubly defined: as a claim of the beneficiary on the bank, and as a claim of the bank on the beneficiary for the loan granted. Modern money is thus neither a good, nor a metal, nor a claim, nor a debt, but an inextricably linked claim/debt or, seen from the other side, a debt/claim. . . . The circulation of this money takes place by means of transfers of writing. . . . Writing is based on writing, an indefinite mechanism for transferring claims. There is no security to guarantee the value carried by the writing, no demonstrable value that is not also, in turn, writing. *Writing of writing of writing of writing*, etc.: such is modern money. . . . Immaterial, but very real, . . . [money] is very precisely a claim on the banks, or a debt from the banks to the actors of the economy. Nothing more, nothing less: no relation at all to any metal whatsoever, gold, silver, or alloy; no material guarantee serves as a backing for this currency. No *vertical* relationship exists any longer between this currency and nature. Money has become a purely and simply human creation.[24]

The result is an inverted relationship between what we call economic reality, made up of the production and exchange of material objects, and money, the only function of which had been considered until now to be facilitating such exchanges. I am calling it inverted because reality follows credit and not the other way around, because credit is an advance drawn on the future. This profoundly modifies the role of monetary circulation, which is often compared to the circulation of blood, seen as a simple flow of liquid that ensures the exchanges between the different organs and parts of the body that perform the organism's various functions. Today we know that the blood itself has very sophisticated functions. And it is the creative function of bank credit that inverts its relationship to the rest of the economy. "A posteriori, we note the existence of buildings, furniture, various objects; in short: the existence of what our senses call *reality*. Reality is like the lime deposited by a river."[25] This new metaphor, then, is the metaphor of a river whose flow leaves various kinds of buildup behind.

The tangible world, the work of human beings, buildings, bridges, roads, objects, is, *in short*, nothing but frozen money, hence the lag in those theories in which money only functions as the medium for exchanges. From this point of view . . . it is but the "great wheel of circulation," as Adam Smith thought, or, following Marx, a great exchanger, a universal equivalent. This perspective on money misses the essential point, though it is very close: money does not adapt to a preexisting reality to which it brings new vitality, in the manner of blood or water; money makes reality possible. Money is an agent. It engenders. It is potential. A force ready to come to fruition. It is virtual reality. . . . Pure credit is something strange. It is money without money, the way we speak of soilless agriculture, agriculture without soil. Coming from nothing, it demands a projection, it is pro-ject, advance. It is the advance and project of society as a whole, which is thus inclined toward this future to come [*a-venir*] which recedes just as we believe we are getting closer to it.[26]

These lines were written in 1993, but the developments of the last few years have only accentuated the phenomenon, leading up to the financial crisis of 2008, which displayed this ungrounded aspect of cash flow for all to see. In the meantime, the investment of "venture capital" in start-ups whose output is far from guaranteed or even predictable, the kind of investment that is at the root of various "bubbles," is a perfect illustration of this precedence of money over the reality it produces.

Nevertheless, this development has not loosened the connection between money and language. *Quite the opposite*, because flows of dematerialized money are nothing but flows of information, just like the billions of bits exchanged every moment in networks for transmitting messages of all kinds. But it is characteristic of this information to be neutral with respect to the meaning or absence of meaning it can transport. As we have known since Shannon,[27] the quantity of information transmitted through communication media and measured in bits is the same for an equal number of letters, whether these letters express a Mallarmé poem, a mathematical theorem or a page from the phone book. The network does not concern itself with the content of the messages that are exchanged within it. But at the same time, such a network can have self-organizing properties, because with information, as with money, *it is not just a matter of trading or exchanging, it is also about creating something new* because of the dynamic of the flow itself. And this is only possible if these flows are without prior meaning, without a referent, unless it is a meaning or a referent that they acquire after the fact by means of the effects of these creations, which are as unforeseeable as they are truly new. Put differently, a non-planned capitalist economy shows some of the properties of natural self-organizing systems,[28] which create newness because of their exposure to the vagaries of existence, which are sometimes destructive but sometimes produce new adaptations. As in a biological structure, new meanings—that is to say, new functions—will appear after the fact to the observer who studies it carefully, provided the system has adapted, that is to say, provided that the crisis has not been fatal to it.

Earlier, we saw how in the sixteenth century it was possible to affirm, following Aristotle, that "the voice is the material of meaning as silver is the material of the coin or the vessel."[29] This clearly implied that coins and vessels were bearers of an a priori meaning, an established value, like the articulated speech of which the voice is the material. But what is transmitted in networks today is neutral information, without meaning because it serves as the basis for all meanings, linguistic and monetary, which may not even appear until after the fact. As for the matter or material on which the information is based, it is doubly neutral in that the matter could be anything—electronic, light, sound, paper, a screen—which is a characteristic of what André Gorz has called an economy of the immaterial.[30]

In a prescient study, Gorz shows the ambivalent character of this dematerialization of the economy. The transition from a post-industrial society to a "knowledge society" or "intelligence society," in what Jacques Robin has called the "information age,"[31] may be the occasion for an uncoupling of market value and wealth, of market value and the intrinsic value of beings and things. The ambivalence arises because this transition cannot take place other than in and by means of capitalism, and yet this capitalism, transforming itself into "cognitive capitalism," not only is a capitalism in crisis but also represents the crisis of capitalism itself. This accounts for the ambivalence of the transition, which is both a source of profound imbalance and crisis and also a new chance for the humanization of societies and for the personal flourishing of an increasing number of people. One condition for the seizing of this chance is the acceptance of the self-organizing nature of these processes: the goal is itself part of the process and cannot be split off from it by being posited in advance by a planned economy or liberal ideology. But of course this is no guarantee of what the end product will be because, essentially, no one can predict what the human content of the process will be made up of.

We can now immediately see what the constant and increasing threat is in this desacralization and the ensuing dematerialization: inflation, monetary inflation but also the inflation of spoken and written words. There is a new aspect, though, the effect of an even more radical second-degree dematerialization, if we may call it that, that the 2008 crisis has caused to appear: the inflation of credit without monetary inflation proper, but with the creation of "bubbles" that are blown up by the wind of loans increasingly disconnected from "real," material, and energy-based goods and that are, for that reason, destined to burst. Taking up Rachline's river metaphor, we may say that such a "bubble" and its bursting correspond (as in the current crisis) to a speeding up of circulation, which, like a torrent, carries all the "deposits," that is to say the wealth and the previously produced goods, with it as it rushes past. At the same time, new possibilities are created, emerging in seemingly spontaneous fashion from financial markets and media exchanges: possibilities of profits for some and losses for others, at the borderline of theft, fraud, and lies, along with new kinds of bluffing and propaganda. Hence the necessity of establishing new boundaries and defining new offenses, such as money laundering, tax evasion, financial crimes, "insider trades" (an information crime!), etc., after the fact, in a kind of high-speed chase in pursuit of the inventive power of the people involved in trades and exchanges. Monetary inflation means that money loses its value. Credit inflation means that money is no longer available. And the inflation of discourse means that words lose their truth-value, diluted in a mass of less and less meaningful information. It is instructive to recall how the perpetrator of a gigantic years-long fraud recently described his activities, a credit scam that took money from new investors to pay fantastic interest rates to old investors in a cavalcade that could only work if it never stopped. He admitted to his collaborators and friends, whose apparently unlimited trust he had abused, that his financial fraud was, as he described it, "a big lie." And yet all he had done was to imitate normal banking activity, albeit crossing a threshold: he had not only usurped the function of a bank but had overstepped the bounds while doing it. A *big* enormous financial fraud, a *big* lie in written and spoken words of trust: that was the crime of which he was guilty.

For the normal situation of the market economy implies quasi-frauds, quasi-lies that almost inevitably accompany the vital and accelerated circulation of moneys and words that must not stop under penalty of the death of the system. This is the world of *ona'ah*, the almost-theft, almost-lie, almost-oppression that accompany the social bond as soon as it ceases to have the purity of the static, almost-fused solidarity that is guaranteed by the god's presence, in which every word is *given* and makes absolute claims on the future and in which loaning without interest is an obligation even if repayment is uncertain. In the reality of postbiblical existence, once the loan at interest has been instituted, a threshold is established with which to distinguish between the charging of legitimate interest, legitimate because recognized as inevitable, and usury, which is always condemned, and of which it can be said that it, too, crosses a line, but, in this case, for the lender. The threshold is established by more or less arbitrary convention, as a function of the interest commonly agreed on on the money market.

Similarly, the Bible's prohibition of any fraud in a transaction involving buying or selling an object is absolute, whereas the Talmud institutes the one-sixth rule, one-sixth being the threshold below which the divergence of a price from the market price is "forgiven": a fraud that is less than one-sixth of the market price is no longer a fraud! The world of *ona'ah* thus instituted acknowledges the necessity of tolerating almost-fraud, almost-deceptive labeling of goods, and the task obviously becomes to establish limits on this in order for it not to devolve into counterfeit money and robbery.

Without limits?

But such limits are harder and harder to establish. Or rather, they must be newly reimagined and reimposed each time as the dematerialization of money progresses. The limits that need to be imposed increasingly resemble the relative limits that must be placed on practices of lying even though it is acknowledged that sometimes lies are inevitable. This, too, is an aspect of things through which we can see money converging with language in ways that are less and less metaphorical. Increasingly, the differences that seemed obvious dissolve into their common function as exchanges of information and symbolic expressions, although we know less and less what it is that the symbols are symbols of. Rachline explains how, once finite quantities of precious materials (gold, silver, and others) no longer serve to guarantee the value of money, nothing a priori opposes an infinite creation of money by virtue of its circulation alone.[32] The natural limit imposed by the finitude of material wealth is thus replaced by a conventional, socially constructed limitation. Immaterial money joins language, with its infinite capacity for the indefinitely renewed creation of words. Here, too, the function as an exchange and as a social bond can be preserved only if the social bond is already established based on some minimum amount of trust, itself resting on a minimum of lies—in the form of the ambiguities and vagueness of natural languages, more or less voluntary misunderstandings, and other lies by omission—all with the knowledge that this minimum cannot be zero if these exchanges are not to come to an end.

The deregulations that are accompanied by financial crises show how fragile this equilibrium is, because it is based on a circle that can easily become vicious. As we have seen in the recent crisis, the very same credit that is indispensable to circulation can in fact turn out to be excessive, exaggerated in relation to the necessarily limited possibilities for creating money if confidence is to be maintained. For credit is based on precisely such confidence in a sort of stable truth of prices and of the market. But this truth is necessarily relative since money is no longer an absolute value . . . by virtue of the very fact of credit and of its interests, which tend to over- or undervalue it. An encyclopedia article on the role of credit in the modern economy[33] does a good job of showing how the distinction between credit and money is obscured once the instruments of credit become substitutes for means of payment, that is to say, for money. The circle is described perfectly: "Debts cannot be defined in terms of money because money must be defined in terms of debts."[34] An imbalance is always possible when the volume of credit goes beyond certain limits, at the same time as those limits are all the more difficult to ascertain because they rest on this confidence in the debts' being paid. Specialists—economists, bankers, government leaders—are constantly inventing new means of regulation meant to keep the "system" functioning, while at the same time that "system," like the system of information exchange on the Internet, is increasingly anonymous, with no meaning other than the profits and losses—in money and in knowledge—of one group or another.

Under these conditions, we see a multiplication of new forms not only of more or less fraudulent cheating but also of mental pathologies: the system itself is denounced as "insane" when it enters a crisis, while individuals develop pathological dependencies, veritable addictions to symbolic and ephemeral exchanges, to words or stock market "values."

It is as though the desacralization of money and speech were unleashing the vengeance of a god—the god that used to guarantee the value of a social bond that was able to maintain a balance between the innermost self, where individual joy and pain is experienced, and the objectivity of collective social structures.

It is thus easy to understand the increasingly apparent need of groups and communities that are still marginal to leave the circle by imagining parallel economies and currencies, along with exchanges that have regained the personal touch, far removed from the anonymity of the global "system."[35] And yet among these groups, we must particularly emphasize the establishment of microcredit, which earned the Bangladeshi economist Muhammad Yunus a Nobel prize. Microcredit was able to reconnect, in a way that had seemed unattainable until then, with the loan of solidarity of ancient societies, directly rooted in the "soil" of a particular and personalized productive activity.

The sacred

It is important to make ourselves aware of the stakes involved in these attempts by reflecting on the role played by the presence of the sacred in money and speech in the ancient world from which we come. It is important not so that we can return to such a world, even if that were possible and desirable (for that world was also not devoid of various individual and collective alienations and pathologies, accompanied by the extreme violence from which modernity has increasingly tended to liberate us), but in order, instead, for us to try to recreate, in this new world of science and technology, the reality of that inner life that the ancients imagined to be the condition of individual salvation (that is to say, of happiness) in their world of gods and prophets. For what is at stake here is a kind of connection that always needs to be rebuilt, a connection between the inner and the outer, between individual, society, and the world, between the private sphere and the public sphere, between the subjectivity of the innermost self and objective, or at least intersubjective, external reality.

Now, since the beginning of time, the intimacy of inner life and the public good that both unites and divides individuals have established close ties with the sacred, ties by means of which the social bond of human communities has differentiated itself from that of animal societies.

Let us recall, first of all, that experiences of the sacred do not come from the God of the theologians but that, on the contrary, all kinds of representations of such experiences have become representations of the divine. At the dawn of humanity, these experiences were induced or at least aided by the use of hallucinogenic plants, which was quickly defined and ritualized, identified as an opening to "another reality" constituted by dreams, the erotic, and death. Monotheism was an attempt to unify these representations, after the fact, in something beyond representation, since the experience of the sacred is at the same time the experience of a majesty, of a possible confinement, of a crushing and an alienation and thus the experience of an invitation to knock down its limits, to a smashing of the idols that is all the more necessary for their being real gods. The great institutionalized religions have repressed the memory and the practice of these experiences in mythical stories like that of the tree of knowledge or that of the effects of *soma* in the Rigveda. But even a Church Father like Tertullian, in the second century, derives the experience of God from the experience of dreams.[36] And the cultures of ancient peoples in the Americas, Asia, and Africa continue to make use of these plants, directly or via shamans who specialize in the art of interpretation, as a door that opens to "the other reality," the world of gods or spirits, the world of the Dream, of the "dreaming" or "dreamtime" of Australia's Aborigines. Elsewhere, I have analyzed the role these experiences played in the origins of religions and of the systems of norms that arose from them and, ultimately, of ethics. One of their effects was to allow for the internalization of the social norm, ritualized at first, in that the sacredness of the ritual made it possible to live out, at the same time, both an external social obligation and an opening onto another world in the most intimate innermost self that is unveiled in these experiences.[37]

Now, language is both internal, an expression of thoughts and affects, and external, a place of exchanges, a set of signs exchanged about a common reality. As for money, which in its function as exchange is also external, it ultimately finds its value in the most intimate and most profound of affects, in *desire*, which is expressed in these exchanges.[38] And the experience of the sacred that accompanies modified states of consciousness, possibly provoked by substances some have called "theophoric" or "entheogenic,"[39] the experience to which the mystics who may or may not have been aided by such substances also testify, allows for the internalization of the collective norm at least as much as does the Reason of the philosophers, often even in association with that Reason. For by itself, each individual's experience of his or her own existence in his or her habitual consciousness of everyday life would not immediately seem to dispose that person to a spontaneous acceptance of the law of the group. Sociobiology has proposed theories for the biological rootedness of the forms of "spontaneous" altruism observed in animal societies. But the transposition of these theories to human societies is far from convincing, among other reasons because of the human capacity for memory and imagination: these are expressed in languages in which the negation of what is, in favor of something imaginary that must be, plays a decisive role. As for functionalist psychosocial theories, we will see that in spite of their undeniable explanatory value they are inadequate, like all functional explanations, in that they explain phenomena by their effects rather than by their causes.[40]

The experience of the sacred, on the other hand, an internal experience but also an external one in that it seems to impose itself from some other place, the shamans' "other reality" or the theologians' "transcendence," allows the individual to truly internalize the laws of the group. To be sure, those who hold power—sorcerer-chiefs, priests and sovereigns, kings by "divine right" and today's representatives, more or less recognized as they are by the "sovereign people"—can always abuse this internalizing function to the advantage of their own power. They have not refrained from doing so, and this is why modern democracies, which guard against such abuses by separating the churches from the state, by separating powers within the state and by limiting their terms, constitute the least bad of political regimes or, to quote a famous phrase, "the worst form of government except all the others that have been tried."[41]

The "Thucydidean moment" of verbal fraud

But political power has always had more than just the privilege of minting money. It also has the privilege of imposing the meaning of words, in an authoritarian way or insidiously. The language it uses, its political and legal language, is the product of a politics of language. And this obviously creates a somewhat loose relationship between public speech and the supposed truth it affirms. This double privilege belongs not only to princes or tyrants but also to the people's representatives in a democracy. But as we will see in chapter 8, there is nonetheless a difference between these different political regimes according to the degree of lying: a difference between total lies and half-truths. Throughout the centuries and in many different contexts, the ambiguity of the relations between power and language has been the subject of a large number of studies. In a 1992 book, Thomas Gustafson presents his work, which is interesting in several respects, on the relations between politics, literature, and language in the United States in the critical years of its history, between 1776 and 1865.[42] He presents his work as fitting into the tradition of a long series of analyses of political language and the politics of language, from Aristotle's and above all Plato's reflections on the rhetoric of the Sophists to contemporary philosophers like Marcuse, Foucault, and Derrida, by way of Montaigne, Hobbes, and Locke, among others, and above all, numerous American authors—politicians, writers, philosophers, and linguists—between 1776 and 1865. These American authors illustrate the ambiguity of the public discourse, which both represents and distorts reality at the same time: *representations-misrepresentations* of the American project—the American "dream." The American democratic revolution was somehow expected to imply a reform of the English language, or at least a reform of its usage, seeking truthful eloquence instead of tortuous rhetoric. But the authors of all sorts who called for such reform, including political leaders like John Adams, were aware of the difficulties associated with it. They saw—and some of them denounced—the tension in political discourse between the founding texts of a new, quasi-messianic social order (the Declaration of Independence, the Constitution) and the rhetoric of violence that transformed and adapted the meaning of words (for example, Native Americans being massacred under the name of "Indians," or slaves, euphemistically named "Persons . . . bound to Service" in the Constitution), culminating in the explosion of the Civil War, both bloody and verbal, that almost swept everything away. But Gustafson emphasizes the fact that many of these authors and their predecessors referred to Thucydides's description, in his *History of the Peloponnesian War*, of the civil war on Corfu, where Athenian and Spartan partisans tore at each other. It is in Hobbes's translation of Thucydides that these writers find a paradigm for the description of the systemic *verbal fraud*, coarse or subtle[43]—in which words, for better or for worse, mean the opposite of what the actions are that they name—that accompanies chaos and social violence, both as cause and as effect. When selfishness, ambition, and special interests win out over a concern with truth and the public good, the corruption of people and language, unrest and political and linguistic violence take hold, inseparably linked together. This is why Gustafson calls this toppling into the perversion of political language and power the "Thucydidean moment"; I for my part will later call this the "worm in the apple" of democracy.[44] But this long series of texts could not itself have been published—and still could not be today—if it were not for the protection of democratic liberties. Thus, in whatever way it might be, these liberties allow for movement and change as opposed to the immobility of dictatorships, a seeming immobility that lasts until the final collapse, unfortunately after much time and suffering. The words of public language that analyze the perversions of public language—words such as *pharmakon*,[45] meaning both poison and remedy—necessarily make things happen and can prevent verbal fraud and corruption from crossing all boundaries of what is tolerable. In fact, the reference to movement brought up by the "Thucydidean moment" in Gustafson and some of the authors he mentions goes along with a reference to an inverse movement, a saving of humanity through the power of words, whose archetype is the myth of Orpheus. It is as though the corrupting power of words were being denounced against the background of a nostalgia for a golden age of divine origin, created by Orpheus with the sound of his lyre and the words of his song, at one and the same time poetry, law, and initiation into the secrets of the gods. It is to Orpheus that the myth attributes the movement out of primitive chaos into civilization, the movement that the "Thucydidean moment" reverses:

Orpheus, the archetypal poet and legislator, was divinized by the ancients of Greece and Rome, and the myth of Orpheus preserves a story of transformation by "forms" that suggests the incomparable value attributed to speech in classical culture. In the beginning there was wildness. But Orpheus, with his lyre, charms the denizens of the woods, or rude and savage men, to a gentler way of life, calling them together in one place, teaching them to build cities, to keep laws, and to embrace virtue. This transformation from chaos to civility is a moment when language and law, poetry and politics combine to create and celebrate the founding of the *polis*.[46]

It is as though the demands of virtue and truth in public life could not but feed on the nostalgia of a mythic discourse of absolute Truth, a kind of revealed speech in the sacred precinct of enlightened political sovereignty, revealed in the announcements and curses of the oracle and the miracle-working philosopher prophet.

Although monarchy by divine right has been replaced with democracy, democracy still seems unable to prevent its practice from generating a sort of nostalgia for the sacred: ideologies and political programs, rather than simply resigning themselves to organizing the management of public exchanges, also claim to "change life," to convince individuals of the "charisma" of leaders who provide not only the institution of a collective existence but also the attainment of individual salvation by means of the participation of each and every person in the secularized ritual of political life. The true separation of the churches—including secular churches—from the state will not be accomplished until leaders, and the intellectuals who support or criticize them, renounce the practice of making voters and, especially, their own campaigners believe that politics is a means of individual salvation, that is, of guaranteed happiness. In the meantime, this nostalgia weakens democracies by increasing the risk that they will turn into ideological totalitarianisms, be they secular or religious.

For the desacralization of money has not detached money from the private sphere and from inner life. It has just made it into an aspect of the private that is reduced to *naked desire*, with no other meaning than that of profit for profit's sake, gain for the sake of gain, as in a casino game. It is this desire that objectively fuels what we call consumer society, where, under the influence of the words of advertising, false or not, in the service of the circulation of money that keeps the "system" going, it is channeled toward objects that are less and less necessary but more and more sought after. Democracy makes consumer society and the economic liberalism that comes with it possible; that is why the critics of unrestrained consumption weaken democracy by reinforcing the nostalgia for a more-or-less-enforced virtue and frugality—unless a "pure" solidarity system of gifts or of interest-free loans limits the wildest desires of the largest number by way of a bad conscience. For a certain form of shame can be useful in the face of the countless numbers who are left behind or unaccounted for, excluded, left by the wayside on the road to development, and in the face of societies that are (still?) underdeveloped. This is how democracy can coexist, in an unstable balance, with a somewhat equitable redistribution of the wealth that the circulation of money—that is to say, of debts and of profits—helps, unequally, to create.

Under different skies

This kind of evolution has not been confined to the history of the West. The example of Japan is particularly interesting. In the seventeenth century, Japan's transition from a pre-monetary economy to a modern economy was accompanied by unexpected consequences for medical practices and for representations of the body. In Japan's Edo period, from the seventeenth to the nineteenth centuries, the birth of an economic society founded on the circulation of wealth and money represented a break with nostalgia for the "purity" of the previous, pre-monetary period, a nostalgia that was nurtured by Chinese Confucian influences, among others. In a remarkable study on "The Life of Money and the Afflictions of the Body,"[47] Shigehisa Kuriyama shows how the emergence of this kind of fluid economy of debts and investments was accompanied by new representations of the body and new medical practices. Here, money no longer seems to share a semantic field with language but shares one with the body instead. The life of the body, like the life of money, can only be maintained through its circulation. A new medicine developed from this model, with new diagnostic practices, in which the search for "stagnation" of the vital flow in the form of "knots" that could be discovered thanks to palpation of the abdomen superimposed itself on Chinese medicine's interpretation of different kinds of pulses.

But here, too, we find a modification of the intimate experience of the innermost self that accompanies the relative desacralization of heaven's static majesty and its irrevocable harmony. The accumulated gold of the palaces represented heaven's sovereignty, and the body was represented in Chinese medicine as a microcosm on the model of that macrocosm. The interactions between organs and the circulation of "energies" between acupuncture points were the reproduction on earth of the relations between the different hierarchical degrees of sovereignty and the cyclical revolutions of the heavenly bodies. In the Edo period, all of this was replaced by the vital circulation of wealth, constantly being displaced by the projection of debts and claims into the future. Nor is the soul, if we may say so, absent from these representations. Indeed, if we transpose Western categories here, we may qualify this cultural and linguistic context as a monism of body and mind. The exploration of the body is above all an exploration of the *hara*, the chest and the abdomen. And the new palpation of the abdomen (*fuku*) imagined by Edo physicians was also called "probing the *hara*," but with the connotation of

"feeling out" . . . private thoughts and aspirations, tactful inquiry into what people, whatever their public pronouncements, tacitly believe or desire. It spoke of fathoming a person's hidden depths. In other words: the *hara* was the object of figurative as well as literal probing, of allusive verbal querying, as well as direct manual kneading.[48]

And this is how Shigehisa Kuriyama explains the development of the palpation of the abdomen (*fukushin*) in the Edo period, which was also the period during which Japan entered into a monetary economy:

[T]he appeal of a technique like *fukushin* is easy to understand: for centuries, the term *hara* named the spiritual bosom as well as the physical chest and abdomen, encompassed both the center of the body and the core of the person. It straddled palpable flesh and invisible thought.[49]

In other words, the medical probing of vital flows was also the probing of desires buried in the depths of the person. And in this way, in Edo-period Japan, there was also an intensification of a desire for wealth, to be spent ostentatiously, which emptied the coffers and threatened the stability of the previous social order. The leaders of the time attempted to limit this desire in authoritarian fashion, but in vain; they had not understood that such regulations could only serve to impoverish their society because it is precisely this desire, this "passion to consume, which drives the circulation of currency, and inspires the industry of merchants and craftsmen."[50]

A guilty conscience and shame

The relationships of money and language with the sacred and with the private sphere become even more obvious when their opposites—deceit, lying—invade them and produce all kinds of breaches of the social bond. What is thereby distorted is not only the propriety and accuracy of exchanges of goods and words but also the way in which these exchanges are specifically human, which affects both the public and the private.

The experience of the sacred fills desire. Without pushing it out of the sphere of the private, it projects desire toward an outside, an internalized public, or even cosmic, good, the order of Nature as with the Stoics or the Word of God of monotheistic mystics or the Word of the Spirits of the shamans and other inhabitants of dreamtime. We see now why the breaking of the social bond does not concern public exchanges alone. It is also an intimate matter, a cheating on desire, a breach of the innermost self, a profound injury, a violation of consciences and affects, an attack on human dignity with all the shame and humiliation that accompany it and which also distinguish the human from the nonhuman.

The semantic loops are closed again when we realize that financial debt, which ensures the "life" of money by making it circulate and by projecting it into the future, has "to be due" as its verbal form.[51] The debtor's duty, at once financial, moral, and legal, is due, just as redress or damages are due from anyone who is at fault. Paradoxically, being too much in debt, especially out of an excessive desire for superfluous luxury, can be as "shameful" as granting excessive credit, speculating on the desires and needs of others. It is as though, just like the circulation of blood in the body, the circulation of money, albeit vital, at the same time created waste in the form of accumulated and indecently ostentatious wealth, which could become a source of shame and a guilty conscience, as if wealth itself constituted a duty—a debt—toward those who possess no wealth and are therefore dispossessed. Hence the identification, in certain popular languages, of accumulated riches with excrement, as Kuriyama reminds us.[52] Olender describes another possible connection of misappropriated money to abusive breaches of the intimate and to shame, in the context of feudal Europe. A feudal prince certainly had the right to coin money, guaranteed by his semidivine seal, but in no instance could that privilege be extended to changing the value of the coinage at his convenience. That would have been considered as indecent an intrusion into the private lives of his subjects as if he had raped their wives.[53]

But we can see how not all injuries are equivalent. Where are we to draw the line between what is decent and what is not? Between excessive, perhaps "shameful," desire and legitimate desire (legitimate in the same way that, in the life of the body, as a metaphor of the circulation of money, some waste is inevitable)? The absolute "purity" of the exchanges of premonetary economies is no longer possible. Yet there must be permissible limits to "impurity," to the quantity of waste. Put differently, a new realm has been created in which verbal deceptions and injuries are inevitable byproducts, collateral damage that is apparently indispensable to the economy of social relations. It is as though a large chunk of the inner life and of the world of its meanings had had to be sacrificed, for the common good, on the altar of economic circulation. It is this realm of admisssible limits to the inevitable divergence from fair prices and from the purity of true and beneficial words that constitutes the world of talmudic *ona'ah*. Let us recall that the biblical prohibition on deceiving one's neighbor in buying or selling, like the prohibition on loaning at interest, was absolute, without any room for tolerance, in the prophetic world of a "pure" economy. It is the Talmud, in its post-prophetic world and even before instituting and providing a framework for loans at interest, that institutes a maximum permissible threshold for commercial fraud proper: as we will see in more detail, false advertising or the deceptive labeling of goods (*ona'ah*) only begins with a difference from the market price of at least one-sixth of that price.

In his commentary on Olender's text, Jean Starobinski rightly remarks that monetary metaphors must not be pushed too far.[54] For cold, hard cash remains quite different from spoken words when these are not covered by writings, signatures, or other signs of guarantee. But this difference between language and money, already mitigated by the dematerialization of money, disappears a little more in their respective negations. Counterfeit money (or the money of a perverted market) and lying (and humiliating) speech come together in the deception and the injuries and damage that they produce, even if monetary fraud is more easily *measurable* than verbal injuries.

4

Technical Objects

Objects of exchange, objects of desire

While the fact that money had been set in motion and that credit had been progressively dematerialized was creating new needs and stimulating desire, which, in turn, amplified and accelerated the process, objects of desire were multiplying thanks to more and more sophisticated production techniques. Technology allowed the third element of the exchange, alongside words and money—namely the exchanged object itself—to undergo an accelerated evolution as well. For before money and probably, from what we can tell from animal behavior, before speech, what was exchanged were objects; certainly not technically processed objects but objects taken from nature and desired for their immediate or deferred consumption value. But here, too, these exchanges created a social bond among individuals, a social bond superimposed on their direct bond with nonhuman nature, which in turn had an effect on desire itself. Desire was no longer limited to physiological needs but transformed by the nature of social relations into mimetic desire in particular, as René Girard has described it, with all its avatars, violence, and conjuring of violence by means of sacrificial rites that are themselves violent to a greater or lesser degree.

This is why exchanged objects have always been invested with various symbolic values of consumption insofar as they are the concrete and visible bearers of the reality of human relations that constitute social organization, as are words and, later, money.

In a parallel development, Homo sapiens also became Homo faber and objects became technical, thereby multiplying the possibilities of exchange. In this way, the technical, in association with words and economic exchange, has become the distinctive trait of the human in social structures.

But it has not, for all that, left nature behind. On the contrary, this is precisely what makes the technical a natural activity of the human species, as are, by the way, all its cultural activities. It is worthwhile to avoid reducing our philosophical reflection on the technical to Heidegger's analyses and to counter those analyses with, in particular, Gilbert Simondon's evolutionary conception.[1] For Simondon, the technical is a process of individuation of objects that are not reduced to their utilitarian functions, a process that follows the individuation of the living and the articulation of individuals with their environment. In this context it is not surprising that technical objects accompanied the evolutions of language and of money in their connections with the sacred, which is itself always in one way or another constitutive of the social imaginary. There have always been close connections between machines and writing. Thus, it is the symbolic investments of technical objects, whether by their inventors and producers or by those who consume and use them, that, in a way, make them "talk." And what these technical objects "say" is saturated with errors, illusions, and lies at least as much as with truths, just like what words themselves say. These objects, too, are taken up in the circle of value because their effects, like those of money and words, can be just as harmful as they are beneficial.

Contrary to what is often said, technical activity is not a direct application of a scientific knowledge whose truth has been established once and for all on the basis of the logical empirical method that would serve as its guarantee. In fact, the technical and theory remained separate for a very long time. Technology, as the putting of scientific knowledge into practice, is a relatively recent phenomenon. We see some expression of this in the proto-science of the Renaissance, in the "natural magic" of the alchemists, astrologists, hermeticists, and cabalists, but the developments of this phenomenon really begin with the scientific, mechanical, and geometric revolution of the seventeenth century. Before then, as in ancient Greece, *theoria* was closer to contemplation while the technical was the work of artisans, carpenters, smiths, and surveyors. Their art, made up of manual dexterity and empirical prescriptions, was an art of cunning reason, the Greeks' *metis*, the Hebrews' serpentine "wisdom of the left side," rather than "right" reason, which descended directly from the world of ideas.² Their murky origins, both sacred and transgressive, were expressed in myths, like the myth of Prometheus stealing the fire; the myth of the biblical Tree of Knowledge, whose fruit was eaten by Adam and Eve under the influence of the snake, "the most cunning of animals"³; or the myth of the father of the smiths in the Bible, who invents both the plow and the sword: as a descendant of Cain, who was the first murderer and the son of Adam, Eve, and the snake, he transmits to humanity the ambivalence of this knowledge. The Heideggerian idea of the human being as a "being-toward-death," "en-framed" by the technical, might be a Christian avatar of this biblical vision in which, following the legend of Genesis, death is instituted as a punishment, a consequence of the Fall, which the Augustinian Christian interpretation of original sin holds to be irremediable in this world. Other readings of the legend of Genesis, on the other hand, see in these biblical texts an announcement of possibilities of overcoming death and of constructing a human "being-toward-life" to the extent that the Tree of Knowledge is also a path toward the Tree of Life. But the transition cannot take place automatically, denying or forgetting the deviousness, devilments, lies, and illusions of cunning reason as it deals with the ambivalences and resistances of nature.

Be that as it may, while Renaissance physicians, alchemists, astrologers, and cabalists like Paracelsus and Giordano Bruno began to "scientize" technologies on the basis of their theoretical knowledge, they still struggled to defend themselves against accusations of sorcery. For there was still a strong tendency to believe that extraordinary-seeming technical feats to which ordinary people were not yet accustomed must have a demonic origin. The legend of Faust is an echo of this. When, with Kepler's laws, the new Copernican science of the stars became mathematical, the projection of the surveyor's geometrical calculation techniques onto the movements of heavenly bodies was itself resisted as a demonic science, in opposition to a "pure" science that has an obligation to remain "qualitative."⁴

Contrary to what one might think, none of this has disappeared with the advent of modern science. The fascinated reaction of the public but also of politicians and even scientists to the extraordinary advances made by molecular genetics and biotechnologies since the nineteen sixties reproduces this mixture of seeing what seems to be a kind of magic, all the more fearsome for working so well, as both divine and diabolical.

Here, too, technical feats precede theory. This was already the case for the beginnings of physics and chemistry. Explanatory theories, sometimes approximate and later revised, followed technical achievements that had established themselves thanks to their efficacy and their usefulness as tools. Pulleys and levers long preceded the laws of mechanics. Metalworking long preceded the development of theoretical chemistry. True, certain theoretical developments in turn suggested technical applications whose efficacy then served as a "validation," if not a "proof," of the truth of the theory in question, even if, later, other empirical observations nonetheless "falsified" the theory. The history of the sciences and of the technical is not linear and the notions of validation, proof, and falsification do not always have the same meaning. It is a fact that the use of nuclear energy encompasses a set of technical applications that would never have existed without the theoretical physics that predicted their reality. The same is true for the applications of the laser, and other examples could be cited as well. Yet the fact remains that, for the moment, the state of the field of biology is characterized by a considerable lead by the technical feats of molecular and cellular biology over the explanatory power of theory.

All this shows that the Heideggerian project of discovering an "essence of technology" is completely illusory. The relationship of the concrete human being to the technical is precisely not on the order of essence but on the order of the contingencies of the human being's connections to the world of nature and of other human beings. The famous "en-framing" [*Ge-stell*][5] of nature by the human technician who is in turn en-framed without being aware of what determines him is in fact a reality, but it is a contingent social reality rather than the result of an essential connection to Being and to a dereliction of modern humankind. When the technical was put to use, by some people, to the detriment of others, in order to subject human beings to machines, it was possible to accuse the technical, in the industrial age, of expressing an intrinsically dehumanizing "essence." It is then easy to contrast technology, or the technical, as an "en-framing" of nature, as Heidegger does in the case of a power station that denatures the Rhine, with a proto-technology that is still natural (?), expressed in a wooden bridge over the very same Rhine. But can we really consider there to be *one* essence of the technical, that is contrasted, among other things, with the essence of Art, in the same way that the "Rhine" imprisoned in the power station is contrasted with the "Rhine" that is celebrated by

Hölderlin?[6] That would be the emblematic image of this essence as a "provocative unconcealment" of what nature has hidden, and in particular of nature's energy that is put in the service of humanity and thus "en-framed," just as the river in the power station is imprisoned in its function of making the turbines turn, thus "brought to reason," summoned, as Bacon announced at the dawn of the mechanical revolution, to "account for itself" with the rest of nature in order better to be dominated and mastered. In that case there would be an essence of the technical, ultimately independent of the real human beings who produce objects and machines because these would also be en-framed by the technical that subjects them.

But this requires us to neglect the diversity of technical objects themselves, of their modes of production, of their purposes, of their intrinsic value as works of art, and above all of the places they occupy in the exchanges between human beings, inextricably linked with language and money.

Heidegger does, admittedly, contrast the artisanal object, which has a certain degree of independence, with the machine, which is entirely engaged, en-framed and en-framing, and in which this all-powerful "essence" is expressed the most. But now we have the case that the new machines of the post-industrial information age are in turn bearers of new dangers precisely because of their supposed "independence." Information-processing machines, more and more intelligent and less and less "robotic," are said to threaten to elude their designers' control. Just as the mechanization of the industrial age resulted in the subjection of human beings, exploited by other human beings, to machines, so too do the new technologies, so-called "artificial intelligence" and "artificial life," threaten to elude the control of most of humanity to the benefit of a few. But to see in this the various manifestations of an ultimately ahistorical essence of the technical is to cheapen other kinds of subjection of human beings by other human beings, like slavery and bondage, that preceded the power station and were contemporaneous with the wooden bridge.

This contrast between old artisanal techniques and modern technosciences is found again today in the contrast between the products of traditional agriculture and animal husbandry on the one hand and un-"natural" genetically modified organisms on the other, as if the former were not themselves the effects of the technical imposed by the human race on the rest of nature and on other species in nature.

If there is an essence, it would instead be the essence of the species whose survival was immediately conditioned by its abilities to manage its environment by producing artificial habitats and tools, that is to say, products of art which are at the same time obviously "natural" as well, in the sense of being adapted to the constraints of nature, like an airplane is artificial while at the same time it is adapted to the laws of gravity. This naturalness of human artifacts is at the same time a humanization of nature; and even more so when this humanization is a product of the sciences, where *theoria*, the contemplation of ideas, expresses capacities of thinking that are in fact characteristic of the human species.

The fact that these are the ideas of mechanisms governing not only the movements of bodies, including the heavenly bodies, and the chemical transformations of bodies into other bodies, but also the functioning of living beings, including human beings, thus conceived of as complex natural machines, does not necessarily imply an "en-framing" of nature and the human being by the technical. That would be as if the discovery of mechanisms, which is after all indispensable to the intelligibility of reality, implied in itself a dehumanization of individuals that turned them into robots and transformed them into technical objects. This is a conception unexpectedly inherited from post-Kantian idealism and vitalism, in which the intelligibility of the living, extended to the human being, necessarily implies the "unconcealment" of the human being as "being-toward-death."

But perhaps this is an echo, more or less secularized, of the biblical curse. Let us recall that the Bible punished man and woman for having ingested the fruit of the Tree of Knowledge by, precisely, committing them to death and, at the same time, to the necessity of arduous labor to ensure their survival and to the pain of childbearing. Without a doubt, the age-old necessity for Homo sapiens to make use of its brain's cognitive and technical capacities to survive is obviously echoed in the myth, which sees in that necessity the effect of a curse and a fall in contrast to the ideal of an Eden dedicated to Life, around the tree also named Tree of Life, without pain or suffering. But not all the interpretive traditions of this biblical myth are the same. Some, especially those inspired by Augustine, see in the divine curse an irreversible state that only God could lift, in a *parousia* not of this world. Others, inspired among other things by the cabalistic notion of *tikkun*, "redress," see in it instead a vocation of the human race to attain wisdom and knowledge in order to transform the world by "redressing" it on the existential as well as the moral level.

Be that as it may, it is better, rather than searching for an eternal essence of the technical, to try to distinguish among the different forms that the relations of subjection or liberation among human beings may take, with their labor and their art, and with their tools and other technical objects, which are at the same time the products and the means of this art and this labor.

This is what Gilbert Simondon attempts with his *genealogy* of the technical. To do this, he begins with an analysis of the genesis of technicality and technical thinking as a relationship of the human being to the world. Starting from the primitive unity of magical thinking, a fusional union of the human being and the world, of subject and object, the technical and religion then began to separate. This original unity had to split into technical thinking and religious thinking in order for the magical mediation between human being and world to "objectify itself in the technical and subjectify itself in religion, bringing about, in the technical object, the first object and, in divinity, the first subject, whereas before there had only been a unity of life and its environment."[7] But the technical and religion do not between them exhaust the objectivity of the world and the subjectivity of the human being "because they are between the human being and the world but do not contain all of the reality of the human being and of the world and cannot completely apply to this reality. Governed by the divergence that exists between these two opposite aspects of mediation, science and ethics deepen the relationship of the human being and the world."[8]

From that starting point, technical thinking and the objects it produces, from the very oldest to the most modern machines, go through several phases in which technicality expresses itself in its existence. But the existence of technicality cannot be separated from either the history of technical objects or the connections between technical thinking and other kinds of thinking, aesthetic, theoretical, or practical, which are themselves derived from their own beginnings in magical thinking and their subsequent divergence into technical activity, religion, science, and ethics. For Simondon, it is the task of philosophy to think about the unity of the relationship of the human being to the world by establishing a true technology, in the proper sense of the word, thanks to the integration of the realities of the technical into universal culture. Philosophy would thereby overcome the old dualism between theory and practice, contemplative knowledge and operative knowledge, precisely by an analysis of "the mode of existence of technical objects" as the unifying element of philosophical thinking. The renewed unity of human and world would not be a return to primitive magical unity, because the transition through scientific knowledge is irreversible. Just as technology is not to be confused with the technical, so "*operational*" knowledge "is not synonymous with *practice*; technical operation is not arbitrary, bent in all directions to the will of the subject according to the chance of immediate utility; technical operation is a pure operation that puts into play the true laws of natural reality."[9]

This observation of Simondon's, fundamental as it was in the nineteen fifties, is even more relevant today, when the technical has taken possession of biology and when biotechnologies now manufacture living artifacts. Up until now, it was only the physical and chemical sciences that produced technical objects. We have long been used to artifacts in the form of tools, machines, and synthetic objects. Biology, the successor of natural history, was a science of observation. But the theoretical and technical efficacy of molecular biology now makes it possible to manufacture biological artifacts. We are only at the beginning of genetically modified organisms, systems biology, and what is called synthetic biology. But the starting signal has been given and that is enough to create both fascination and dread in the face of the possible invasion of these new artificial objects, which quite clearly concern not only microbes, plants, and animals but also human beings as members of the mammalian species Homo sapiens. Yet what is forgotten is the observation we have already made, which concerns the biotechnologies as much as physical technical objects: all these artifacts are possible only insofar as they, too, are natural. Airplanes could only be built starting with the laws of gravity, and the same is true for steam engines and thermodynamics, computers and electronics. As Simondon puts it so well, "the artificial is the generated natural, not the false or the human mistaken for the natural."[10] The opposition between natural and artificial, though it is not erased by the human technical activity that creates artifacts, is not relevant as either an ethical or a religious norm. Contemporary biology's erasure of the absolute barriers between the living and the nonliving, between human and nonhuman, or rather the transformation of these barriers into evolutionary progressions, leads to a naturalization of the human and at the same time a humanization of nature. Through its artifacts, human nature expresses itself in its specificity and allows human beings to liberate themselves from nature without leaving it behind, all the while being totally imbued with nature.

It is for this very reason that technical activity, insofar as it can be the source of both liberation and alienation, requires norms, just like other human activities.

Open machines: The information age

Simondon and Heidegger both see the industrial mechanization of the nineteenth century as an era in which the human being is erased by the technical. But instead of seeing in this the unconcealing of an essence, as Heidegger does, Simondon sees it as one phase of an evolution. The eighteenth century had been fueled by an optimistic idea of progress and of the continual improvement of humanity's fate. But before machines, the only technical objects were tools, and the machine took the place of the human being because up until then, the human being had performed "a machine function as bearer of tools."[11] This is the age of thermal engines and the energy sciences that accompany them, in which technical progress is expressed in a hubris that seems to crush everything in its path, including the human beings it has subjected. But this age of thermodynamics ends in the first half of the twentieth century, when the information age arrives to begin replacing it. The nature of machines undergoes a change. They become open because of the indeterminacy that characterizes the way they deal with information. In this, they are no longer hostile to the human being because they express the properties of the (human) life that gave birth to them. Thus

> the development of the technical seems to be a guarantee of stability. The machine . . . becomes that which augments the quantity of information, increases negentropy, and opposes the degradation of energy. The machine, a work of organization and information, is like life, and with life, it opposes the disorder and the leveling out of all things, which tend to deprive the universe of its powers of change. The machine is that by which the human being opposes the death of the universe; it slows down, as life does, the degradation of energy, and stabilizes the world.[12]

It is noteworthy that as early as the nineteen fifties, Simondon already had a vision of self-organizing machines that reproduce the properties of biological self-organization, especially as concerns their openness, that is to say, their ability to integrate indeterminacy—what I would later call organizational noise or randomness—into their functioning.[13] In fact, the artificial joins the natural in that living organisms—including human organisms—are now perceived as natural machines, and artificial machines—conceived and fabricated by human organisms—as their products, which simulate them and prolong some of their achievements. Simondon thus restores, in the twentieth century, the optimism of the eighteenth, amplified by his vision of the new information age, of which we can say, in the twenty-first century, that its resonance goes beyond anything he could have imagined.

Simondon, writing in 1958, already saw a world of humanized machines:

> The true perfecting of machines, of which we can say that it raises the degree of technicality, has nothing to do with an increase of the automatism but, on the contrary, has to do with the fact that the functioning of the machine conceals a certain margin of indetermination. This margin allows for the machine's sensitivity to outside information. It is by means of this sensitivity to information on the part of machines, much more than through any enhancement of the automatism, that a technical whole [*ensemble*] can come to be. A purely automatic machine, completely closed in on itself in a predetermined operation, could only provide perfunctory results. The machine endowed with superior technicality is an open machine, and the ensemble of open machines presupposes human beings as permanent organizers and as living interpreters of relationships between machines. Far from being supervisors of a squad of slaves, human beings are the permanent organizers of a society of technical objects that need them as much as musicians in an orchestra need a conductor. The conductor can direct her musicians only because, like them, and with similar intensity, she plays the piece of music performed; she curbs them or edges them on but is also curbed or edged on by them. . . . This is how human beings function as permanent inventors and coordinators of the machines around them. They are *among* the machines that work with them. The presence of human beings to machines is invention perpetuated. What resides within machines is human reality, human gestures fixed and crystallized in structures that function.[14]

But Simondon was surely too optimistic, for today it is precisely the self-organizing properties shared by the new artificial machines and the natural machines (that are our bodies) that worry us and make our alarm bells go off. The worry is that our future is predetermined to be a reign of autonomous machines that have completely escaped control and imposed themselves on a trans-humanity and a post-humanity generated by humanity with its own brains and fabricated with its own hands. These of course are the fantastic visions that have long fueled science fiction, but as it happens, some researchers think that they are going to be able to take the work of their laboratories in these directions. And it is a fact that the technologies of the twentieth century performed feats that had only seemed possible in the imagination of science fiction.

In fact, this suggests that the relative independence of technical objects, old and new, from their human inventors and users is not a sufficient criterion for serving as the norm of the good and the evil, the benefits and the harm that they bring to humanity. As always, ever since the human species began using its brains and its hands in order to survive thanks to its technical activity, the dangers of mastering fire—from the first flames to nuclear fire, via the cooled-down fires of DNA chemistry—are not to be found in the technical objects themselves. What transforms them into sources of life or death, or of life for some and of death for others, is the nature of the exchanges between human beings and the role of technical objects in these exchanges. And this is still the case in the information age into which we have entered, despite apocalyptic descriptions of an anonymous global regime of digital networks that make decisions about our future in our stead, automatically. In particular, the very nature of its openness means that the self-organizing processing of information is always limited by the question of its potentially infinite meanings, which are created by those who receive and use the information.

As in the stone age and the age of fire, and as in the age of thermodynamics, the effects of new technical objects depend on the power relations between the human beings who exchange and use them. Information circulates in exchanges and is associated with language, money, and the other technical objects that convey it, objects that tomorrow will be produced by genetics and the neurosciences. Because of this, information fuels power relations in that it can be used as a weapon, in the same way that the technologies and tools that work with energy can be. But the information age also brings about a radical novelty compared to the age of material objects and the energy age: although information, too, is an object of mimetic desire, it can easily elude Girardean mimetic *violence* because it is not limited by a law of conservation. Its value does not depend on its rarity because it can be easily and almost infinitely duplicated; transmitting a piece of information or even stealing it does not mean that its initial owner loses possession of it, unlike the case of material objects or sources of energy. But it can nonetheless deprive the owner of *exclusive* possession, which may in turn be a source of value and of possible violence.

In fact, Simondon's analysis of the nature of technical objects forms part of a much broader philosophical project in which the analysis cannot be reduced to a Manichaean dichotomy between technophobia and technophilia. The different phases of the technical form part of what Simondon calls a process of "psychic and collective individuation." This process produces the individuals that constitute the world, from the simplest atoms and particles to the most complex natural and artificial compounds, human ones in particular. But the process that precedes individuals (insofar as it produces them) unifies them at the same time that it differentiates them and at the same time that it is an object of knowledge. Relationships come first, and it is their meaning that determines the meaning of individual and collective behaviors, which therefore always refer back to the necessity of an ethical environment, of moral and even ritual rules. Such an environment already existed in the magical unity that characterized technical activity at the beginning of time. We have seen that this was also the case for language and for money in their connections with the sacred, with divination, and with Scripture.

This amounts to saying that the independence of technical objects, or at least their autonomy, in a way their hierarchization, remains an unavoidable question even if it does not by itself provide the basis for a norm of good and evil by which to judge the value of those technical objects. For through its autonomous existence, the technical object acquires an intrinsic value, which in the past was often sacred and today is aesthetic and affective, that is not to be confused with its utilitarian value.

The autonomy and the repose of technical objects

At the point where magical and philosophical thinking are joined, in the ancient Hebrew world where this transition was articulated in the talmudic academies, the thought of the Mishnah dwells on this question of the independence of technical objects. It does so in the context of the laws that govern the Sabbath, or *shabbat*, which are such that the weekly rest not only is an interruption in the human condition, dedicated to arduous labor, but also becomes an experience of inner liberation; hence, among other things, the cessation of writing activity and commercial exchanges as well as of the transportation of objects in public spaces. But this is extended to the larger family:

[T]he seventh day is Sabbath to YHVH, your God; you shall not do any work—you, your son, your daughter, your slave, your maidservant, your ox, your donkey, and your every animal, and your stranger within your gates, in order that your slave and your maidservant may rest like you. And you shall remember that you were a slave in the land of Egypt. . . . [15]

This extension of the group to which the rule of resting applies provides the occasion for raising the question of the autonomy of tools and mechanical devices of various degrees of elaborateness.[16] In other words, must the obligation of resting on the Sabbath also apply to tools and machines the way it does to their owner as well as to his slaves and animals? Obviously, the question comes up because machines and fires can be activated before the Sabbath and continue to work autonomously. The result is that the nature of the relation to these objects changes by virtue of the fact of this autonomy, an autonomy that in a way humanizes the objects, like a slave, or at least renders them alive, like an animal.

Let us recall that Aristotle, on the contrary, considers the slave to be an "animate" tool or "instrument," since for him, there are human beings whose "nature" is to be the executors of actions on behalf of other human beings who command them. Among the executors, moreover, slaves, like tools, are acquired goods. That is the way in which their status is that of animate tools.[17]

In the Talmud, the question is debated and finally decided in favor of those who do not extend the prohibition on laboring to tools and machines. But now we can understand that the question itself brings out this particular and double status of objects precisely at the moment when their autonomous labor is put to use on the day on which for us, the prohibition of labor is a condition of liberation. These objects thus remain different from slaves and animals. But at the same time, even when we do not make them work, we are led, by the very fact of their possible autonomy, to look at them differently than on the other days of the week, when they cannot be anything other than simple tools that extend our hands, *neutral* objects close at hand, without individual existence.

Use value and intrinsic value

This question of the autonomy of technical objects continues to come up to this day, again and again, as robotics, which makes such objects seem closer and closer to the animals and slaves they imitate, progresses. This reinforces the usual duality of our way of perceiving them, in terms of their intrinsic or their utilitarian value. The intrinsic value of an object and its functional value are obviously not the same; for one thing, they separate the material of an object from its form. A silver cup does not have the same value as a plastic cup.

But at the same time, and this is what is new, objects, like money and words, are swept up in runaway production that devalues them as individual objects. *Inflation* carries them away, transforming them into disposable objects, reduced, in the one-time use they are destined for, to their functional value. This utility can be very high,[18] but it is completely dissociated from the intrinsic value, which has been reduced to zero, of the object that is thrown away after use. Even if the objects are not immediately disposable after a single use and are very sophisticated, like digital or computerized machines, for example, whose autonomy is more and more obvious, the acceleration and inflation of their production makes them more and more rapidly obsolete. Their intrinsic value can then reappear when they are transformed into collector's items, like vintage cars or vintage computers. And like the inflation of money and of words, the inflation of technical objects skews the truth of exchanges. Lines that must not be crossed have to be established in order to carve out a certain space of tolerance, not zero, but not too large either.

When it comes to technical activity, then, just as with money and language, in the exchanges between human beings, the question of truth remains the stumbling block, the search for a good measure between absolute purity and the too large, too systematic lie. At issue here is the truth of prices in relation to the value of objects, the truth of speech in what is said about the properties of objects—this is the question of advertising that is, to a greater or lesser degree, deceptive—and, finally, the truth of power relations and relations of conflict between human beings, the question of propaganda as a greater or lesser perversion of political speech.

We are still talking about the world of *ona'ah*, where it is a matter of framing this vital interval—"between crystal and smoke"?—between the absolute truth that kills and the limitless lie that kills in a different way. In order to do this, we need to invent rules in the three places of exchange, namely words, money, and technical objects, while knowing full well that this is not always possible!

It is this network of prohibitions and of minimal but not zero tolerance that is staged in talmudic discussions of the world of *ona'ah*, where legend meets law.

One of the central stories in this system concerns, precisely, the status of a technical object, a singular oven whose intrinsic value and use value are called into question.

Is a broken vase still a vase when its pieces have been glued back together? Yes, from the strictly functional point of view, whereas the vase's intrinsic value has almost disappeared. As is the case with disposable functional objects of all kinds, its intrinsic value can be considered to be zero even if the vase has conserved its material and its form.

In the biblical world, where the sacred was organized in concentric circles around the Holy of Holies in the Temple in Jerusalem, the rituals that separated life from death extended from people and animals to fabricated objects. Different degrees of "impurity," that is to say, of death, were transmitted from corpses to people and to objects that then, for a time, carried with them a kind of death, until a purification ritual rid them of it. This expressed both the desire to associate the sacred with life by separating it from death and the acknowledgment that death is ever-present and linked with life.[19] In certain cases, the object that had become impure could not be reclaimed—for instance, if it was made of clay—and had to be broken. But can a broken vase whose pieces have been glued back together acquire impurity in the same way that an unbroken vase in one piece can? Is not the breaking of the vase its death, the loss of its intrinsic quality, a loss that is not made up for by the reclaiming of its function in gluing the pieces together? Can the fragments of a vase that is broken, even though they have been glued back together, acquire impurity when they are, in a way, already "dead"? The recuperation of the vase's function could be seen here as a snake's devilry, making us believe that the vase is still alive when it is already dead! But we could also say that this attitude is too "purist" in its all-or-nothing attitude, refusing to consider that life is always more or less a death. The question is all the more diabolical when it no longer concerns the gluing back together of a the pieces of a broken vase but, rather, a vessel that has been deliberately constructed by gluing pieces together.

We will see how this question, which was posed about a clay oven made of glued pieces, was the subject of a series of verbal injuries, one of which ended up being fatal.

5

The Strange Story of an Oven

The snake oven

An oven called the Oven of Akhnai was built as follows:[1] rings of clay were placed one on top of the other, with sand in between to cement them together. Akhnai was probably the name of the oven's inventor, but the name also means "snake." Rabbi Eliezer, acknowledged to be one of the greatest, if not *the* greatest master, or teacher, in the Assembly of Sages, or Great Assembly, considered this "snake oven" to be made of broken pieces and therefore incapable of becoming impure. Only utensils, tools, or vessels that are whole are able to receive impurity from direct or indirect contact with death.

But he was the only one to hold that opinion. All the other sages considered the snake oven to be whole because it was functional and because the cement guaranteed its unity. In consequence, they declared that the oven could become impure. The practical consequence was that such ovens became unusable and had to be smashed when they became impure. Rabbi Eliezer, on the other hand, held the view that they could continue to be used since they were unable to acquire impurity. The question of a broken utensil and its pure or impure status necessarily invokes the cabalistic schema of broken vessels, even if this theme is not explicitly developed until much later, in sixteenth-century Safed, by the school of Isaac Luria, nicknamed "the Ari." In fact, impurity always has a direct or indirect connection with death. But it is also a relative notion: only a being or object whose level of "life" is sufficiently elevated in the first place can be reached by a source of impurity and in turn become impure itself. The issue is thus a drop in the level of life that might be reparable—though not always, notably in the case of clay objects—with the help of various treatments, particularly immersion. The legend of the broken vessels presents the fragments of these vessels as having fallen into an inferior world, into a kind of death, waiting for the cosmic drama to be redressed by the progressive formation of new vessels capable of receiving and containing their light without shattering like their predecessors. We can see how a broken vessel, in a way already dead, cannot acquire an impurity that would cause it to die even more. That is Rabbi Eliezer's opinion. But for his opponents, a reconstituted oven, or an oven constructed from pieces glued together, is the equivalent of the repair of the shattering of the vessels, and the oven is considered to be reinstated at a level of life that is capable of being rendered impure. According to this interpretation, what is at stake in the controversy has to do with whether the shattering of the vessels and the shattering of evil in the world that, according to the legend, derives from it, is absolute or whether it is relative, operational in a way, in which case the reestablishment of functionality would suffice for the evil to be redressed. For Rabbi Eliezer, only a redress in the very being of things is a true redress, and that can only be conceived within an eschatological reality that is redressed in its entirety, "in heaven" or in a world to come. For his opponents, a functional redress in our world just as it is, "on earth," is already a redress. The practical consequences seem paradoxical here since Rabbi Eliezer's extreme stringency—which characterizes him on other occasions as well, when he most often follows the most rigorous opinion—leads him to consider objects to be pure and, thus, to permit their use when the other sages prohibit their use. It is as though he were abandoning these broken vessels to their earthly fate, vessels that are already impure in any case and cannot become more shattered and impure than they already are. Can we see in this some attraction to the kind of Gnostic or Christian attitude of which Roman authorities will later, under different circumstances, accuse him? In order to answer this question, we will need to outline some of the character traits of this complex personality as revealed in his history as it is related in talmudic tradition.

The confrontation between Rabbi Eliezer and his colleagues and disciples is tense and full of reversals, and it ends in drama. His opponents begin by using all kinds of arguments to "encircle him as with a snake"[2] and to render the oven impure. The story tells us that this is how the "snake oven" got its name. This may be an indication that nothing but the cunning of a snake could have created so perverse a situation, in which the law is circumvented and the status of the object left undetermined. It is as though the object had been made just for the purpose of destabilizing the Great Assembly in its search for the rightful ruling. And it is only through the arguments of an equally cunning and serpentine rhetoric that that search could be brought to its conclusion in spite of the destabilization.

Rabbi Eliezer will not let himself be convinced and he, in turn, brings up all possible arguments for why the oven is pure under all circumstances. But the others do not accept his arguments. He then changes registers, leaving behind argumentation proper and appealing instead to divine intervention by performing miracles that are supposed to testify to the rightness of his position. And this provides the occasion for the following dialogue:

"If the *halakha* [the law that determines the way in which the *mitzvoth*, the commandments of the Torah, Teaching and Law, are to be applied—HA] agrees with me, let this carob tree prove it!"

Thereupon the carob tree was torn a hundred cubits out of its place—others affirm, four hundred cubits.

"No proof can be brought from a carob tree," they retorted.

Again he said to them: "If the *halakha* agrees with me, let the stream of water prove it!"

Whereupon the stream of water flowed backwards.

"No proof can be brought from a stream of water," they rejoined.

Again he urged: "If the *halakha* agrees with me, let the walls of the schoolhouse prove it," whereupon the walls inclined to fall.

But R. Joshua rebuked them, saying: "When scholars are engaged in a *halakhic* dispute, what have you to interfere?"

Hence they did not fall, in honor of R. Joshua, nor did they resume the upright, in honor of R. Eliezer; and they are still standing thus inclined.

Again he said to them: "If the *halakha* agrees with me, let it be proved from Heaven!"

Whereupon a Heavenly Voice cried out: "Why do you dispute with R. Eliezer, seeing that in all matters the *halakha* agrees with him!"
But R. Joshua arose and exclaimed: "It is not in heaven."[3]

What does this mean? Rabbi Jeremiah's response is to see in it the foundation of majority rule as an answer of sorts to the voice of God: "[T]he Torah had already been given at Mount Sinai; we pay no attention to a Heavenly Voice, because You have long since written in the Torah at Mount Sinai, 'After the majority one must incline.'"[4]

The scenery of the talmudic narrative now changes, as an encounter between Rabbi Nathan and the prophet Elijah is recounted in order to evoke another form of heavenly revelation. As the Book of Kings tells us, Elijah the prophet did not die but was taken to heaven in a chariot. According to tradition, he returns on certain occasions, in visions or in various disguises, and reveals things hidden in the upper worlds. Rabbi Nathan, it seems, thus meets him and recognizes him. Indeed, he asks him about the events we just described: "'What did the Holy One, Blessed be He, do in that hour?'—'He laughed [with joy],' [Elijah] replied, 'saying, My sons have defeated Me, My sons have defeated Me.'"[5]

In the best-known version, the story ends here, with this apparently very simple moral: miracles have no place in human affairs. The law is the sages' business: they exercise their judgment and in cases of disagreement decide by a majority. This conclusion is rendered even more vivid by the knowledge that on another occasion, in a fitting inversion, Rabbi Joshua, who in this case is the leader of the majority, finds himself in the minority and bows to its rule.[6] The subject of the dispute on that occasion is the calculation of the calendar and the fixing of the date of Yom Kippur, the Day of Atonement. The assembly has determined the day as falling on a different date than the one Rabbi Joshua has calculated. The president of the assembly, Rabban Gamliel, summons Joshua to come to him, with his staff and his traveling bag, on the day that Joshua has determined to be Yom Kippur. Rabbi Joshua obeys, thereby violating the prohibitions associated with the day according to his own conviction but testifying to his submission to majority rule. And so even though the Law is called the "Word of God," and even if a sage is inspired like Rabbi Eliezer and able to make God's Word heard through signs and wonders, if he finds himself in the minority on a question of law, his judgment is rejected. For in this postbiblical context, the nature of the "Word of God" has changed. From the Sinai epiphany that formally established it, its content has now become something that passes through the mouths of men, "students of the sages" in a sincere search for truth, because "a wise man is superior even to a prophet."[7] And when irreducible disagreements arise despite the good faith and disinterestedness of both parties, practical decisions are taken by a majority vote without the minority opinions being devalued for all that, because they, too, are "words of God." As we read elsewhere on the subject of direct confrontations between two schools: "These and those both are the words of the living god[s]."[8]

But although it is entirely pertinent, this moral to the story, on the whole reassuring and demystifying, ignores at least two questions. On the one hand, how are we to understand the role of the successive miracle-working actors in the gradation of their interventions? For Rabbi Eliezer's opponents do not contest the reality of these interventions; they do not banish them to the domain of illusion, yet they are all the more opposed to their playing a role in any supernatural revelation of the Law.

On another note, this story is told at the end of long discussions dedicated to *ona'ah*, fraud and the harm that results from it in both commercial exchanges and exchanges of words. The question also arises of the connection between the story and this context of *ona'at dvarim*, injurious "fraudulent words."

We can already say that this is a matter of "serpentine" verbal contrasts, as we have seen, where what is at stake is the emergence of a truth that does not manage to be shared. But we will see how the rest of the story and its dramatic epilogue, which is just as fantastic, bring out unexpected illustrations of the potentially catastrophic effects of verbal injuries.

Traditional commentary on the first question, as with other talmudic legends, is divided between those who take the narrative at face value and those who discover symbolic meanings in it. For the Maharal of Prague, it is not necessary to picture these events as if they had taken place in the tangible world, but only as if they had taken place in the minds of the protagonists.[9] The signs that are invoked one after the other as "proofs" now appear to be so many elements of a coded dialogue. It is no longer a question of countering specific arguments but of establishing or rejecting the superior authority of a teacher who has been invested a priori as a bearer of the truth "in all places." What makes it all the more complicated is that Rabbi Eliezer's opponents (most of whom, by the way, are his students) recognize the eminence of his teaching due to his exceptional abilities, to which other traditions, as reported by the Talmud and the Midrash, testify as well.[10]

In this way, the four signs produced by Rabbi Eliezer are interpreted as four allusions to different levels of teaching, affirming his mastery across an entire spectrum that is supposed to be convincing from any point of view whatsoever in the common search for truth.

The carob tree is solidly rooted, very resistant, and does not bear fruit until it is seventy years old. It represents the knowledge transmitted by tradition from one generation to another by way of the mouths of the "elders." But the testimony of tradition in favor of Rabbi Eliezer is rejected: the "old tree" is not a proof, since it could have forgotten. What is more, its "uprooting" could testify to the opposite, as an allusion to the upsetting of tradition that the master's opinion would produce. As for its displacement by four hundred cubits, rather than by one hundred, as some would have it, that alludes to a more radical upheaval, one way or the other, having to do with the four stages of the traditional transmission of knowledge starting with Moses, who received it on Sinai and passed it on to Joshua, who passed it on to the prophets, who passed it on to the elders.[11] Another commentator sees the carob tree, through its name, 'haruv, which shares an etymological root with "destruction," as alluding to the destructive effects of the judgment of the other sages: considering Akhnai ovens to be whole and capable of becoming impure implies their destruction when they become impure, as with all clay objects and unlike objects made of metal or glass, whose possible impurity is not irreversible. Thus, paradoxically, considering them to be already broken and therefore unable to become impure implies a more constructive attitude.[12]

The second sign, the water and its current, is an allusion to reasoning, which is what moves the study of Torah, often compared to living water, forward. Here, too, we have a testimony to the superiority of Rabbi Eliezer. But this testimony "is not a proof" either because reasoning is not in itself immune to error. Furthermore, flowing against the current can also be seen in the opposite way, as a sign of having gone astray.

As for the walls of the schoolhouse, they evoke the context and the entirety of the formal and material conditions that allow study, in all its forms, to progress and to deepen thanks to the interactions between the sages and their students (who are all designated by the generic term "students of the sages," *talmidei hakhamim*). This time, the testimony is not so easily rejected. One of the teachers, Rabbi Joshua, takes the lead in the resistance and refuses to accept the confusion between the content and the container. The conditions of study cannot interfere with controversies about the contents of that study, or support one side or the other, because it is they that ensure the very existence of these controversies. That is why, in the end, their testimony respects both parties: the walls do not collapse, but neither do they stand up straight again. They remain inclined in this compromise to this day.

Finally, in desperation, Rabbi Eliezer appeals directly to the testimony of the divine world. Now he tries to establish his superiority in the realm of hidden wisdom, which is revealed through inspiration, visions, and voices, like the ancient prophecies, which have residual forms in heavenly voices, Elijah's revelations, and sometimes dreams in this disenchanted postbiblical world, from which prophecy strictly speaking has disappeared. And the voice does in fact make itself heard, this time testifying explicitly to Rabbi Eliezer's superiority in this domain as "in all places."

Given that they, too, have access to the realm of hidden wisdom, the others do not in any way contest either the origin of this voice or the content of its speech. But the same Rabbi Joshua, in a radical innovation, sends it back to heaven. He puts forward another heavenly voice to oppose it, the voice whose words and commandments were written down in the Torah of Moses and thus acquired the permanence of the written word. The *halakha*, he says, that is to say the Torah as a source of legal obligations, "is not in heaven" or, rather, "is no longer in heaven," following the interpretation of the verse from this same written Torah that he then invokes. The heavenly voice that Rabbi Eliezer causes to be heard testifies that the divine word is indeed what he says it is. But it finds itself in opposition to another divine word, the word of the God who speaks in the Torah of Moses and says, precisely, that "it is not in heaven." Of course it comes from heaven, more precisely from "Mount Sinai," but it is now on earth, and it is through the mouths of the sages who make it speak that it is the "word of the living god[s]."[13] In fact, this Torah that is developed through research, interpretation, and discussion among the students of the sages is called the *oral* Torah. As the place where the Torah was renewed as infinite wisdom, this oral Torah was only put into writing, in the accounts of discussions that make up the Talmud, out of necessity, for fear that exile and dispersion would cause it to be forgotten. And now majority rule, presented here as applicable to these discussions, is opposed to quasi-prophetic revelation in the very name of the supreme written text of prophetic revelation, the revelation to Moses at Mount Sinai. We understand, then, the reason for God's (ironic?) smile as he finds himself defeated by his children: he is forbidden to intervene in the development of the oral Torah—which nonetheless sees itself as a continuation of the voice heard and even "seen" on Mount Sinai—in the very name of his written word derived from that voice. It is as though the Word of God were forbidding any appeal to the Word of God to settle legal questions, in the name of this very same Word of God! In fact, the opposition is between words that appear to be of timeless and absolute origin, heard by inspiration, and other words, established according to other criteria, social context in particular. To be sure, "these and those both are the words of the living god[s]," but the god of the teacher whose understanding is the broadest and deepest nonetheless finds himself defeated by the god of the community made up of the other teachers, a community that is the custodian of the truth it constructs thanks to its investiture by the first written Torah, the Torah of the Sinai. . . .

But it is important to see that all of this is only possible through the dialectic of sacred writing and its endlessly renewed oral interpretation. And sometimes, the price to be paid is the more or less extensive distortion that interpretation inflicts on a verse or verse fragment taken out of context. This is already apparent in the case of "it is not in heaven." It is even more obvious in the case of the explication that follows, in which Rabbi Jeremiah invokes another verse, taken from an entirely different context, to show majority rule. In fact, "it is not in heaven" appears in the context[14] of Moses exhorting Israel to "listen to the voice of YHVH, your God, to observe His commandments and His decrees, that are written in this Book of the Torah." The aim here is to prevent an appeal claiming that this task is too difficult:

For this commandment that I command you today—it is not hidden from you and it is not distant. *It is not in heaven,* [for you] to say, "Who can ascend to the heaven for us and take it for us, so that we can listen to it and perform it?" Nor is it across the sea. . . . Rather, the matter is very near to you—in your mouth and in your heart—to perform it.[15]

We can see how these verses acquire a different, very particular meaning after the fact, when they are transposed into the postbiblical context that is concerned with establishing the law: what we have now is an a priori rejection of all prophetic revelation, which is far from the meaning that these verses have in their original context.

The role of interpretation is even more obvious in what comes next, where the concern is with establishing majority rule. In this case, what we have is a relatively obscure verse taken from a different context[16] about the functioning of courts called on to decide equitably between litigants and to judge the accused fairly, without deviating from the truth of the judgment in one direction or the other, by falling into the trap of the perversions of language.[17] The biblical text is about "*not be[ing] a follower* of the majority for evil" and, for judges, not allowing themselves to be influenced against their conscience by following such a majority. Hence the idea that, by contrast, one must follow the majority when it is for the good. This interpretation is transposed into our context, it being understood that the Great Assembly in its deliberations, with its majority vote, is obviously oriented toward the good. Thus a prescription *not to follow the majority* in a very particular case of the workings of a court is turned into majority rule in the establishment of the *halakha*, potentially even against a minority of which one has every reason to believe that it is defending, from its point of view, a just position founded on a truth that is possibly "purer." This underlines the truth stakes in verbal exchanges, along with the injuries that can accompany them, which is the subject of the chapter of the Talmud in which the story of the oven is told.

Verbal injuries: Words, of life and of death

In this story of the snake oven, one can very well see the extent to which words become fraudulent and cause injuries in all directions. These injuries are not intentional and certainly not ad hominem; and this only accentuates their dramatic character. For they penetrate minds and affect them in a way that is sometimes indelible and irreparable, whereas from the beginning, the concern is with establishing a common truth about the status of a technical object that stands in a symbolic relationship with life and death. Verbal *ona'ah* causes injuries in every direction. On the one hand, there is the teacher who is unable to convince his students, who have become teachers or masters themselves, and then argues from authority, crushing his opponents with his charismatic radiance and his authority "in all places." On the other hand, we have his students, making use of the fraud of interpretation—because interpretation is speech that does violence to other speech. The interpretive technique called *drash* appeals to the text or, rather, "demands" of it a meaning that is explicitly absent from it.[18] As we have seen, interpretive discourse can be a veritable transgression of the text of a verse, an injury to the words which offer themselves to be read, but in some way for its own good. Like psychoanalytic interpretation, which hears in a conscious negation the denial of what one actually wants to affirm, without knowing it, the interpretation of the speech conveyed in a verse manages to make it say the opposite of what it says: for all the right reasons, of course, and in the name of a deeper, less trivial, more interesting, more universal truth, of which the author of the text was probably unaware. This situation, furthermore, is described explicitly in the context of Moses, when the Midrash tells us that Moses did not understand Rabbi Akiba's words of Torah even though Rabbi Akiba himself justified them to his students, who doubted their origin, by saying that they were *halakha le Moshe mi-Sinai*, "a *halakha* given unto Moses from Sinai."[19] Now we can understand the vision of a God who is defeated by his own self, and by his unconscious as revealed through the mouths of his children—and who delights in that defeat.

But this story, which in its best-known version concludes with this happy ending, does not in fact end there. Verbal injuries leave traces. Their consequence is a cosmic evil that is amplified to the point of tragedy.

It all begins with the destruction and burning of all the objects that Rabbi Eliezer has declared to be pure. After this, the assembly votes to exclude him. His favorite student, Rabbi Akiba, volunteers to tell him so that someone else will not do so inappropriately, thereby "bringing about the destruction of the world." Rabbi Akiba first makes the announcement without words, by showing up dressed in black and staying at a distance, in a ritual of grief and of exclusion. When Rabbi Eliezer asks him what could have happened that day, he tells him: "Master, it seems your fellows have separated from you," as though it were they who had been excluded from his assembly instead of the other way around. Now Rabbi Eliezer in turn begins to grieve and his eyes begin to cry. "The world was not destroyed then, but it was smitten: a third of the olive crop, a third of the wheat, and a third of the barley crop. Some say, the dough in women's hands swelled up. Great was the calamity that befell that day, for everything at which R. Eliezer cast his eyes was burned up." Finally, Rabban Gamliel, as president of the assembly that had voted for the exclusion, enters the scene. Finding himself on a boat that threatens to be carried off by a storm, he understands (as did Jonah, who refused to listen to the divine Word) that the storm is directed against him on account of the injury inflicted on Rabbi Eliezer. The sea becomes calm when he addresses the master of the universe: "You know full well that I have not acted for my honor, nor for the honor of my paternal house, but for Yours, so that strife may not multiply in Israel!" Rabban Gamliel thus escapes death because he underscores the unintentional and disinterested nature of the injury for which he must take responsibility.[20]

But still this does not end it because the wound remains open and the tears of Rabbi Eliezer can, at any moment, sow death. In fact, we have been told earlier that "[s]ince the destruction of the Temple, the gates of prayer are locked" but that "the gates of tears are not," and also that "[a]ll gates are locked, excepting the gates of *ona'ah*."[21] Rabbi Eliezer's wife, who is also Rabban Gamliel's sister, knows all this and fears the devastating effects that could result from awakening her husband's pain. Her name is *Ima-Shalom* (which can be approximately translated as "mother of peace") and she knows that her brother is still in danger. Rabbi Eliezer obviously does not intend to kill him. But his pain runs the risk of being awoken if he speaks certain ritual words of anguish that are normally associated with the daily prayers. These words express a form of anguish that every human being feels in his everyday existence, faced with his own finiteness as opposed to the infinity in whose service he lifts himself up in the ritual. Ima-Shalom wants to avoid having her husband find himself in that state because she knows that the wound, once reopened, will trigger her brother's death. Yet these words are only spoken on ordinary days and not during the rituals for holidays and for the new moon. She is thus careful to keep him from saying them when he ordinarily would have to do so. But it eventually happens that she makes a mistake with the calendar and confuses the last day of the month with the new moon. According to another version of the story, a poor man comes to the door and she leaves the house to give him some bread at the very moment at which she is preparing to prevent her husband from saying those words of anguish: in the first version, a human error on the part of Ima-Shalom, despite her goodwill; or worse, in the second version, a good deed that leads to the catastrophe. She cannot, therefore, prevent Rabbi Eliezer from "falling on his face,"[22] to use the expression that designates this ritual. When she sees him, she understands that it is too late and tells him to get up because he has just "killed his brother." And indeed, Rabban Gamaliel's death is announced at that moment.

When Rabbi Eliezer asks his wife how she knew the danger these words of anguish harbored for her brother's life, she says she drew the knowledge from a tradition of her father's house (a tradition, it seems, that Rabbi Eliezer did not know!): "All gates are locked, excepting the gates of *ona'ah*."[23]

This is the end of the story. We can now understand, after the fact, the place that this story holds in the chapter: the whole long story of the oven now appears to be a particularly rich, multifaceted illustration of the conclusion to the drama that is related by Ima-Shalom.

This affirmation is already to be found in the introduction, in the form of a saying of Rav Hisda's, which precedes the story, in a group of aphorisms about the extraordinary effects of verbal *ona'ah*.[24] And the story of the oven shows us the degree to which the consequences of these injuries—even when they are involuntary, even when they are an inevitable by-product in the course of disinterested exchanges in the service of the search for truth and for the good—are incalculable, beyond measure, irreparable.

Later, we will have to ask ourselves about the relations between the "*ona'ah* in buying and selling," which can be measured with respect to a fair price, and this "*ona'ah* in words," whose devastating effects are beyond measure. We will see that the latter produces harm in the intimacy of one's being, which can in principle be measured but is, in practice, inaccessible to any such measurement because it would imply an infinite knowledge of the interiority of each and every person, a knowledge only a god would be capable of. Hence a curious verse that Rav Hisda quotes in the same lines in which he affirms that all gates are locked except those of *ona'ah*: in it we see the God of Israel using a measure of uprightness, "a plumb line,"[25] to judge that which is at stake in the articulation between the interior and the exterior. This image of God with a plumb line would imply, in this interpretation, that "[a]ll compensation is made indirectly through an intermediary, except [the compensation of] *ona'ah*."[26]

The story of the oven is thus framed by numerous commentaries on the biblical warning "do not hurt your neighbor." In the commentaries that precede the story, the "neighbor" (*'amit*) is interpreted in different ways: as "your wife" or, based on a play on words (*amitekha*: "with you"), as the one who, like you and with you, receives and studies the Torah. The importance of not hurting one's own wife, guardian of the household and of its prosperity, is underscored just before the story of the Oven of Akhnai, perhaps to introduce the role that Ima-Shalom, who appears later, will play.

The commentaries that follow the story end this passage of the Talmud by returning to the insistent prohibition on injuring strangers in particular, a prohibition that is as important as, if not more important than, the prohibition on oppressing them: the prohibition on hurting one's neighbor (*'amit*) also concerns strangers, because "the stranger is included in the neighbor."[27] Thus we encounter Rabbi Eliezer once more, by way of a reminder of one of his teachings on this insistence. He explains the repetition, over and over, of this prohibition through the fear that the humiliation of strangers might set them more easily on the path of evil. Finally, this is all concluded with a reminder of the very Bible verse that justifies this particularized prohibition: "You shall not wound or oppress a stranger, *for you were strangers in the land of Egypt.*"[28] At the same time as the stranger is singled out, he is also identified with everyone else, because this particular status is, in fact, everyone's status. We are all strangers, and it is because we have had the experience of being strangers that we can and must share the extreme sensitivity to hurtful words, even the most indirect. Or, as Rabbi Nathan—the same Rabbi Nathan who asked the prophet Elijah about what God was doing during the discussion—puts it: "do not talk to your fellow man about a flaw that is also yours." In hurting him, it is yourself that you hurt when you recall an ancient wound you both share. And finally, in order to end on a less sinister note, a humorous parable is given as an example of this type of humiliation, the Aramaic equivalent of the proverb "don't speak of the rope in a hanged man's house."[29]

6

More or Less than One-Sixth

A threshold

Let us go back to the beginning of the chapter of the Talmud that institutes a threshold of tolerance (of one-sixth) for *ona'ah*, the harm suffered by a partner in a transaction because of a divergence from the fair price in a purchase or sale.[1] As we have seen, this is an innovation with respect to the biblical injunction, which in no way imagines such a threshold. In fact, it is this very threshold that ends up defining *ona'ah*, strictly speaking, as a reparable harm, different from a larger or smaller divergence. We will also have to look into the similarities and differences between that *ona'ah* and verbal *ona'ah*, another innovation introduced later in the same chapter: "Just as there is fraud in buying and selling so there is fraud in spoken words." In chapter 2,[2] we saw how the Talmud's interpretive method makes it possible to formally derive this analogy from a redundancy of the biblical text, which does not mention it explicitly. Yet this interpretation puts the analogy to work in both directions: in its extension from the commercial domain to that of speech, *ona'ah* receives a surplus of meaning. The discussions of the threshold established for commercial *ona'ah* gain new meaning after the fact in light of what we can understand about verbal *ona'ah*, although the latter is not measurable and obviously does not allow for any threshold whatsoever.

Let us note from the start that it is the same guiding thread that leads us through the problems both of commercial exchanges and of words: both types of exchanges bring out tensions between the interests of individuals in their subjectivity and the interests of society, organized around shared rules. The market is also the *agora*. Whatever is exchanged there, whether it be goods or words, the stakes are double, both individual and social. If the exchange is distorted, the harm that results affects both the injured individual and the community in the shared organization of exchanges that ensures its stability. A coin, with its two faces, expresses this double role of the relations between individuals in their subjectivity and of the guarantee of the social bond, with, in addition, a nod to the sacredness of the royal person—or of the republic—in which the individual in his or her interiority and the exteriority of social reality are said to be reconciled. For there is a need for such a reconciliation, since the flourishing of the individual often seems to be thwarted by the law of the group and the social order is threatened by individual desire.

The Talmud's discussions of the threshold for acceptable damages bring out different situations that are all aspects of the analysis of the individual and collective implications of fraud, with a concern for compromise in order to safeguard, as far as possible, the legitimate but sometimes contradictory interests of the individual and of society. It is as though the economy could not be thought of in an exclusively "objective" manner, without referring to the human nature of language and of affects, with its own reality including the ever-present possibility of verbal injuries.

Let us recall that, to begin with, the question is one of knowing how to transcribe the biblical injunction into the law and how to apply this injunction, which is repeated several times in different forms: "When you make a sale to your fellow or make a purchase from the hand of your fellow, do not hurt one another." "Each of you shall not hurt his fellow, and you shall fear YHVH, your god." "You shall not hurt or oppress a stranger, for you were strangers in the land of Egypt." The phrases "Do not defraud, . . . ," "do not deceive, . . ." and "do not hurt . . ." are all ways of translating the expression *al townu*, from which the word *ona'ah* derives and which designates at the same time both the deception and the harm suffered by the person deceived.

Two preoccupations in the spirit of the law, which sometimes contradict each other, appear in the questions that are brought up. One concerns the direct relation between two people when one of them has been injured or deceived by the other—intentionally or not. The other has to do with the transaction itself and the *fair price* or market price. A threshold is imposed (one-sixth) beneath which there is no *ona'ah* strictly speaking. Even if somebody has been injured by buying at a higher price or selling at a lower price than the market price, the injury (or deception, or fraud, according once again to how one translates *ona'ah*) is said to be "forgiven" if the divergence from the market price is less than one-sixth. But above the one-sixth threshold there is also no *ona'ah* because the transaction is then automatically annulled. The principle of the rule of *ona'ah* is as follows: there is only "injury" if the difference is equal to exactly one-sixth of the fair price. That injury can be redressed by payment of the difference or by annulment of the transaction if the person harmed so decides.

Why a threshold? And why one-sixth?

A threshold is indispensable for maintaining at least a minimum of stability and of agreement in exchanges. In fact, it is very difficult to define the fair price or market price with absolute precision. Small fluctuations that are always present necessarily create a certain amount of play, in the space of which the seller or the buyer can injure or be injured. It is only when the price paid goes beyond the market price by a large amount that we consider that deception—voluntary or involuntary—has occurred and that the transaction must be voided, applying the biblical law so that neither partner is injured.

The purchase and sale of land is an extreme case. The talmudic rule stipulates that "there is no *ona'ah* for land" because each piece of land may have a different price than any other due to its own particular characteristics and because an "objective" fair price is practically impossible to determine. Therefore, the price of the land is determined by the agreement between the seller and the buyer . . . unless there is an "enormous gap," estimated to be about half the price.

So it is movable goods for which the threshold for *ona'ah* is fixed at one-sixth of the market price; a period of deliberation is also provided for before the cancellation of the sale to give the buyer—and possibly the seller—time to gather information on the market price. But completely aside from the question, to which we will return, of whether the value of the threshold is arbitrary or not, the very existence of the threshold creates a particular situation when the price paid is *exactly* equal to one-sixth above or below market price. In fact, the conclusion at the end of the discussion is that it is only in this very particular case that there truly is *ona'ah*, or fraud in its strict definition which must be redressed, since above that threshold the transaction is canceled (and thus there is no longer any fraud) and below the threshold the transaction is validated and "forgiven" (and thus there is not yet any fraud). Only in this one particular case can the injured person choose between either canceling the sale or else validating it by receiving the difference between the price paid and the fair price. The threshold and the rule that applies to it thus create a particular situation in which the two preoccupations come together, the one concerning subjective interpersonal stakes aimed at preventing one person from inflicting harm on another, the other one to do with objective economic stakes aimed at facilitating transactions that are as fair as possible by means of regulation.

This particular role of the threshold that defines *ona'ah*, or fraud strictly defined, is underscored by an opinion given by a famous teacher in the *Mishnah*—Rabbi Tarfon—according to which the threshold is to be fixed not at one-sixth but at one-third of the fair price. According to one interpretation, this would imply that *ona'ah* strictly speaking would in fact be defined not by a single value but by a range between one-sixth and one-third.

This is a minority opinion, and it is not adopted, even though we are told that it was to the liking of the merchants of Lod, Rabbi Tarfon's city, because they saw in it a way of reducing the number of canceled sales. It is interesting to note that Rabbi Tarfon was known not only for his great wisdom but also for his wealth, which might explain his concern with maintaining the validity of a larger number of transactions. But he was also noted for his concern that an entire day be allowed after a transaction as a deliberation period in which the sale could be canceled or the *ona'ah* made up for, instead of just the actual time necessary for verifying the fair price on the market or with a close adviser. This obviously was no longer to the liking of the merchants of the town who, finally, preferred the rule of one-sixth, with its shorter delay, that was favored by the majority! Even though these contradictory views of the merchants of Lod with respect to Rabbi Tarfon's opinion may seem to be purely anecdotal, a careful discussion of the implications of their initial satisfaction and later dissatisfaction will serve to analyze different options for who decides to cancel, to forgive, or to make reparation for the amount of the damage, depending on the scenario, of an *ona'ah* that is, respectively, greater than, less than, or equal to one-sixth. Following the technique of talmudic discussion, a practical decision (a *halakha*) is adopted only after all possible options have been analyzed. But the terms of the discussion continue to be present in the background and serve as reminders of the theoretical advantages of the options that have been discarded.

A first question obviously concerns the establishment of the fair price. The assumption is that there is an "objective" market price for the object that was bought and that both protagonists are understood to have access to that price. A deliberation period is granted between the transaction and the reparation of the potential injury in order to give the buyer time to go show the object in the marketplace and to make sure of its price and to give the seller time to go show an identical object (because the object is no longer in his possession). But particular personal situations are discussed that differ according to whether the person injured is the seller or the buyer and whether they are private persons or professional merchants who are more naturally familiar with market conditions.

Another question concerns two different ways of calculating this divergence from the fair price by one-sixth. Should it be calculated on the basis of the value of the object or on the basis of the price paid at the time of the transaction? In the first case, if an object worth six dollars is bought for five dollars or seven dollars, the situation is certainly one of strictly defined *ona'ah*, with a divergence of exactly one-sixth. And if an object worth five dollars is bought for six, the divergence is now one-fifth of the fair price if calculated on the basis of the value of the object and not of the price paid. This difference of one-fifth is larger than one-sixth and the transaction has to be canceled. In the same way, if an object worth seven dollars is bought for six, that is a difference of one-seventh, therefore less than one-sixth, and the transaction is validated, "forgiven." If, on the other hand, the calculation is made on the basis of the price paid in these last two cases, we end up in both instances with a divergence from the fair price of exactly one-sixth, up or down. In a way, the answer to the question brings the two options together: the transaction is neither canceled nor "forgiven" unless the divergence is, respectively, larger or smaller than one-sixth, whatever the basis of the calculation, whether it be the value of the object or the price paid.

In another discussion, we again find this tension between the objective and subjective characteristics of the injury, depending on whether one's primary concern is with the intrinsic value of the transaction or with a sense that either or both of the partners to the transaction has of injuring or being injured. The issue here is whether the rules of cancellation, of validation, and of redress for divergences from the fair price are automatic or not. Does the cancellation of the sale if the price paid diverges from the fair price by more than one-sixth, its validation without redress (its "forgiving") when the divergence is less than one-sixth, or its validation with redress (restitution of the amount overpaid or additional payment to make up for the amount underpaid) take effect automatically (under the responsibility of the tribunal)? Or are these actions left to the judgment of the injured person, who "has the upper hand" over the other party in that he or she can, in all cases, decide whether or not to validate the transaction, with or without redress?

The conclusion of the discussion highlights once again the particular status of the divergence of exactly one-sixth. It is only in this case that the choice—of whether to cancel the sale or to have the amount of the fraud made up, that is, one-sixth of the market price—is left to the person harmed. In fact, it is only in this case, as we have seen, that *ona'ah* even occurs, since the sale is automatically either canceled or validated if the divergence is, respectively, greater than or less than one-sixth.

Following this, particular situations are imagined, all of which bring out the tension between the subjective and moral character of the biblical injunction ("you shall not hurt . . .") and the more impersonal, economic objectivity of the transaction. Thus, for example, if the seller and the buyer agree on a price that is injurious to one of them and if the injured one accepts the price knowingly, the rules of *ona'ah* do not apply. Furthermore, these rules do not concern all transactions: real estate (land), slaves, and contracts (where the object sold does not concretely pass "into the hands" of the buyer) are not affected. Finally, deceptions about weights and measures and about money itself are treated differently, in ways that bring them closer to theft. We shall return to this.

All of this tends to single out situations of *ona'ah* within the general context of economic exchanges, and it is as though the ground were being readied for extending these situations, as will indeed be the case, to *ona'at dvarim*, verbal fraud or injury, whose effects pass through words. But, as we will see, the question of the one-sixth will then have to be put in an entirely different way.

And finally, why one-sixth rather than some other fraction of the fair price? As happens very often, the question of the particular meaning of any given injunction is not even explicitly brought up in the Talmud. In many cases, we have to turn to cabalistic commentaries to find an answer. And here, again, as we shall discover, these commentaries shed unexpected light on this rule of one-sixth.

Let us note, first, that several reasons can be cited in favor of the choice of one-sixth over some other fraction, such as, for example, one-tenth. As is the case with the Sumerians and the Babylonians, for instance, six is often used in numbering, along with its multiple, sixty, in sexagesimal numbering systems.[3] Something of this remains in our divisions of time into hours of sixty minutes and minutes of sixty seconds. Its origins are not very clear; they are sometimes attributed to the six directions of space that are thus present, indirectly, in measurements of time, notably on sundials, which are separated into twelve hours to cover one day. As it happens, these six directions of space are also associated, in cabalistic typology, with the six *sefirot* that correspond to the "affective" part of the human body, from which the "head," with its three *sefirot* of wisdom, intelligence, and knowledge, is separated.

In the talmudic tradition, one-sixtieth is a small fraction tending towards zero, like our modern epsilon. Hence the expression *batel be shishim*, "canceled in sixty," to designate a dilution or a mixture of one body in another such that the dissolved body is considered canceled, or annulled, once it falls below a concentration of one-sixtieth. Along the same lines, on a more abstract level, certain experiences of our existence undergo a change in nature even as they retain a trace of their original nature outside of our world and of the order of the sacred, of which they are no longer more than just one-sixtieth: "Fire is one-sixtieth part of Gehinnom. Honey is one-sixtieth part of manna. Sabbath is one-sixtieth part of the world to come. Sleep is one-sixtieth part of death. A dream is one-sixtieth part of prophecy."[4]

Six hundred thousand, finally, is the canonical number of "souls" in the community of Israel that was present at the base of Mount Sinai, the community that is supposedly reconstituted in one way or another from generation to generation in the individuals—who have, however, become much more numerous—who have historically constituted the people of Israel.

So it seems as though this base six designates a spatial multiplicity, dispersed, one might say, "to the four corners—or rather, the six corners—of the world." But its multiplications into tens, hundreds, and thousands tend to unify it. In fact, the unpronounceable abstract *unity* of *aleph* reproduces itself in base ten and returns in the *eleph* ("thousand") and the thousands of thousands (*alphei alaphim*). This base-ten multiplication is superimposed onto the spatial dispersion of base six. It thus produces a kind of unified multiplicity that we also find in the relativity of passing time, where "a thousand years in Your eyes are but a bygone yesterday."[5]

Whatever the case may be with these symbolic meanings, the decimal numbering system seems to have prevailed almost universally, probably starting with our ten fingers, but bases six, or sixty, or twelve are not without their advantages, notably where their multiples and submultiples are concerned. The number six is the only number whose value is the sum of its divisors (one, two, and three). The numerous divisors of twelve and sixty allow for games of submultiples that are much richer than is possible with those of ten, which is divisible only by two or five. And currency systems have long used duodecimal numbering.

Let us also note that the Talmud itself gives us an indication in that the rule of one-sixth of the fair price is introduced in the Mishnah with an explicit reference to a currency, the *sela*, which is divided into 24 *ma'ot*, perhaps on the model of the *dinar* (which is divided into 24 *issars*), a Roman currency utilized at the time and worth a quarter of a *sela*. All of this could provide a relatively simple explanation for the choice of one-sixth as the value of the threshold.

And yet, it turns out that the *sela* is equated with the shekel, the ancient biblical currency, which has twenty submultiples (Leviticus 27:25) rather than twenty-four. And Rashi observes in his commentary that "our masters *added one-sixth* such that six *ma'ot* make one *dinar* and four *dinars* make one *sela*." The Talmud, therefore, introduces one more innovation as compared to the biblical text, by adding one-sixth of the very value of the monetary unit. As in the case of the divergence that defines the threshold of *ona'ah* instituted by the teachers of the Talmud, this divergence of one-sixth is one that appears here between the sacred currency of the biblical world, to which the perfection of base ten is appropriate, in the image of the Law falling from heaven, and the approximation of the currency of the post-prophetic world, in which "the Law is not in heaven." Here, we can already see an allusion to the esoteric meaning of this entire story, which we will now present in outline form: a meaning that revolves entirely around the distance between twenty-six, the value of the name of being (YHWH) in its unity and its perfection, and twenty-four, as that multiple of six that is closest to it.

One-eighteenth of being

There is—now is the time to say it—a common denominator shared by commercial fraud and fraudulent speech: the damage they cause, though measurable in one case and not in the other, is gauged in a context that is marked by two shared properties. On the one hand, a certain degree of fraud, of divergence from the fair price or involuntary verbal deception, cannot be avoided. On the other hand, everything must be done to limit the damage to a minimum even if establishing that minimum—one-sixth of the fair price—can seem arbitrary in the case of commercial exchange and impossible in the case of verbal injury.

Yet the question of this minimum is formally regulated in cabalistic commentary,[6] in which what is at stake is explicitly neither a commercial exchange nor an exchange of words but rather the constitution of a being whose structure is progressively organized on the model of the human body. To anticipate the conclusion, this dynamic process implies the step of a division of the value of the being into three whole parts, although this being in its unity is indivisible. The minimum divergence—which includes *ona'ah*—from an equitable division thus appears to be one-sixth of one-third, which is to say one-eighteenth of being!

This schema takes up a classical sefirotic structure for a being in the form of a human body. Each *sefira*, or category corresponding to a part of the body, itself reproduces the same structure in nine categories, discharged onto the tenth, which completes them. The one corresponding to the torso has a special status because of its central position: it is the transition point between the head and arms above and the legs and sexual organs below, and its own structure of nine categories is divided into three parts. The upper third, above the diaphragm, is the place of intellectual and emotional outpourings, which remain hidden, buried in the "heart." The lower two-thirds are revealed to be potential receptacles for these outpourings as they descend and are transformed into motors of the union—the *da'at* or "knowledge"—with the feminine being, constructed from the tenth, global *sefira*. This schema is used to represent an exchange between the upper third and the lower two-thirds that includes the possibility of *ona'ah*, that is to say, of unequal division and of "injury" to one of the parties resulting from the exchange. At stake here, then, is the status of the being itself that is constructed on the model of a human body. This construction is represented as an exchange between the upper third, which "sells" these outpourings, and the lower two-thirds, which "buy" them. And here, too, an *ona'ah*, a divergence from the fair "price," along with the damage that results, is unavoidable. As we shall see, this comes from an arithmetic particularity of the name of being, the tetragrammaton YHVH, where we find, unexpectedly, the function of the threshold of damage that is not to be crossed attributed to the portion one-sixth.

This commentary introduces a more profound dimension into the rule of one-sixth at the same time as it establishes a connection with the other *ona'ah*, verbal *ona'ah*, whose damage within the victim's interior self and within that of the author of the *ona'ah* is a priori immeasurable. In fact, we are told here of a harm produced by an inevitable inequity in an exchange that is constitutive of a developing being whose name is none other than the tetragrammaton YHVH. The use of Hebrew letters and the traditional attribution of a numeric value to them—yet another kind of numbering system—makes it possible to quantify this name of being in some way, along with the arithmetic consequences that flow from this. Made up of the tenth letter, the fifth, the sixth, and once again the fifth letter of the alphabet, the name of being therefore has a numeric value of twenty-six. *Yet it turns out that twenty-six is not divisible by three.* In this, it significantly diverges from the multiples of six and twelve, of which twenty-four is the closest. Unlike twenty-four, which has numerous divisors (two, three, four, six, eight, twelve), twenty-six is reducible only to two times thirteen, in other words a unit that is a doubling up of the prime number thirteen, which itself is the numeric value of "one" (*é'had*) and "love" (*ahavah*).

The commentary carries out a noteworthy reversal compared to the talmudic rule. It provides a very general formal interpretation, in which the one-sixth rule receives an ontological foundation, so to speak, thanks to a kind of quantification of being. In the Talmud's exposition, the value of one-sixth is presented as an obvious given, without justification, as the threshold for a divergence from the fair price of a transaction that requires reparation. In this context, it is admitted that it is impossible to avoid harming one of the parties, and the task is therefore to reduce the harm thus produced to a minimum, to an admissible, "forgiven," divergence from the fair price. But the cabalistic commentary leaves behind the literal context of a commercial exchange and situates itself, from the start, within a process that constructs a being. It represents the transaction as a transmission, the division of an outpouring of "light" from one level of the being to another, across the upper third, where the light is hidden in the thorax and held back by the screen of the diaphragm, and the lower two-thirds of the torso, which are open to the eye. In the symbolism of "figures" (*partsufim*) in the Lurianic Kabbalah, this is a generation in which the stakes involve the construction of a human figure, that of a "son" whose "brains" are not yet completed, who receives from the "father" (wisdom) and from the "mother" (intelligence) that which allows him to "know" the "daughter" or "spouse of the son" by constructing in her his capacity for "knowledge." This diffusion passes through the constitution of a "knowledge" at the top, in the "heart" of the son, on the basis of what he has received from the father and mother. The influence of the mother, an inescapable passage, is present in the son like the influence of the female bird hatching her young.[7] As we shall see, the outpouring from the mother to the son, "knowledge from above," must pass through the screen of the diaphragm so that the rind that envelops the male sexual organ (the foreskin) will not prevent "knowledge from below" from being carried out correctly. In a parallel move, an inverse causality, moving up from below, has the "circumcision of the heart" depend on the "circumcision of the flesh."[8]

In this representation of the exchange, the upper third thus plays the role of "the seller" and the lower two-thirds that of the "buyer"; the transaction is fair if each of the three parts receives its due, that is to say, one-third. But that is impossible for reasons that are intrinsic to the very nature of being, namely its numerical value of twenty-six, which is not divisible by three. The division of twenty-six into three whole parts is necessarily unequal, advantageous to some of the parties and disadvantageous to others. This is what distorts the exchange in a way and makes it inequitable. In fact, the ways of dividing twenty-six into three whole parts that most closely approximate an equitable division produce unequal parts distributed in the relations eight, nine, nine, or nine, nine, eight, or ten, eight, eight. (Whereas an ideal division into three equal parts would produce fractional parts each equal to eight and two-thirds.) Of these three distributions, the first implies injury to the upper third, the "seller," which receives only eight parts, i.e. two-thirds less than what it would have received in an equal division. In the other two distributions, on the other hand, the seller receives, respectively, one-third and one and one-third *more*, which implies therefore that it is the lower two-thirds, the "buyer," that is injured.

We can verify that in all three distributions the divergence between the whole parts [and the fair fractional portion] is less than one-sixth of eight and two-thirds (the exact fractional value of one-third of twenty-six).[9] And yet, although the three unequal divisions are admissible according to the rule of *ona'ah*, because the injury is always "less than one-sixth," it is the first division that is considered to be the most "normal," since the resulting surplus of outpouring for the lower part takes place from top to bottom, in the right direction for the constitution of being.

Therefore, it is as though a kind of construction flaw were unavoidable. Compared to what would be a static perfection, given once and for all, the construction of a developing being implies a certain initial imperfection compared to its subsequent completion. The perfect indivisible unity of the one (thirteen), reinforced in the loving otherness of two "ones" (twenty-six), collides with the necessary differentiation between the top, bottom, and middle parts; the static duality is overcome and mobilized by the arrival of a third term, a putting into motion of the nutritious outpourings that is indispensable for the construction of individual beings. But this construction flaw must be reduced to a minimum, and the minimum reveals itself to be equal to one-sixth of one-third, that is to say one-eighteenth of this being, by the very fact of its arithmetic properties.

But matters don't end there, because the inequality that favors the "buyer" attains the threshold of one-sixth and even surpasses it, albeit temporarily, and must therefore be subsequently redressed according to the rules of *ona'ah* that is equal to or greater than one-sixth. And here the cabalist, in a way that is unexpected at first, sees in the back-and-forth of this division not only the *sod*, or esoteric "hidden" meaning of the talmudic rules concerning *ona'ah*, but also the *sod* of circumcision.[10]

Circumcision, of the heart and of the flesh

As is often the case, this level of interpretation of the "hidden meaning" or *sod*,[11] which is characteristic of cabalistic writing, is presented using a technical, formal vocabulary that seems far removed from the text and the context to which it is applied. An interpretation of the interpretation can be useful. In the present case, we suggest the following way of roughly understanding what lies behind the technique of numeric analogies used by the author of *Etz Hayyim*.

The construction of the developing being is accomplished only when the male sexual organ, which is initially prevented from uniting itself in an unfettered way with the female by the "rind" that covers it, is unveiled. The unveiling is a manifestation of the very act of knowledge through both intellect and sex. For knowledge is both the unveiling of what was hidden and the experience of a reunion between the knower and the known and with knowledge itself, to use the classical expression that is taken up by Maimonides, Spinoza, and certain cabalists. But in order for this to be accomplished, according to the author of the *Etz Hayyim*, the static unity that has been achieved through the compromise of unequal division—in which the inevitable inequality has been reduced to an unavoidable minimum, "less than one-sixth"—must be shaken up a little more. In fact, the upper third, which includes the "heart," in which, as we have seen, the source of knowledge that is the "mother" is hidden, must unveil itself and its light must pour through the screen of the diaphragm into the lower part of the body, down to the male or female sexual organ.

We must note that in this way of looking at it, as opposed to the thorax, where the light of the "father" and the "mother" (wisdom and intelligence) remain hidden, the lower part that corresponds to the abdomen is, from the outset, where the unveiling is situated that is necessary to the initial construction of a body that is still immature, before this body can grow and make itself into a receptacle for "knowledge," the product of the union of wisdom and intelligence. This structure is astonishing because it seems as though the covering ought to be reversed and involve instead the lower parts of the body, according to the pretty much universally established rules of modesty. But the covering here is not the covering of clothing. The "nudity" covered by clothing, at the minimum a penis sheath or a fig leaf, is indeed the nudity of the skin. But the skin is itself an opaque covering. Behind the evidence of its exposition, the interiority of the subject is hidden and its transparency rejected, in a more or less nostalgic Edenic ideal. On the other hand, according to the story of Genesis, the clothing that, in turn, covers the skin of the subject, ever since the expulsion from Eden, allows for a certain unveiling of the individual and social personality of the one who wears it. The body that is at the center of this abstract representation, however, is a body of "glory," if we may call it that, whose skin is itself "light," shining and transparent, as it was on Adam and Eve according to the Midrash—before it became opaque when they fell.[12] For this archetypal body, modesty has to do, instead, with the concepts of a subtle knowledge whose truth always runs the risk of being deformed when it is exposed too brutally, without the veils that make it possible to perceive its depth.[13] It is this modesty, rather than the modesty connected to the nudity of the skin of the body, that is the subject of the *Sifra ditsni'uata*, the "Book of Modesty," a treatise of the *Zohar* that describes the major elements of the structure of the worlds for the cabalist tradition.

In this context, in which the lower part of the body is normally uncovered, the sexual organ is an exception in that the "rind" of the foreskin covers it, creating a screen between the male and the female. This screen reproduces, on the lower level, the screen created by the diaphragm between the hidden upper third and the uncovered lower two-thirds. The circumcision that is represented in this commentary consists in eliminating these screens on the two levels, each one conditioning the other, from top to bottom and from bottom to top. The upper third, then, uncovers even more than the minimum that, as we have seen, was necessary for getting the process going and constituted the injury that was, for this reason, allowed and "forgiven." This additional uncovering thus implies a greater "injury" for the upper third, the "seller," which at first loses *exactly* one-sixth, and then even more than one-sixth, of the portion that would be its due in an equal division. It is this additional outpouring that was initially held back by various envelopes and screens at various levels, to prevent this injury and not exceed the normally acceptable threshold. There are thus a variety of correlated and interdependent levels of "uncircumcision," as is indicated by the biblical expressions not only for the sexual organ, but also for affects, the intellect, language . . . and even trees.[14] The commentary with which we are concerned here is explicitly discussing the two levels of the heart, hidden and covered in the thorax, and of the sexual organ, covered by its foreskin. The heart refers not only to the affects—one also speaks of a "heart of stone" or a "heart of flesh"[15]—but, in addition, to the intellect of the "mother," *bina*, the "intelligence that understands," in the classical cabalistic typology of *sefirot*.

Even though this is not made explicit in the commentary, we may also associate the foreskin with the organs of language. Moses's "foreskin of the lips" (Exodus 12 and 30) prevents his words from coming out freely, to the extent that he must appeal to his brother Aaron as his "prophet" to transmit his speech (Exodus 7:1). The "foreskin of the ear" of which

Jeremiah speaks (6:10) when he talks about the people and which he elsewhere also qualifies as a "foreskin of the heart" (9:25) keeps words from being heard. As for the foreskin of fruit-bearing trees, we may refer it to the analogy in which "man is the tree of the field" (Deuteronomy 20:19). This analogy is presented in the context of a prohibition on destroying fruit trees during the siege of an enemy town, which is extended by the rabbinic tradition to the premature destruction of all natural or manufactured goods.[16] But there are some cabalistic interpretations that see in this the image of the just (as in, for example, the commentary *Maor vashemesh* on this verse from Deuteronomy), woman for her part being represented in the *Zohar* by "the field of the sacred apples." Finally, all of this also refers us back to the nature of the two trees at the center of the Garden of Eden. The Tree (*'etz*) of Life and of Knowledge is a concrete instance of *'etza*, "counsel," and the ingestion of its fruit produced the effects with which we are all familiar.[17]

Be that as it may, the additional outpouring across the screens now rendered necessary by the construction of the adult body implies a crossing of the threshold of injury of "less than one-sixth" that is normally allowable.

Hence the idea, at first unexpected, that the talmudic rules of *ona'ah*, in their cabalistic interpretations, refer back to the *sod*, the esoteric "hidden" meaning of the ritual of circumcision. The construction flaw implied by the opposition between the unity of being that is given in its initial static perfection and the putting into movement of its becoming, across the history in which it must construct itself by multiplying itself, now exceeds the allowable limits. It is then, in a way, separated into two stages. The injury begins by attaining and even exceeding the allowable threshold, but it can be redressed according to the rules foreseen for this case. And yet this redress necessarily implies a certain delay. It therefore does not eliminate the historical reality of the injury before it has had time to be redressed. Whether the issue is the reimbursement of the divergence from the fair price that has injured one of the parties or the pure and simple cancellation of the transaction, redress is not immediate and thus does not eliminate the reality of this transaction, not even temporarily. This time lag is obviously also the subject of the talmudic discussions surrounding *ona'ah*. A certain amount of time, long or short, may pass and *during that time* the transaction is a reality. It is as though the loss produced by the injury were a forced, involuntary loan that will, of course, be repaid, but only later. In other words, there is something irreparable after all that remains in the measurable and reparable *ona'ah* which brings it closer to verbal *ona'ah*, which is not measurable and which is not eliminated by a potential pardon.

Of course the real, concrete circumcision of the male sexual organ is irreversible and therefore not temporary. But its symbolic effects, that is to say, the opening to knowledge both "from above" and "from below" and to the union with the feminine, are pushed back to a later time. Furthermore, unlike the union of the figures of the "father" and the "mother," which is a permanent union on the model of the intricate union that entangles wisdom in intelligence and intelligence in wisdom, the union of the masculine and the feminine at the level of the "son" and "daughter" who represent man and woman is not permanent. In the Bible, material circumcision as a ritual of sexual initiation is a "sign" of Abraham's alliance for the future, which assures him of numerous offspring in a "multitude of nations" after he has been exhorted to be "perfect" and after his name, too, has been completed.[18] As with every alliance, this one has more to do with the future of promises than with the present of an encounter that we know to be temporary. Let us recall that, in biblical Hebrew, every alliance that is concluded is said to be "cut" in that it is not a fusion. It is precisely because the alliance is concluded between two parties that remain separate that the parties need the alliance, in order to make claims on the future as a promise despite their separation. The alliance of circumcision, which announces the future and intermittent union of masculine and feminine through knowledge, is thus sealed by a cut as well. This is already the case with YHVH's promise to Abram (before his name is changed), sealed in a ritual of alliance in which sacrificed animals are cut in half and the two partners walk between the pieces.[19]

Let us note that for the author of this commentary, there are other circumstances in which the same formal model is reproduced. The issue is still an additional outpouring of the upper third that allows the lower two-thirds to construct themselves, an outpouring that is the basis of an injury to the "seller" and exceeds the normally allowable threshold. As in the preceding case, the transaction is only temporarily in effect before it is either canceled or compensated for in reparation of the injury. But its influence endures because the *canceled exchange* is not the same thing as the absence of an exchange in the being that it has contributed to bringing about. In addition to the symbolic meaning of circumcision, this model is also applied in order to give an account of the hidden meaning of the story of the construction of woman in Genesis. To put it roughly, after the man Adam, initially a hermaphrodite, has grown, the hidden presence of the "mother" in his heart is no longer necessary; her influence of "intelligence" works on him through the brain in his head. The mother is then occupied with making the daughter grow in turn. The same model is applied to the meaning that *shabbat* has for the cabalist: the being of the son has grown and receives knowledge from above in his head, while the girl or the wife of the son has also grown and their union between adults can now be consummated. Finally, the story of the sale of Joseph by his brothers in Genesis is also interpreted in this commentary as a paradigm of the theft constituted by an injury greater than one-sixth during the time when it has not been canceled.[20]

If we now return to the commercial context of real buyers and sellers, the threshold of one-sixth as a way to define *ona'ah* no longer appears, in the light of this commentary, as an arbitrary fact but as the projection of an intrinsic property of a formally quantified being into the realm of commerce. The circle is closing: verbal *ona'ah* certainly reaches the person directly, in a manner that is apparently not measurable and cannot be redressed, in contradistinction to the measurable and reparable kind that only extends to goods. But this measure and its redress are calculated using an arithmetic of being, in which the person is a dynamic process, under construction part by part, whose essence is constantly modified along the way. Exchanges of goods and of money now take place on the model of exchanges in which beings are constructed, and not the other way around, as one might be led to believe by simply reading the talmudic sayings one after the other.

Measures and values

In chapter 1, we saw that value is caught in the circle of its truth and of the value of truth. But it is also caught in a permanent tension with the question of its measure. For "values" are, in principle, beyond all measure. A "true" value is priceless and beyond measure, even infinite, as, for example, the value of human life. Yet in certain cases, the value of an object or of the general equivalent that is money is supposed to determine a fair price. This tension is the basis of the apparently endless analyses in a treatise of the Talmud entitled, in fact, "Values," *'Arakhim*. But the singular of this word designates an evaluation (*'erekh*) that is sometimes approximate, thus unlike precise measures. Many pages of the treatise are in fact dedicated to evaluating the price of a human person in the particular context of a vow that consecrates a given person to the service of the sanctuary. A certain amount of money representing the value of the person then has to be paid to fulfill this promise. A general "evaluation" of the amount is then made based on age and sex, following a very precise scale already established by the biblical text.[21] But the Talmud's interpretation extends the biblical injunction's field of application to the vows of consecration of people whose price is not fixed a priori by this general rule of evaluation, independent of their physical or mental state. On the contrary, their price needs to be estimated according to their particular trade value in the potential situation, even if that possibility is purely hypothetical, of the person being sold as a slave in the marketplace![22] Furthermore, we find in the same treatise the most radical affirmations of the infinite value of a person's dignity, which can be trampled by slanderous speech. The immoderate nature of humiliation and of the harm it inflicts is thus expressed in the infinite measure of the evil of which the slanderer becomes guilty.[23] In general, measures in the sense of precise magnitudes, as opposed to valuations, are designated by the word *midot*. But this word also designates logical categories and qualities such as generosity, justice, harmony, perseverance, and beauty, that is to say, that which constitutes the intellectual and moral *value* of human beings. Finally, the "gates" (*shé'arim*) also designate "measures" in the sense of quantities of products, while the verb derived from the word designates the act of making an estimate.

This is all brought together on the subject of *ona'ah* in an expression we have already encountered, at the end of the story of the oven, an expression of the excessive character of *ona'at dvarim*, verbal fraud or injury: "All gates are locked, excepting the gates of *ona'ah*."[24] Curiously, as is so often the case in the talmudic Midrash, this teaching of Rav Hisda's rests on a verse from the book of Amos (7:7) that is itself enigmatic: "Behold, the Lord standing on a plumbed [*anakh*] wall with a plumb line [*anakh*] in His hand." The same verse also serves to support Rabbi Elazar's teaching: "All compensation is made indirectly through an intermediary, except [the compensation of] *ona'ah*, as it is said 'with a plumb line in His hand.'"[25] This "plumbing" of the wall and this "plumb line" expressed by one and the same word, *anakh*, which is repeated in the verse, obviously have suggested numerous commentaries. But it seems that here we are referred back to the question of measuring that which is not measurable. Only a god possesses the standard tool of measurement, the "plumb line" to measure the divergence, the deviousness, of verbal fraud. For neither the malice of the one who does harm—because he may have been unaware of the effect of his words—nor the extent of the damage—because it is damage to the dignity of a being and not to what it owns—can be measured.

As we saw earlier, in our discussion of the one-sixth rule, it is this immeasurability of the verbal injury that is projected, in part, onto commercial fraud by the institution of a space between a minimum below which it is "forgiven" and the maximum beyond which it is redressed by the cancellation of the transaction. It is as though the being (of the seller and of the buyer) is also engaged in the exchange of the object and something immeasurable is superimposed on the fair price, on the "value" of what one has.

In the verse from the book of Amos, the god of Israel appears to the prophet on a perimeter wall, between the interior and the exterior. Talmudic interpretation sees in this the place from which everything is visible, the interior as well as the exterior, the interiority of moral life and of its hidden intentions, good and bad, and the objective exteriority of behaviors, where the standard of measurement of an equitable justice is to be found. The god of Israel appears to the prophet, who is concerned with what will become of his people, holding this standard, which will also be the expression of the judgment and of the devastations that will follow from it. In fact, we read in the next verse: "Behold, I am placing a plumb line in the midst of My nation Israel [in order to measure its faults]; I will no longer continue to forbear them."[26]

It is this dialectic between interior and exterior, being and having, immeasurable value and objective measure that talmudic interpretation projects onto verbal injuries, both inflicted and suffered. It is the same dialectic that led to the institution of the world of *ona'ah*, the irreducible interval between the interior and the exterior, in the objective exchanges themselves, with a view, as we have seen, to reconciling individual integrity with the interest of the collective.

In fact, the chapter of the Talmud began with a long discussion of the applications of a principle that governs every purchase of an object: a transaction is considered to be definitive and irrevocable only once the object is in the hands of the buyer. As long as this is not the case, even if the money has been paid to the seller, the transaction can be revoked and the money returned. And here we find the same dialectic between the legal realm, with its objectivity, and the moral subjectivity of inner life. For this principle obviously leaves room for a certain bad faith as to the agreement concluded and the commitment of the two parties. But the court is not in a position to estimate this commitment in the case of litigation and harm caused by the withdrawal of one of the parties. Here, too, it is reduced to relying on the works of a god who is now hidden to take the responsibility for moral subjectivity and to ensure payment for the harm caused by the words of a broken commitment, even one without legal value. A curse by the Assembly appeals here to the model of the divine interventions that struck the authors of particularly wicked actions in the Bible: "He who punished the generation of the flood and the generation of the Tower of Babel, He will take vengeance of him who does not stand by his word."[27]

Elsewhere, Rabbi Shimon appeals to the one who made "the inhabitants of Sodom and Gomorrah and the Egyptians on the Red Sea" pay. And he adds the more general principle of a moral condemnation with no legal sanction (not even the sanction of a "curse"): "[H]e who enters into a verbal transaction effects no title, yet he who retracts therefrom, the spirit of the Sages is displeased with him."[28]

But it is in the cabalistic commentary on the rule of one-sixth that this opposition between measure and excess is projected onto both having and being, divisible and indivisible, through the formalism of the four-letter name and its multiplications. We have seen how the rule of one-sixth that defines *ona'ah*, with its interval of tolerance, is interpreted as expressing the impossibility of exact measurement in the domain of being at the same time as it expresses the projection of this same impossibility onto possessions; as though something of being were also exchanged in the trading of objects.

And yet, contrasting with the world of *ona'ah* with its inevitable interval of tolerance, there is the world of the trilogy of "weight, count, and measure."[29]

This interpretation again appeals to the arithmetic analysis of the divisibility of the tetragrammaton YHVH and of its numerical value, twenty-six. Let us recall that the transaction between the "seller" and the "buyer" is interpreted in this commentary as representing an outpouring that constitutes being in the form of a human body, an outpouring that starts from the upper third, the source of life hidden above the diaphragm, and moves toward the lower two-thirds, where the outpouring unveils itself in mobility and sexual activity. And, as we have seen, this symbolic representation comes up against the indivisibility into three equal and whole parts of the numerical value twenty-six of the name of being. Hence the impossibility of avoiding an inequality, of surplus or of lack, with injury either to the upper third compared to the lower thirds or vice versa.

Yet this impossibility is opposed to other instances in which a division into three equal parts is possible. This associates the world of *ona'ah* with the world of precise measurement expressed in the operations of *weighing*, of *counting*, and of *measuring* in general. And yet the issue still involves operations on the same tetragrammaton. But one of the most frequent interpretive models in the Lurianic Kabbalah consists in declining this name in different ways following the method of *writing the name's four letters* by spelling out *their names*, then doing the same with the names of the letters in each of those names, and so on. The result is a multiplication process that resembles a Neoplatonic emanation from the One to the multiple. For, on the one hand, the tetragrammaton written *simply* with its four letters, Y, H, V, H, is the name of the being whose unity is proclaimed in Moses's exhortation to the people, *Shema Israel* . . . ("Hear, Israel, YHVH [is] our *elohim*, YHVH [is] one"), commonly considered to be the monotheistic credo. Unity is already expressed here in different ways, in which letters and numbers blend: its only possible division, into two times thirteen, refers to two times *e'had* ("one") or two times *ahavah* ("love"), for each of which the numerical value is thirteen, as if this unity were even more accomplished thanks to the loving union of two "ones."

But, on the other hand, these four letters can be written in a different way, "fully" as it is called, by spelling out the names of the letters, that is to say, the words that are themselves used to name these letters in the alphabet: *yod* for Y, *hey* for H, *vav* for V, and again *hey* for H. The same process can be repeated, and each of the letters that spell the words that name the four letters can in turn be written "fully." The result is that the tetragrammaton can itself be multiplied into a larger number of letters. Its numerical value is then multiplied as well and becomes, among other possibilities, seventy-two (three times twenty-four), two hundred and sixteen (three times seventy-two), or forty-two (three times fourteen), according to different ways of writing it, "fully" or "full of fullness." The commentary associates these values with various divisions into three equal parts that, unlike in the world of *ona'ah* and its interval of tolerance, characterize the world "of measurement [*mida*], of weight [*mishkal*] and of the count [*miniane*]." Here, there is no tolerance for false weights, for false measurements, or for inexact counts. Since each "third" can receive its exact share, every deviation can and must be redressed exactly, under punishment of being charged with theft or inadmissible deception, however small, on the model of counterfeit money. We are thus no longer in the world of *ona'ah*, fraud that is admissible at less than one-sixth of the fair price, even though the symbolic model remains derived from an arithmetic analysis of the name of being. But it is as though the transition from the One to the multiple, from the simple being to the multiplied being, whether it takes place in being or possessions, which now merge in their ontological reality, implied a transition from the world of *ona'ah*, partially irreparable in objects and totally irreparable in the simple being, to the world of exact measurements, reparable in principle at least.

In this world of multiplicities, fraud assumes the form of counterfeit currency, that is to say of theft, deception, and lying beyond the limits that are compatible with the social bond. In his analysis of the relations between language and money, Olender cites the treatise *De moneta*, written in the fourteenth century by Nicole Oresme, mathematician, physicist, and bishop of Lisieux, in which these relations are made explicit:

True money must have an appropriate name. . . . Oresme reminds us that the [biblical] shekel is both the name of a currency and the name of a weight: *shekel* comes, in fact, from the verb "to weigh." . . . As for counterfeit money, it is characterized by an alteration of its weight, by the composition of an illicit alloy, or by the mutation of names, by false appellation. We cannot call "gold what is not gold and pound what is not a known pound." . . . That would mean the reign of the illicit alloy, of "black money" (*nigra moneta*). The more imperceptible it is, the more cunning and "sophisticated" the fraud. "Black money," a nuisance that injures the community, damages the very name of *moneta*. In these pages, Oresme stresses that money is the ultimate sign of that which does not deceive. . . . Its semantic power is such that its common name guarantees it: *moneta* "advises" that there is no fraud since "money" comes from *moneo*, "I advise." . . . Money fraud, the violation of the integrity of the name, sows confusion and disturbs the order of the world. For to deceive about the composition of the matter being exchanged, about weights and measures, is to violate "God [who made] all things in measure, in weight, and the number." . . . This supreme evil [in the community and especially for a prince who renders himself guilty of it] results from monetary fraud. Such a "mutation of money" in fact leads to an inevitable "scandal." The scandal gives rise to a disorder that befalls not only the monetary affair but the entirety of the system of religious, political, and emotional values from which this common measure draws its legitimacy.[30]

Thus we find here, again, the triad "measure, weight, and number" mentioned in the commentary of *Etz Hayyim*. Like what lying does to the moral attitude that Jankélévitch describes as purist, deceptions about measure, weight, and number are the supreme evil in that they destroy the order of the world in all its dimensions, they disturb the community all the more for their ability to be invisible and befall the "intimate."[31]

This is not the case, as we have seen, in the talmudic institution of the world of *ona'ah*, which posits an interval of tolerance as an inevitable evil due to the very fact that it is impossible to measure. This impossibility can be objective, technical in a way, when we are dealing with the objects of buying and selling and the fair price, the market price, cannot be defined with absolute precision. But it can also be ontological when the evil is beyond any measure in that it befalls the intimacy of a being, as is the case with injurious speech. Hence we see, in the arithmetic of the names of being presented in the cabalistic interpretation of this institution, that the priceless value beyond all measure and the measuring, despite everything, of that which has no price refer to one another, like the simple unity and the complex multiplicity of being. Although in practice, persons must be distinguished from exchangeable objects and that which can be redressed from harm without price, all of this evokes the intuition of a deeper and more "hidden" substantial unity of the One and the multiple.

Hence the symmetrical temptations of that which lies beyond the limit, the *sacred* and the absolute on one side, and the unbridledness of the total *dissolution* of the true on the other.

7

The Crystallized Sacred

The nature, function, and genealogy of experiences of the sacred

The notion of the sacred must not be analyzed retrospectively through the prism of the history of institutionalized religions. We must instead appeal to a relatively new field of anthropology, enriched by what we can learn from ethnobotany.

"Between Crystal and Smoke"[1]: this is the name I once gave to the "in-between" that characterizes living organizations—between the repetitive order of crystal and the disorder of smoke; between two kinds of death, the rigidity of the corpse and the chaos of dissolution. In the preface to that book, I made reference to the association evoked by this image, unconsciously at first for its author but not for his companion: the association with the two moments of exterminating death that were Kristallnacht (the Night of Broken Glass, the expression of the false purity of the false Aryan "race) and the smoke of the crematories.

But it is another "in-between" I want to talk about here, between two more subtle forms of death than the destruction of bodies, two extremes that I will call the "crystallized sacred" and the "diluted sacred." At stake here is the status of truth, which can kill in two ways as well, by an excess of purity and by a dissolution into systemic fraud. Human societies have always been confronted with this back-and-forth whose institution is none other than the institution of the sacred: it is there, indeed, that the imaginary and violence come together, along with the truth or lies of their expressions, the constitutive elements of the bonds by which human beings unite within a group and confront those that are outside the group. At least since Émile Durkheim,[2] the function of the sacred as a stabilizer of the social bond has been the subject of all sorts of sociological and anthropological analyses. René Girard has analyzed the relationship between the sacred and violence as a foundational ambivalence: for him, sacrificial violence done to the scapegoat, the deputized victim, whether human or animal, protects against the initial mimetic violence of each against all.[3] Jean-Pierre Dupuy has shown that not only do these analyses pertain to ancient societies but that expressions of this sacred are to be found in modern societies as well, albeit without explicit sacrificial rituals.[4] Omnipresent natural violence, human and nonhuman intermingled, is "treated" by way of collective representations and behaviors that provide practical and symbolic answers, which are appropriate, to greater or lesser degrees, to the catastrophes of the past and those that appear on the horizon for the future. The nuclear threat, in which planetary catastrophe has been avoided in the past by games of deterrence whereas future catastrophes continue to be likely, serves as a paradigm for this.

The role of the imaginary in the representations that societies create of themselves has already been analyzed by Cornelius Castoriadis in *The Imaginary Institution of Society*.[5] Maurice Godelier has recently shown its original and creative foundational force, along with the bonds established by the exchanges of goods and of signs in both modern and ancient societies.[6] We saw in chapter 3 that the exchanges themselves, especially through the role played by money, are imbued with this dimension of the sacred, even if the sacred has evolved from the ancient times of "hieratic"—that is to say, sacralized—expressions of authority to the current, apparently desacralized, forms of mass demonstrations, secular communions around an exceptional political or sporting event, a concert, commemoration, or any other collective expression of joy or sadness that brings crowds of people together.

But most often, these analyses sin by omission, a major omission. They neglect the individual neuropsychic aspect of the phenomenon, without which the order of the sacred would have no means, whatever its form, of taking root in the bodies and minds that make up societies. This is above all the case for those analyses that use the logic of functional explanations: they describe the sacred and explain its pervasiveness by way of the functions it performs in establishing and stabilizing the social bond. Without denying the importance of these functions, we can still say that the problem with these explanations lies in their teleological character, producing, as they do, final causes that are supposed to account for the existence and the structures of the sacred. For to be able to play such a role, to exercise such a function, it is at least initially necessary that its force and its structures be given, rooted in the reality of the bodies and minds of the individuals that constitute the group, even if those structures can then in turn be reinforced and possibly modified by the effects of society on the individuals. In other words, an ability to experience the sacred must be part of human nature, in the same way as the capacity for language, for opposable thumbs, for toolmaking, and even for the very constitution of human societies themselves, with all their specificities compared to animal societies. When it *is* taken into account, this individual reality of the order of the sacred is most often associated with the phenomenon of religion and even with its theological expressions: it is described as having to do with belief in gods or in God, with ritual and its accompanying priests being its collective expression. But with the exception of certain ethnologists and ethnobotanists, most modern authors writing about sociology or philosophy have trouble imagining these categories outside of the framework of the religion that dominates their own culture, that is to say, Christianity.[7]

I have already mentioned, in our discussion of money, this insufficiency in the analyses that overlook the archaic rootedness of experiences of the sacred in the neurophysiology of dreams and of shamanic hallucinoses, both spontaneous and provoked. It is not a matter of explaining religious phenomena, to which the experience of the sacred is most often reduced, by way of either the specific brain activity, including its explicit contents, that brain-exploration techniques allow us to identify or the naïve theories (whose insufficiency Jean-Pierre Dupuy has recently, and rightly, denounced) that are sometimes suggested by the cognitive sciences.[8] But neither can we be satisfied with functional sociological explanations. Like all teleological explanations of social phenomena, they lack any rootedness in a phenomenology of individual experiences to which the social can certainly not be reduced but without which the social could not exist.

Furthermore, many of these theories rest on the highly questionable hypothesis[9] of an initial human nature of chaotic violence of each against all, of the human being who, in Hobbes's famous formulation, is "a wolf to man." This egotistical wild-animal nature of human beings is said to have made it necessary for culture, at first inseparable from religion, to impose laws capable of socializing them. Yet we know, on the one hand, that wild animals are not all, nor always, egotistical and violent and that, in fact, some of them have developed forms of social organization. On the other hand, there is no reason for us to suppose that this initial "state of nature" of humanity ever existed. Quite the contrary: the human nature of Homo sapiens, from the moment it appears, seems to be inseparable from the elements of its culture with all their diversity. Human beings' representations of themselves, of others, of their vegetal and animal environment, and of the universe, through their activities and their experiences, notably of death, but also through their dreams, their spontaneous or induced visions, their historical-mythical stories and the rituals that perpetuated them, formed part of their nature as much as did their anatomy and physiology. But it is true that the philosophically and religiously dominant culture in the West, which has been progressively desacralized for two and a half thousand years, was accompanied by a spiritualization that was rapidly followed by a disincarnation and by the reassignment of bodies to this supposed animal nature. Modern biologism, for its part, has reinforced this idea by relegating the nonscientific productions of the human mind to the domain of fables without substance. In a fair reversal, animal nature today seems to carry with it elements of socialization.

So instead, we must look for descriptions of this neuropsychic rootedness that is at the origin of experiences of the sacred in the work of ethnobotanists and of certain anthropologists, philosophers, writers, and psychologists, still in the minority, who have attempted a phenomenology of altered states of consciousness[10] as independently as possible of their own cultural context.[11]

For there is a great difference between the original sacred, the "true" sacred if you will, and the diluted sacred that emerges here and there, partially repressed, in the modern and postmodern world, the end of a long process of desacralization. The original sacred was a presence that was both individual and social, rooted in these experiences of what has been called "another reality," which is related to our everyday reality in the same way that the world of dreams and hallucinoses is related to the reality of waking life. Elsewhere, I have written about the role these experiences play in ancient rituals and in the genealogy of ethics.[12] It is very likely that they allowed for the direct internalization of norms experienced as both individual and collective, independently of the social functions of the sacred which may have then developed on their foundations, as described by sociologists and anthropologists. The direct impression they make on individuals' minds gradually weakens over the course of the historical evolution of human nature, which is described in different ways: as the end of prophecy and of sacrifices in the ancient Hebrew world; the development of Buddhism as a replacement for Indian sacrificial rituals; the development of Confucianism after the *I Ching*; the invention of Greco-Latin philosophy built on top of the traces of ancient mythology and polytheistic cults on the coasts of the Mediterranean. The reality of these experiences was repressed into the domain of pathology[13] or of the "mystical." While shamanic cultures have, in the practice of their rituals, continued to this day to preserve at least the memory of this reality, in the modern world it has ceded its place[14] to "religion," which is based on the mysterious act of individual faith and subsequently rationalized by theology and institutional churches.

This is not to say that the "sacred" is still a central core shared by all current religions. Institutionalized religions, the monotheisms in particularly, have separated themselves much too much from these original experiences. The only exceptions are some somewhat marginal minority currents, considered to be "mystical" and sometimes charged with heresy. Current religions in fact have undergone the very same process of desacralization that led from the ancient to the modern world. And in this world, remainders of this sacred—sometimes degenerated, sometimes sublime—can be observed in expressions that are just as often secular as they are religious.

In modern, so-called "disenchanted," societies, there are traces of the diluted sacred that can be seen, alongside the nostalgia of disenchantment, in remnants of modified states of consciousness that are given, if not to everyone, then at least to many. Other than individual or convivial intoxication and psychedelic "trips" that go to varying lengths and involve a varying amount of danger, we may list as examples the erotic, music, and the practice of sports at a very high level. Like the hallucinoses of the original sacred, these effects are probably accompanied by modifications of the blood flow to certain areas of the brain that can sometimes be seen on brain imaging, although these measures can obviously not, for all that, tell us much that is pertinent about the quality of the feelings associated with them.

Between two extremes

The world of *ona'ah* is, as we have seen, an in-between contained between two extremes: on the one hand absolute truth in price, value, speech, with no deviation by even one iota, under any circumstances whatsoever, and on the other hand systemic relativism, a realm of lies, deception, and theft.

These extremes turn out to be more than just two moral and philosophical postures. They can also be observed at the two stages of this historical evolution: the one in antiquity, inventing philosophy which is still rooted in mythology, the other characterizing modernity and postmodernity.

The thaumaturgist philosophers, like Pythagoras and Orpheus, stand at the beginning of the long transition from myth to philosophy. In his person, Orpheus combines music that charms both humans and gods, the ultimate experiences of Eros and Thanatos, and the sacred language of incantations and initiations into the secrets of the gods. It is not surprising to see that myth has attributed to him the transition from chaos to order and to social peace at the origins of humanity. As we saw in chapter 3, on the spectrum that starts with the truth and the harmony revealed to humanity by Orpheus's lyre, we find at the other end systemic verbal fraud and social corruption, both of them inextricably linked with what Thomas Gustafson has called the "Thucydidean moment," of which modern democracies are the heirs.

Situated between these two extremes, the scientific adventure seems, from the point of view of its relationship to truth, to correspond (perhaps after the fact and from a distance) to this in-between of *ona'ah*, in which approximation and the cunning of modesty appear as the least bad guarantees of a truth that is under construction.

Athens and Jerusalem

The contrast between these extremes, represented by the figure of Orpheus on the one hand and "Thucydidean" modernity and postmodernity on the other, must not be confused with the contrast between Athens and Jerusalem to which, in modern thought, we have become accustomed. This way of thinking has us see Athens as the birthplace of reason and Jerusalem as the birthplace of faith, yet this is a mistaken perspective stemming from the fact that Christianity arose in Jerusalem, out of Judaism, and then was able to impose itself, by becoming the official religion of the Roman Empire, against the philosophical schools. In fact, however, the postbiblical Judaism of the Babylonian and Jerusalem Talmuds, which was first imbued with Babylonian culture and then later heavily Hellenized, was itself made up of philosophical schools or "sects," as the historian Flavius Josephus, who was their contemporary, calls them. The primitive Christian church developed as one of these schools, derived perhaps from the Essene school. But all of these schools, just like the ones in Athens, faced the same problem: what to make of this turning point in history and how to adapt to this new world, in which human beings were less and less exposed to the presence of the gods? In its later evolution, Christianity, unlike the other Greek and Jewish schools, moved away from this context thanks to two interdependent innovations. The first of these was the proselytizing nature of Christianity's mission and the conversions of barbarian peoples that followed on the conversions of Rome and Athens. The other innovation, on which the first depended, was the replacement of the law, as the path to happiness and salvation in this world as well as in the world to come, with faith, which left the earthly realm to Caesar while reserving the Kingdom of Heaven for God. This original feature of Christianity compared to all other cultures has led some to speak of Christianity as the "religion of the end of religions." In particular, this is the interpretation given by Jean-Pierre Dupuy,[15] in which he follows René Girard, who sees in Christianity the only possibility of getting out of the contradiction between the impossibility for any society of surviving without channeling violence onto a scapegoat or deputized victim and the supposed—but far from obvious[16]—impossibility in modern societies of making this scapegoating mechanism work, even in a symbolic and ritualized manner, for the simple reason that the mechanism has been revealed. Alternatively, we may ask whether the originality of Christianity is not rather to be found in its *invention of religion* by the institution of a single culture that is, at least in its aspirations, denaturalized and purely spiritual. Paradoxically, it is Christianity's temporal success, its intellectual and material extension to every continent, that has transformed its singular character into the paradigm of the religious in general as a phenomenon organized around faith. For once the Roman Empire had seized it, the two poles became a triangle, Athens-Rome-Jerusalem, which, in the words of Arnaldo Momigliano, "is still at the center and is likely to stay at the center as long as Christianity remains the religion of the West."[17] But because of this very political success and the resulting reign of the Christian churches, Christianity could not avoid falling back into the ambivalence of the sacred: because the explicit social content of faith could not remain buried in the inexpressible subjectivity of the individual, it necessarily had to express itself in a theology that was to some degree dogmatic and that drew on its origins, that is to say, on Greek philosophy! Hence a return to the ambivalence of the original sacred, albeit in a way that is different from that of overtly sacrificial religions. It is Christianity that, in inventing religion, instituted Faith as the rival of Reason, despite recurring attempts to reconcile theology and philosophy. Islam was a newcomer that took up the baton of revelation a few centuries later in lands that had been pagan until then, and which faced the same problems in some of these same lands; Islam's role in these attempts to reconcile theology and philosophy is well known and obviously not to be neglected. And finally, Jewish philosophy as theology followed suit, for better or for worse.

But I want to look for the origins of the problems posed by what we may call the transition from the crystallized sacred of the presence of the gods to the diluted sacred of a world without gods, and I will be looking for these origins well before the development of the history I have just summarized. Even though this transition was experienced differently in different cultures, we will limit ourselves here to Athens and Jerusalem, but not from the point of view of the opposition between Reason and Faith, which has become a conventional opposition. Quite on the contrary, we shall see how these two emblematic places together faced the same transformation of the world, albeit in different languages and with different customs.

Yet there is a third way, Leo Strauss's way, of comparing Athens and Jerusalem that we must briefly examine.[18] Strauss, following other philosophers, notably Hermann Cohen, takes up this conventional opposition in an original way that also pushes it back to its premodern origins: as has conventionally been done, he, too, contrasts the two in a competition for Truth between revelation and philosophy, reason and faith, biblical wisdom and Greek wisdom, Socrates and the prophets. But he does so in an original way, namely by transposing this opposition into the history of contemporary Judaism. Nevertheless, he does not neglect the Christian origin of the problem, remarking in particular that simply posing the problem in these terms already implies that one is situating oneself within the perspective of philosophy as it has developed in the West, that is to say, in Christianity, up until modern times. But for Strauss, who is not only a twentieth-century philosopher and heir to German idealism but also a participating witness to contemporary Jewish history, this is an opposition between "orthodoxy and atheism," which in a way de-Christianizes the conflict. In fact, what is at stake is not so much faith but what Strauss, interpreting Spinoza, calls "rites," which he contrasts with the "foundations of religion" and which are the very "*spirit* of the Law . . . the latter are to be discarded, while the former are to be retained."[19] The impasse of modernity and of modern rationalism, for him, lies in its abandonment of divine Law. Here he follows his interpretation of Spinoza, for whom Jewish religion in exile weakens the people while ritual preserves and strengthens it, just as Machiavelli holds Christianity responsible for the decay of the virtue of the Romans.[20] For him, the theological-political is the great issue of our times, with Spinoza as an inescapable obstacle that must be read both as a source of radical Enlightenment and as inspiring a reprise of the quarrel between the ancients and the moderns. Convinced of the self-destruction of modern reason but equally convinced of the weakness of religion, Strauss hopes to start again on new foundations, the foundations of a premodern rationalism that found its sources in the Jewish and Arab philosophy of the Middle Ages, where Spinoza's opposition (notably to Maimonides) would be entirely pertinent.[21]

It seems to me that we must not stop here, on such a promising path, but keep going to trace these origins back even further.

The world of oracles and prophecy

In the fifth century BCE, Plato tells the story of how Socrates indirectly receives an oracle (a mission?) from Apollo. The god speaks to one of Socrates's companions through the mouth of the Pythia at Delphi and tells him that there is no wiser man than Socrates.[22] Since the oracle of the god cannot be anything other than words of truth, Socrates feels obliged to decipher it and to seek a hidden sense in it because it contradicts his experience of being neither wise nor learned (*sophos*). In fact, Socrates goes out to look for other men who are supposed to be wise and learned: politicians, poets, and artisans. Yet he discovers that despite their gifts of, respectively, oratory, inspiration, and technical skill, they do not know what they think they know. The god was right: Socrates is superior to them in wisdom because he does not imagine himself to be wise and has found in this, precisely, the incentive to go look for wisdom. A new beginning for philosophy is born of this, philosophy as search for wisdom rather than as wisdom itself, which belongs only to the gods. Pythagoras, dedicating himself to the study of numbers and of nature, had already invented the name of philosopher, "friend of wisdom," to differentiate himself from the sages of ancient times, such as the Seven Sages of ancient Greece and the Homeric heroes Ulysses and Nestor, who draw their wisdom from their direct relations with the gods. Socrates renews the project by applying it to human affairs and to the search for the highest good.

Six centuries later, the Platonic philosopher Plutarch, priest of Apollo at the Delphi sanctuary, wonders about the disappearance of oracles.

At the dawn of the civilizations that we recognize as such, we find the reign of an absolute truth, guaranteed by its divine origin. This is the time of gods, prophecy, oracular knowledge, and shamanism. Here, the circle of value discussed earlier is resolved rather simply: the truth of the oracle and the value of truth are both guaranteed by the oracle's divine origin, and the potential verification of the oracle is but a confirmation of the presence of the god and a sign of the value of its carrier. As Heraclitus said: "The lord whose oracle is in Delphi neither declares nor conceals, but gives a sign."[23] For what makes an oracle an oracle is not necessarily speech. Divination techniques that work with dreams, omens, harbingers, birdsongs, and the drawing of lots, not to mention astrology and palmistry, aimed—and still aim—at obtaining signs supposed to bring knowledge about the hidden things that are commonly ignored. Oracular and prophetic speech, furthermore, is itself often enigmatic, so that the question of interpreting signs always arises, and this question occupied much of the time of many of the philosophers of antiquity, who, with the possible exception of the Epicureans, were far from purely and simply rejecting all of this as fables and delusions. This is where the use of reason was to intervene, associated with traditions received from previous generations that were themselves supposed to be of divine origin. *Logos* and *mythos*, reason and myth, provided they were used well, complemented divination as a source of philosophical knowledge in ancient Greece and in the entire Roman Empire until at least the first centuries of the Christian era.

The ubiquity of these practices in antiquity is well documented.[24] In particular, the connections among ancient Hebrew prophecy, divination among the Greeks, and shamanism in general appear to be much tighter than is usually supposed, despite the conventional contrast between monotheism, united around its unique sanctuary at Jerusalem, and polytheism, dispersed across multiple sites for cults and sacrifices.[25] But there are many fewer studies that manage to account for the particular phenomenon of their cessation, that is to say, the disappearance of divination and prophecy as means of access to a revealed truth.

This question is also the question of the *nature* of prophecy, which is the subject of what has been called the prophetology of theologians and philosophers up until the Middle Ages. Spinoza asks the question at the beginning of his *Theological-Political Treatise*, but he declares that he has no answer about the nature of the process by which the imagination of the prophets gave them access to the revealed Law. He observes biblical prophecy as a fact of the history of antiquity and confines himself to analyzing the structures and contents of the prophets' words because he grants them a moral value, at any rate, while at the same time denying them all value as objective truth. I have tried to find elements of an answer to this question of the nature of prophecy by resituating it in the larger context of shamanism and of "modified states of consciousness." This, unlike Spinoza's procedure, will obviously not tell us anything about the contents and functions of the words of the prophets. Yet we cannot ignore the legislative function of the prophet, the intermediary who pronounces a "divine law" for the kind of ideal city that Plato already called for. This is what Leo Strauss has shown so well in his first works on the prophetology of medieval Jewish and Muslim philosophers. Spinoza could not grant the biblical prophets the status of true philosophers guided by reason and the light of nature, but for these medieval philosophers, the prophet-legislator, like Plato's "prophet-king," was the "philosopher-statesman-seer[-thaumaturge] in one."[26]

We will return to these questions when we discuss two exemplary contemporaries at the end of the first and the beginning of the second century: one Greek, who wondered about the disappearance of the oracles, the other Jewish, whose prophetic revelations were rejected by his colleagues and disciples.

For the first philosophers, in fact, reason itself came from heaven and the truth of its teachings was proven by the commonality of their character, shared by means of dialogues and debates and not limited to the opinion of individuals alone.[27] That is why the teachings of the greatest masters, which imposed themselves on the largest number of people by the force of conviction, were themselves conceived of as being of divine origin, like the teachings of Pythagoras or Plato.

Legends about the "barbarian" traditions[28] that inspired these teachings, about Egyptian priests and about Chaldean, Indian, and Hebrew sorcerers and prophets, told by Diogenes Laertius among others—legends concerning the origin of philosophy in particular[29]—only reinforced this idea of a divine, creative, "spermatic" Logos, especially among the pre-Socratics, Plato, and the Stoics, or of a (just as creative) agent intellect in Aristotle, fueling the mind and reason of sages and philosophers, as a guarantee of the truth of their teachings. It is as though the experience of the sacred and/or of divinity were a dimension of the human condition that could not be eliminated. All that remains is to define its contents, to understand the stakes of its hidden realities. Ethnobotany is a discipline that can provide a likely natural neuropsychological origin for it, stressing, as we have seen, the role of modified states of consciousness, perhaps ritually induced with hallucinogenic plants, such as the Australian Aborigines' dreamtime, the American Indians' "other reality," or the Rigveda's *soma*.[30]

In this context, as we have seen and will see again, the divine metaphor of money as a vehicle and a sign of exchange, with its sacred character, recurs often, as if what was at issue here was more than a metaphor: truly an identification, a true presence of the divine in that which guarantees the truth of exchanges, of words as much as of goods. Magic, initiation practices that are to greater or lesser degrees occult, commerce with demons, and the consultation of oracles were, like prophecy, the vehicles by which communications and exchanges were established between the pure and immortal divine world and the world of human beings, of generation and corruption. Even Epicurus, the ultimate philosopher of nature, although he was said to be a "materialist," was also considered to be "divine," albeit mortal, at least by his disciples. Lucretius invokes his master's "godlike mind" thanks to whose "power nature everywhere in every part lies open; all her secrets are laid bare." Epicurus's "doctrine of truth" concerning the principles of the universe and the nature of the gods denounces illusions about "the superstitious element" and makes it possible for human beings to liberate themselves and to achieve a life "worthy of the gods." For, in fact, even if the Epicureans consider the gods to be indifferent to the conduct of human beings, they do not deny their existence, if only as sources of inspiration and as models for a liberated human life.[31] But most of the philosophers of Greco-Roman antiquity agree on the reality of the experiences of divination and prophecy. What divides them are the questions that then inevitably arise about the nature of the gods and the nature of the process of revelation.

In his treatise *On Divination*, Cicero asks this very question, the question of the nature of the gods *on the basis of* the experience of people who "are sleeping or mentally inspired" who "see things that do not exist anywhere."[32] Experiences of divination and of dreams, which are associated with divination, are thus the concrete starting point for "theological" questions about the gods, the visible and invisible worlds, and what is hidden, including things to come that destiny might have in store for us.

On the basis of this experience, there are three points that, for Cicero,

> will stand firm: the gods exist, by their foresight the world is governed, and they are concerned with human affairs, not only in general but also in particular. If we maintain this, which to me seems unassailable, it surely follows that the gods give to men signs of what is to come.[33]

Are the gods identical with the heavenly bodies whose names they share, Apollo and the Sun, Venus and the Star, etc., as Stoic immanentism would lead one to suppose? Or are they different, as the soul is different from the body, according to Platonic idealism? So many questions on which the different schools are divided. As for the mechanisms by means of which the gods talk to or make signs for human beings, they are the subject of endless speculations and traditions about the nature of oracles and the role of different kinds of demons and other fiery, terrestrial, and heavenly forces that act as intermediaries between gods and human beings.

This phenomenon of the reciprocal impregnation of reason and myth, of philosophy and prophecy is not limited to the Greco-Roman world. We also observe it among those who, in that universe, are called "barbarians," notably in India and in the Jewish world. Furthermore, we also observe, at about the same time (from the fifth century BCE to the third century CE), the evolution that is so astonishing that some have wanted to call it, in so far as Greece is concerned, the "Greek miracle": the evolution in which rational philosophy separates itself from mythology. It is the disappearance of oracles or the end of prophecy, along with the disappearance of the gods and their progressive replacement by the

Christian god. In the ancient Hebrew world, postbiblical rabbinic Judaism replaces prophetic Hebraism and invents new expressions—such as the Place, the Master of the World, the Sacred who is Blessed, then the Infinite—to name the one god in whom the different biblical names of the godhead are unified. At the juncture of the Jewish and the Greek worlds, the beginnings of Christianity contribute to this evolution.[34] But there is a long transition period before philosophy, and then science, separate themselves, at least in part, from mythology and then from the monotheistic theologies that followed it. This period is marked by the extraordinary eclecticism of a philosophy and science steeped in occultism, demonology, magic, and astrology, expressed in Greek, Christian, and "barbarian" terms all at the same time.

The "masters" or "teachers" (rabbis) of talmudic Judaism, who expressed themselves in Hebrew but also in Aramaic, the vernacular of that time, participated in the spirit of the times even though they were concerned with ensuring the continuity, in spite of everything, of the organization of their people around the laws of Moses and the books of the prophets. Not only were they not prophets, they believed that henceforth, "a wise man is even superior to a prophet."[35] Themselves they generally called the "students of the sages" (*talmidei ḥakhamim*) and sometimes only "sages" (*ḥakhamim*), notably when certain ones of them collectively expressed a judgment or an opinion that they shared. Considered to be "barbarian philosophers" in the eyes of the Greeks, they could easily be confused, whether in praising or deprecating them, with the Chaldean Magi, with whom they shared at least a language.[36]

In this somewhat imaginary context, among the barbarian philosophers from which Greek philosophy was said to have drawn, the Jews were sometimes compared to the philosophers of India. Josephus Flavius even relates a legend according to which "Jews" (or "Judeans," '*ioudaios*) is the name Syrians give to philosophers, like the name *kallanoi*, "philosophers," used by the Indians.[37] Describing the four groups, parties, or "sects" into which the Jewish people were divided at the beginning of the first century, the same Flavius Josephus, writing this time as a historian and a contemporary, characterizes the doctrines taught and practiced by three of these groups as "philosophies." In this he distinguishes them from the fourth group, the Zealots or *sicarii*, a theological and nationalist messianic party that preached revolt against Rome. According to Flavius Josephus, these latter constitute "a sect of their own, having nothing in common with the others. Jewish philosophy, in fact, takes three forms."[38] He then describes the philosophy of what he calls these three "sects" using language that reminds us of the philosophical schools of his time, especially of the Stoics where the Pharisees are concerned. It is from this school that historical Judaism will later emerge, when the priestly party of the Sadducees has practically disappeared following the destruction of the sanctuary in Jerusalem; the Essenes, whose philosophy has "a reputation for cultivating a particularly pious life,"[39] have joined either certain pharisaic currents or the Christian communities; and the Zealots have been crushed and massacred by the Romans.

A little closer to us, the teachers and students of the schools of Judea and Babylon, the subjects and authors of the reviews and discussions that constitute the Talmuds that have come down to us, forcefully and thoroughly rejected everything that could evoke the customs and pagan cults of the societies in which they lived by encircling the biblical precepts with a "hedge for the Torah." But they shared a cultural, spatial, and temporal environment with the philosophical schools of these societies, and many among them knew their languages. In this shared environment, what was experienced by some as "the end of prophecy" and by others as "the disappearance of the oracles" was a major anthropological event. Elsewhere, I have analyzed the likely nature of this event from a strictly anthropological point of view as an evolution, both psychophysical and sociocultural, of human nature. The neuropsychologist Julian Jaynes has a thesis about the evolution of the psychological meanings of the communications between the right and left brain—as an internalization of the right brain's "voices," which had previously been interpreted as being received from elsewhere, from gods and from god-kings—that accords with the results of studies in comparative mythology. In the most recent biblical texts, an evolution can be observed in what he calls the "psychological thickness" of the characters, with more obvious expressions of what we might call their inner life, when compared to the older texts. An analogous evolution, well-known to Hellenists and studied especially by James Redfield, shows the appearance of the *myself* in the Homeric characters of the *Odyssey*, whereas the characters of the *Iliad*, possessed and acted upon by the gods, seem to be devoid of the capacity for inner dialogue.[40] This is a historical phenomenon that is probably more general than the one habitually ascribed in the West to the birth of modern philosophy and theology, situating them in a period that stretches from Plato to Saint Augustine.

Be that as it may, this evolution profoundly changed everyone's relationship to truth, albeit in different ways due to differences in language, tradition, myths, history, and customs. As far as ancient Greece is concerned, Jean-Pierre Vernant compares this phenomenon to a "mental mutation" followed by an evolution of several centuries in the form of what is said and what is written, at the same time as the power of god-kings is being replaced by the power of citizens. This "mental mutation," as he calls it, appears to be linked to transformations that take place between the seventh and the fifth centuries BCE at all levels of Greek societies: in the political institutions of the city, in law, in economic life, and in money.[41]

I, for my part, have shown an example of this transition in the Jewish world of the same period, involving the desacralization of chance and of the oracles during the progressive transition from the prophetic biblical world of ancient Hebraism to the postbiblical world of talmudic and rabbinic Judaism.[42]

Two extraordinary characters, contemporaries at the end of the first and the beginning of the second century of the Christian era, express this transition, in a tragic way, in their lives and in their teachings. One of them, Plutarch, is Greek, a philosopher and priest of Apollo at the Delphi sanctuary; the other, Rabbi Eliezer, is Jewish, a master and teacher of the *Mishnah* in Palestine and a contemporary of the destruction of the second sanctuary of Jerusalem, whom we have already met in the story of the Oven of Akhnai.

Plutarch and the Pythia

Plutarch is the heir to the long tradition of Greco-Roman philosophical schools, from the pre-Socratics of ancient Greece to the Stoics, Epicureans, and Neoplatonists of the Roman Empire. Although he himself is a Platonist, his writings—including his best-known book, *Lives of Illustrious Men*—testify to a close proximity to other philosophical doctrines, the most ancient as well as those of the schools of his time, with which he sometimes argues. But he was also a priest of Apollo, in charge of the sanctuary at Delphi and of the sacrificial and oracular practices during which the Pythia was questioned.

Plutarch thus had to assume a position that, due to his twofold activity as philosopher and as priest, may have been uncomfortable, at least intellectually, but may also not have been that uncomfortable after all. For there was nothing exceptional about linking the practice of philosophy with official religious services and administrative responsibilities. The practice of theurgy and magic was commonplace, especially among the Neoplatonists. A remarkable study by Renée Koch[43] shows how even Epicurus's disciples submitted to civic responsibilities, which included their participation in the services of the gods, even to the point of providing esoteric teaching, in which everything was assigned various symbolic meanings, in their school for internal use.

But Plutarch, by virtue of his function at Delphi, had to confront a new cognitive situation that could not but challenge his practice of philosophical questioning. The oracles of the Pythia had gone through a period of disaffection during which their truth was strongly doubted, before they simply disappeared. The oracle at the sanctuary of Apollo, like the oracles at other temples, had stopped speaking some decades earlier. In addition, before even becoming a priest at Delphi, Plutarch had wondered, as a philosopher, about this phenomenon. He wrote a text in the manner of Plato's dialogues about "the disappearance of the oracles," which is usually combined with two later texts to form the Pythian dialogues. For the sanctuary had been restored, and when he was named priest there, worship services were held there once again, with their sacrifices and their oracles. But it is easy to see how, in the meantime, certainties could have been undermined. To be sure, the Pythia is once again questioned under the responsibility of the priest, but in a different way. Different questions are asked, more private than political, or even cosmic, than before. And the answers are simpler. This is what emerges from the Pythian dialogues, in which Plutarch takes up the question again, this time from the standpoint of the evolutions that he has observed in the form and the contents of prophetic revelations. Hence the composition of two other dialogues, one about the meaning of the inscription of an *epsilon* that greeted visitors to the temple, the other on "Why are the Pythian Responses no longer given in verse." In these dialogues, he confronts the tension between a divine origin for oracular knowledge, whose truth should be as timeless and immortal as the divinity itself, and the reality of divination, which appears to be subjected to the vagaries of history and the place of its practice.

The first question concerns the relation between the immortal god and the mortal and changing carriers of his words. To try to respond to this question, to challenge the Epicurean negation of any relation whatsoever between the gods and human beings, it is not too much to convene the arguments of several philosophical schools (those of Pythagoras, Heraclitus, Plato, Aristotle, and the Stoics). Cicero had already wondered about the depreciation of the oracles of Delphi, and he observed that the Epicureans were the only ones who denied their reality and attributed their results to human credulity alone.[44] For Plutarch, it must now be possible at least to rationally conjecture about the nature of the processes of prophetic revelation that guarantee the truth of knowledge about the world and about the gods.

For divination, for the philosopher, does not concern the nature of the gods alone; it is not only a question of "theology" in the ancient meaning of the term (as it is used, for example, in the Neoplatonist treatise *Elements of Theology* by Proclus), which is quite different from the monotheistic theology of the Middle Ages. The questions asked by divination also have to do with their relation to the world and through that to all elements of what a true revealed knowledge about the world itself, human and nonhuman, would be. Later, after the gods have departed or at least become silent, these elements will, quite simply, make up the natural sciences.

In other words, the question of the oracles through which the words of the god make themselves heard is the question of the reality and nature of a divine providence that extends to everything that happens in the universe. In fact, if one admits that the gods are involved in human affairs and determine them and thus know the future, one can conceive of the possibility of a revelation. Everyone but Epicurus and his school agreed on this reality. Only the Epicureans conceived of the possibility that nature might produce itself in the infinite totality of its worlds and in the fortuitous events that happen there. They were, in consequence, the only ones to consider that things in nature, including human affairs, take place by chance; that is not to say for no reason, but without intentionality or final causes. For Plutarch and for all the other non-Epicureans, on the other hand, every event had to have an obvious or hidden meaning. Prophetic revelation unveiled the hidden meaning of things and events, as Heraclitus said about the oracle at Delphi whose function was to "signify." Even with all of this, however, questions were obviously still raised about the *how* of oracular revelations. Very roughly, the idea that comes out of the Pythian dialogues is what Frédérique Ildefonse very rightly, in the introduction to her translation of the dialogues into French, calls their "double causality":[45] the god is the cause of the revelation and guarantees its truth, but there are several intermediaries before it arrives at the trance or delirium of the Pythia. Among these intermediaries, demons, which are sometimes almost confused with the gods themselves, play a determining role, although the demonologies we find in practically all philosophical schools of the time are not always in agreement. In addition to and associated with the demon that possesses the oracle and makes it talk, there are other elements that also come in, such as auguries transmitted through the cries of birds or the behavior of the sacrificed goat that will indicate whether or not the oracle to come is true. The most important, however, is the property of the place, the exhalation or "breath" that comes out of the ground, the earthy *pneuma* that penetrates the soul, the *pneuma* of the Pythia, who is predisposed to this reception and to entering a trance. We see that between the god and the pronouncement of the oracle, each of the intermediaries can modulate its effects up or down: the demon can leave the scene and the earth—for various reasons that could be connected to climate but also to the depopulation of a given region where the demand for an oracle then disappeared—can stop producing its exhalation. Finally, all of this can also result in changes in the nature of the questions the oracle is asked and the responses that it gives. The oracle answered the old questions, about major events that affected entire cities, in verse, whose meanings, like the meanings of prophetic dreams, were often enigmatic and needed qualified interpreters. In Plutarch's time, however, relatively simple, prose answers were given to limited questions concerning one aspect or another of the lives of particular individuals. This is the conclusion reached by the protagonists of the dialogue when they ask why the Pythia no longer gives her oracles in verse.

But be that as it may, one of the things at stake in these dialogues, aside from the nature of the gods and of their relations with the world, has to do with access to a true knowledge about hidden things, of which predicting the future is only one particular case. In this regard, Plutarch stands in the tradition of Plato, for whom oracular revelation, far from being in opposition to philosophical reflection, is complemented by it. For what is expressed in trances, visions, and the capacity of the soul to receive images needs to be controlled by reason, so much so that only those who respond to this need are called "prophets." Here again, we find the ambivalence of divination in relation to truth that Plato already developed in the *Timaeus*. On the one hand, "the organ of divination" has been placed in the human being "so that it might have some grasp of truth." It is because of the "disability of human reason" that God "gave divination as a gift" in order "to make the mortal race as excellent as possible" by rectifying even its weak side. For "while he is in his right mind no one [no mortal—HA] engages in divination, however divinely inspired and true it may be, but only when his power of understanding is bound in sleep or by sickness, or when some sort of possession works a change in him." But on the other hand, it is not the role of the person who is in a trance state to judge what has appeared to or been uttered by him or her. On the contrary, it is up to "a man who has his wits about him" to use reasoning to discuss and interpret its meanings. That is "the reason why it is customary practice to appoint interpreters to render judgment on an inspired divination," whom it would be wrong to confuse with the "diviners" themselves. That would be to misunderstand the fact that they are only the interpreters of "utterances or visions communicated through riddles. . . . Instead of 'diviners,' the correct thing to call them is, 'prophets of things divined.'"[46] The balancing of the two is remarkable: on the one hand, the words and visions produced by the enthusiasm of the divination, which alone can unveil some truth of which the prophets are "only" the interpreters; on the other hand, the insufficiency of the same words and visions to mean anything without the help of reason despite its "disability."

Thus, in Plutarch as in Plato, divination, far from being self-sufficient, activates philosophical questioning and reasoning by contributing to the "wonder," the *thauma* that is their starting point.[47] In this way, the *origin* of knowledge remains divine and its truth is guaranteed. This is far from modern ideas of "methodic doubt" and of the "clean slate" of traditional knowledge.

In fact, it seems that even among the disciples of Epicurus, who seem to be the closest to the moderns from this point of view, the divine origin of philosophical knowledge is not questioned, so much so that even the master himself partakes of a divine nature. In this way, Epicurus with his "godlike mind"[48] for them replaces "divine Plato."

This might be an explanation for the curious Epicurean doctrine about the gods: it does not deny their existence, contrary to the commonly accepted idea of Epicurus's atheism, yet it denies any interest on their part in human affairs. What purpose, then, do these gods serve, confined to an existence in the interstices of the universe, indifferent to what happens there? The simple fact of their existence provides an assurance that certain mortals, such as Epicurus himself, will also have the possibility of elevating themselves and participating in the nature of the gods. Plutarch makes fun of this position, evoking, as counterparts to the "prophets of Apollo," the "prophets of Epicurus" who deny the reality of oracles and explain the coincidences between different events, of which some are interpreted as presaging and announcing others, by "chance or accident."[49]

Prosaic truths and monetary metaphors of desacralized language

Be that as it may, it is remarkable that the metaphor of speech as currency returns, as we will see, in Plutarch's argument seeking to explain the evolution of the oracle's poetic language and its replacement with prose. For once the oracle uses language, the question arises of the status of this language, a language that is used in response to the ritual of the temple, a language that is both human speech and speech of the god who possesses the Pythia, in whom an exchange between the divine and the human worlds takes place. At stake in this exchange is the truth of this speech because, as always and as in the case of money, error and deception cannot be ruled out. While opposing the Epicureans and their negation of this exchange, Plutarch also opposes a form of Stoic immanentism, which sees the god as directly penetrating each thing and each being in our world. He thus has to take the status of the intermediary in the exchange into account and must explain the change that comes about in the intermediary's nature once the verses of the "ancient Pythias" have been replaced by prose.

Hence Plutarch's attachment to a double causality, which allows him not to "make divination godless or irrational" and to explain the possibility of changes in the declarations of the oracles and even the possibility of their disappearance:

To sum up, then: while every form of creation has, as I say, two causes, the very earliest theological writers and poets chose to heed only the superior one [Zeus, the origin and common principle of all things—HA]; but as yet they made no approach towards the compelling and natural causes. On the other hand the younger generation which followed them, and are called physicists or natural philosophers, reverse the procedure of the older school in their aberration from the beautiful and divine origin, and ascribe everything to bodies and their behavior, to clashes, transmutations, and combinations. Hence the reasoning of both parties is deficient in what is essential to it, since the one ignores or omits the intermediary and the agent, the other the source and the means.

Plutarch, on the other hand, associates the two causes and therefore does

not make divination godless or irrational when we assign to it as its material the soul of a human being, and assign the spirit of inspiration and the exhalation as an instrument or plectrum for playing on it. For, in the first place, the earth, which generates the exhalation, and the sun, which endows the earth with all its power of tempering and transmutation, are, by the usage of our fathers, gods for us. Secondly, if we leave demigods as overseers, watchmen, and guardians of this tempered constitution, as if it were a kind of harmony, slackening here and tightening there on occasion, taking from it its too distracting and disturbing elements and incorporating those that are painless and harmless to the users, we shall not appear to be doing anything irrational or impossible.[50]

The core of the position taken by Plutarch, priest of Apollo and Platonist philosopher, is on display here in its different aspects, including his reference to the traditions of the ancestors. In this context, the use of myth, as a place of exchange or even as a means of access to a truth that is both indirect and to be controlled, is not precluded either. This emerges, in particular, in the story that opens a dialogue about the true and the plausible, which seems to be a digression on cosmogonic questions of the unity or the finite or infinite multiplicity of worlds. One of the protagonists of the dialogue attributes this story to a "barbarian" and compares the story to foreign currency as a locus of exchange and verification: "But there is set before us for general use a bowl of myths and stories combined, and where could one meet with more kindly listeners for testing these stories, even as one tests coins from foreign lands? So I do not hesitate to favor you with a narrative about a man, not a Greek [*barbárou*]."[51]

Thus, for the priest to be able to explain how the Pythia at Delphi speaks in a state of "enthusiasm," that is to say with "the god inside her," the philosopher must approach the issue from both sides: on the one hand, a physics and metaphysics of providence, that is to say, of the possible relations between the divinity and the world or worlds; on the other hand, the mechanisms that make it possible to represent to oneself how divination and prophetic speech operate in general, accounting at the same time both for its "divine," that is to say, permanent and incorruptible, character and for the disruptions to its modalities, possibly even its disappearance, due to the human and mundane character of its reception. To this end,

Plutarch calls on all the resources of the philosophy and sciences of his time, from Pythagorean numerology and Chaldean astrology to a demonology whose elements are drawn from practically all the philosophers, yet without depriving himself of mythological narratives or of metaphors of all kinds, as we have seen, such as the metaphor of music, of the instrument, and of the musician. Among these metaphors, the metaphor of money, too, imposes itself. It is the general equivalent for value that, because of that, has sacred origins, but it is problematic in its use since, like speech, it can be distorted or counterfeited. And the metaphor of money returns in the same text with even more force precisely on the subject of the changes that have occurred in the language of the oracle, which is content with prose and leaves verse to the ancient myths of Homer:

What statement, then, shall we make about the priestesses of former days? . . . [T]hat era produced personal temperaments and natures which had an easy fluency and a bent towards composing poetry, and to them were given also zest and eagerness and readiness of mind abundantly, thus creating an alertness which needed but a slight initial stimulus from without and a prompting of the imagination, with the result that not only were astronomers and philosophers, as Philinus says, attracted at once to their special subjects, but when men came under the influence of abundant wine or emotion, as some note of sadness crept in or some joy befell, a poet would slip into 'tuneful utterance'; their convivial gatherings were filled with amatory verses and their books with such writings. . . . Wine mixes with the manners of each guest, and as he drinks, prophetic inspiration, like that of love, makes use of the abilities that it finds ready at hand, and moves each of them that receive it according to the nature of each.

    If, however, we take into consideration the workings of the god and of divine providence, we shall see that the change has been for the better. For the use of language is like the currency of coinage in trade: the coinage which is familiar and well known is also acceptable, although it takes on a different value at different times. *There was, then, a time when men used as the coinage of speech verses and tunes and songs*, and reduced to poetic and musical form all history and philosophy and, in a word, every experience and action that required a more impressive utterance. . . . Indeed, owing to this aptitude for poetic composition, most men through lyre and song admonished, spoke out frankly, or exhorted; they attained their ends by the use of myths and proverbs, and besides composed hymns, prayers, and paeans in honor of the gods in verse and music, some through their natural talent, others because it was the prevailing custom. Accordingly, the god did not begrudge to the art of prophecy adornment and pleasing grace . . . and helped in prompting impressiveness and eloquence as something fitting and admirable. But, as life took on a change along with the change in men's fortunes and their natures, when usage banished the unusual and did away with the golden topknots and dressing in soft robes, and, on occasion, cut off the stately long hair and caused the buskin to be no longer worn, men accustomed themselves (nor was it a bad thing) to oppose expensive outlay by adorning themselves with economy, and to rate as decorative the plain and simple rather than the ornate and elaborate. So, as language also underwent a change and put off its finery, history descended from its vehicle of versification, and went on foot in prose, whereby the truth was mostly sifted from the fabulous. Philosophy welcomed clearness and teachability in preference to creating amazement, and pursued its investigations through the medium of everyday language.... When [the god] had taken away from the oracles epic versification, strange words, circumlocutions, and vagueness, he had thus made them ready to talk to his consultants as the laws talk to States, or as kings meet with common people, or as pupils listen to teachers, since he adapted the language to what was intelligible and convincing.[52]

Rabbi Eliezer

Eliezer ben Hyrcanus, also known as Rabbi Eliezer "the Great," is another exemplary figure of this departure from the ancient world of divine presence, this time in the Jewish society of first-century Palestine. The transition here is between the biblical world of prophecy and sacred writings and the postbiblical world of wisdom and its students in which the rabbinical Judaism of the two Talmuds develops. This transition, like the transition from mythology to wisdom and to Greek philosophy, is also progressive: the presence of the god of Israel to his people, solely concentrated here in the Temple of Jerusalem, becomes attenuated as the centuries go by. The biblical world with its writings expresses an absolute whose partly mythical content serves as a starting point and as a reference. The world that follows sees the development of the use of reason in renewed interpretations and teachings. Absolute truth no longer falls from the sky but is henceforth dedicated to "sprouting from earth."[53]

Rabbi Eliezer, like many other teachers of his time, still found himself between these two worlds. We saw the role he played in the story of the Oven of Akhnai. The quarrels he had with his colleagues and students, culminating in his exclusion in that story, show that he was still leaning towards heaven. In another context, however, and in line with the conclusion of these debates, Rabbi Ishmael, a student and classmate who was an opponent of his, simply affirmed that in certain cases the *halakha*, decided "on earth" by a majority, is applied differently than suggested by a biblical injunction and nonetheless supersedes that injunction.[54] Another example of the relative detachment of the talmudic masters from the explicit meaning of the biblical texts is provided by a story related in the Babylonian Talmud's treatise *Abodah Zarah*. A member of a heretical sect, probably a Christian one, is making fun of the fact that Rav Safra, considered to be one of the greatest teachers of his time, has no answer to a question about the meaning of a verse from the Bible. Rabbi Abbahu, for his part, who has himself called this teacher the greatest, has no difficulty in responding to the question. To his astonished interlocutor he points out that in speaking of Rav Safra's knowledge, he meant not his knowledge of Scripture but his knowledge of *Mishnah*, that is to say, of oral Torah. As for his own knowledge of the Bible, Abbahu explains that because Rav Safra lives in Babylon and does not need it, he does not have to engage with it as much as do the other teachers who, like Abbahu himself, live in Palestine and have to engage with Scripture in order to be able to respond to heretics, as he has just done.[55]

But Rabbi Eliezer appears in several stories, aside from the story of the oven, as a complex personality, as the defender of a purist attitude in the name of an absolute truth. He wants this truth to be indisputable in its theoretical content and efficacious as a magical means of acting on the natural elements, like the ideal of a complete science whose truth would prove itself not only in efficacious applications but also in statements of indisputable, definitive teachings.

Eliezer, the son of Hyrcanus, abandoned his destiny as a rich heir in order to give himself over to studies in the academy that Rabbi Johanan ben Zakkai founded at Yavne after his escape from the siege of Jerusalem and the destruction of its temple by the Romans. Rabbi Eliezer was, it seems, gifted with a phenomenal memory, deemed "supernatural" by some, which his teacher compared to "a watertight cistern that never loses a drop."[56] But once he had become a teacher himself, Rabbi Eliezer used this ability to prohibit himself from teaching anything new that he had not received from his own teacher. This is what he says about himself, at any rate, on the subject of questions of *halakha* on the correct manner of celebrating Sukkot (the Feast of Tabernacles), which he does not answer because he has not learned any answers to them.[57] This conservative attitude of passive reception contrasts with the attitude of his classmate Rabbi Eleazar ben Arakh, who produced all sorts of wisdom on his own and was for that reason compared by their common teacher to "a source that becomes stronger."[58] Yet his conservative and passive attitude did not, for all that, keep Eliezer from listening to and appreciating teachings from elsewhere, as is shown in a curious episode that was to cost him dearly.[59]

Eliezer, Christianizing?

Eliezer is, in fact, arrested by the Roman authorities and accused of heresy, at a time when the early Christians were persecuted much more than the Jews. He gets out of this, but he suffers from the fact that such a suspicion could have fallen on him. When he wonders whether he may have deserved it after all, by entertaining heretical ideas, if only in thought, his student Rabbi Akiba suggests to him that perhaps he has only found a certain pleasure in listening to a heretical speech. He then recalls that that had indeed been the case. A "disciple of Jesus of Nazareth" had related to him one of his master's teachings on the biblical prohibition on using money gained from prostitution in the service of the Temple.[60] To the curious question, "what is one to do with it?" he had responded: "use it for the high priest's toilet" (because the priest had to live in the Temple during the week preceding Yom Kippur to prepare for it)! Although several later commentators would contest the pertinence of the question (!) and of the answer, Rabbi Eliezer says nothing but appreciates them in his innermost self; in particular, it seems, because of the use of a verse from Micah, which serves to "ground" the answer in the purest style of talmudic explanations. In the context of the prophetic writings that compare idolatrous Israel to an adulterous woman and to a prostitute, the verse speaks of gifts to idols that "were collected as harlot's hire, and they will revert to harlot's hire."[61] Rabbi Eliezer, known for the severity of his teachings aimed at protecting Israel from idolatry,[62] must obviously have appreciated not only this comparison but also the use that is made of it in the idea that, according to his interlocutor's interpretation, the prostitute's pay "returns" to the world of waste. For the world is still the world of the sacred, because this is still the Temple in Jerusalem. One can imagine that what he sees there and appreciates is a certain mystical way of recuperating waste in a sacredness from which prostitution has been expelled by the biblical prohibition. We must in fact recall that verse 19 of chapter 23 of Deuteronomy, which prohibits the use of a prostitute's pay for offerings at the Temple, follows the prohibition of sacred prostitution, which was long widespread in the temples of pagan antiquity, for the "daughters and sons of Israel." This appears clearly in the immediately preceding verse 18, which uses the terms *kadesha* and *kadesh*, directly derived from *kadosh* ("sacred"), to designate a female and a male prostitute, respectively. The expression "harlot's hire" in verse 19, on the other hand, refers to a more general kind of prostitution, in a way "secular," designated by the word *zona*, which invokes the need for food rather than the sacred. Finally, let us also recall that this is all just a theoretical question since it seems that the Temple has already been destroyed.

The same story is repeated in the Midrash, but there it is followed by the narrative of an episode in which Rabbi Eliezer's intransigence resurfaces;[63] here, too, this intransigence is opposed by Rabbi Joshua, one of his opponents in the story of the oven, who had ended the discussion by affirming that "Torah is not in heaven."[64] A woman wants to convert (or to rejoin the path of Torah). When Rabbi Eliezer questions her and she tells him that she has had an incestuous son with her own oldest son, he rejects her request. But Rabbi Joshua decides to accept it.

It is clear that being accused of heresy himself must have been a serious shock for Rabbi Eliezer. But while the story tells us how he appreciates "in his heart" and without saying anything the teaching of his interlocutor and how, in his own eyes, this could justify his deserving to be suspected, we are not told anything about the objective reasons that have brought the Roman authorities to accuse him. We might conjecture that it was because of his ascetic way of life, which may have brought him closer to the Essenes. It is also possible that he was suspected of being associated with the Gnostic sects, because a little later, along with other masters of the *Mishnah*, he was the hero of a mystical story called "the Prince of Torah," associated with the so-called *hekhalot* ("palaces") literature that constitutes the texts of the oldest Kabbalah. The relationship between these stories of voyages of initiation and the Gnosis have been discussed numerous times.[66] But be that as it may, in the course of these voyages, revelations of all kinds were common currency, if we may say so, even if they were sometimes dangerous. But is it real or counterfeit currency, as in the time of the prophets: prophecy of the truth or of lies? Obviously that is always the question. But these revelations concerned not only questions of Torah but also teachings of magic, of which we know that they constituted contemporary science at least until the Renaissance. That was the case for Rabbi Eliezer, of whom we may suppose that, like his master Rabbi Johahan ben Zakkai, he "spoke with angels and demons."[66] His competence in this domain led his colleagues and students to consider him equal if not superior to the best magicians.

Magic and cucurbit plants

This reputation of Rabbi Eliezer's is what we learn, among other things, from the story of his death and of his last encounter with those who had excluded him from the academy. This is the story that concludes the part of the treatise, *Sanhedrin*, that examines the biblical prohibitions on giving oneself over to different kinds of sorcery and magic.[67] In this story, we encounter the protagonists of the story of the Oven of Akhnai once again, especially Rabbi Akiba and Rabbi Joshua. They visit their teacher before his death and end up annulling the decree of exclusion. But before that, we witness one last exchange, which is very interesting as well.

Rabbi Eliezer is bitter about having been prevented from teaching as he could have and, in the process, predicts unnatural deaths for them. For Rabbi Akiba, who is worrying about his fate, he predicts an even worse death.[70]

Lamenting the fact that he had only been able to learn an exceedingly small part of their Torah from his teachers, he is at least equally bitter about himself not having transmitted more than an exceedingly small part of his own knowledge, in turn. He says that he has produced, among other teachings, "three hundred (or, as others state, three thousand laws) about the planting of cucumbers" without anyone having been interested, with the exception of Rabbi Akiba.[70] This is what different sorts of natural magic were called, and we thus learn that Rabbi Eliezer was an expert in them. In fact, he recalls that he responded to the request of his student by first showing him how, with the help of a speech, he covered the entire field with cucumbers; and then showing him how, still with the help of his speech, he gathered them all up.

We have seen how the "miracles" attributed to Rabbi Eliezer in the story of the oven give rise to several symbolic interpretations. Similarly, this story can also be interpreted by relating it to the use Rabbi Eliezer makes of cucumbers (and of gourds, another variety of cucurbit) in a parable about the commandments of the Torah. These cucumbers, a sort of melon, were, it seems, a much-appreciated fruit. They are mentioned in the biblical story, along with watermelons and some vegetables, among the dishes the Hebrews sorely missed in the desert[70] when their food was reduced to manna, even though manna was said to taste very good! But the status of these cucumbers in the Talmud is more equivocal. On the one hand, here too they are considered to be a sought-after dish, the proof of this being that they are always to be found on the table of two famous aristocratic dining companions, even out of season.[71] One of these men was Roman and the other Jewish; their meetings, which were characterized by mutual respect, were also the occasion of philosophical exchanges on various subjects. The first was the Emperor Antoninus Pius, the second was Rabbi Yehuda HaNasi, president of the Sanhedrin and editor of the *Mishnah*. Their dialogues, on several questions debated in the Talmud, are reported in a variety of places. On the other hand, cucumbers were held by some, in the school of Rabbi Ishmael, to be unhealthy, hence their Hebrew name *kishuim*, from the root *kashe*, "tough" (for the body). On this question, strictly speaking a question of food hygiene, the contradiction was resolved by the observation that there were two different varieties, one large and bad for one's health, the other small and good for one's health. But we may speculate about this ambivalent "toughness," which inspired Rabbi Eliezer in the parable in which he compared the commandments of the Torah to a dish filled with cucumbers and gourds. This episode is also very instructive about the status of his relations with his colleagues, apparently at a time before his rejection and isolation at the conclusion of the story of the Oven of Akhnai. Here, once again, we encounter Rabbi Joshua as Rabbi Eliezer's opponent on the question of measure and excess. This time, their disagreement is about the relative value of the rules of *halakha*, decrees concerning the application of the laws of Torah, which had previously been issued by the rival schools of Shammai and Hillel. In general, the Shammai school was much stricter in its concern with constructing "a hedge around the Torah," a pretty rigorous set of extra prescriptions intended (for fear of what we now call a slippery slope, the idea of which is back in the public eye these days because of questions of biomedical ethics) to prevent one from getting into a position to reach the heart, that is to say, to transgress the *mitzvot* of Torah themselves. But it was the gentler rules of the second school, Hillel's school, that were more often adopted and constituted the generally accepted *halakha*. And yet, on one occasion, which becomes famous for this reason, Shammai's school wins the vote and eighteen of its rules are instituted.[72] Afterwards, Rabbi Eliezer and

Rabbi Joshua render contrasting judgments about the event. Rabbi Eliezer sees in it a "going beyond measure," certainly, but in a positive way, and compares the *mitzvot* of Torah to a full measure of cucumbers and gourds such that the addition of a supplementary condiment, like mustard, only reinforces their effect. Rabbi Joshua, however, sees the event as counterproductive, leading to a negative effect by which the excess will in the end lead to a "decrease in measure" because a law that is too severe cannot be accepted by all and will necessarily bring about a transgression of the commandments of the Torah itself. He compares these commandments to a dish filled with honey, in which the addition of extra items such as nuts or pomegranates would only make it overflow and thus diminish the initial measure. The difference between the analogies is the contrast between the hardness of solid fruit and the softness of liquid honey.[73]

To return to Rabbi Eliezer's magic and its effects on the cucumber field: this is the context in which his teaching is cited according to which the death penalty prescribed by the Bible for every sorcerer in Israel[74] only applied to "really making plants grow" and not to making people believe, by some illusionist's trick, that one had done so. But according to an even more general principle, we then learn, we must distinguish among three kinds of magic, of decreasing seriousness: the first truly effective and punishable by death; the second playing on illusion, a priori forbidden but not punished; and the third entirely permitted!

This permitted magic was the magic used by certain teachers to create artificial animals (and even an artificial human being), with the help, as we learn elsewhere,[75] of combinations of letters. The essential difference between this kind of magic and the first kind lies in its context, its finality, and the orientation of the intentions that accompany it: in the case of this permitted magic, toward a "unification of the name" and not, as in the case of the magic that is punishable by death, with an eye to an egotistical and dispersed mastery of the forces of nature. For it is understood that even if an action is extraordinary and seems to be supernatural, it cannot escape the power of the Creator for the simple reason that it is possible. That, in any case, is the thesis defended by Rabbi Hanina, another great master of magic as well as a great sage, differing in this opinion from those who see in magic an offense to the Creator and to the "family on high."[76]

As far as Rabbi Eliezer is concerned, one nonetheless wonders at the end of this episode how he was able to violate the prohibition, and the response is that the prohibition does not concern actions undertaken with the sole aim of learning or teaching. Obviously, that only strengthens one's appreciation of his knowledge because it is thus concerned with all kinds of techniques for magical action in a given field, techniques both real and working with illusions.

Holy or sacred?

Emmanuel Lévinas, it turns out, has produced a precise translation of this passage, accompanied by a detailed, subtle, and profound commentary that is characteristic of his well-known talmudic readings. The lesson here is a reading of pages 67a–68b of the treatise *Sanhedrin*, the pages that include this text; the lesson is entitled "Desacralization and Disenchantment" and, as the author explains in his preface, it is because of this lesson that the collection of readings in which it appears is named "From the Sacred to the Holy."[77] The general theme of the lesson is the warning against the charms of enchantment, remainders of the sacred in modern societies. It is worth dwelling on for a moment.

For Lévinas, the sacred is suspect from the beginning. It is characteristic of pagan idolatries and practices of sorcery. "Sorcery, first cousin, perhaps even sister, of the sacred, is the mistress of appearance." He contrasts "sacredness" with "holiness." "The sacred is in fact the half light in which the sorcery the Jewish tradition abhors flourishes . . . the sacred adorns itself with the prestige of prestiges. Revelation refuses these bad secrets. . . ."[78] This is why the desacralization of the modern world can be seen as an atheism of the "mortal God."[79] It is an opportunity and even a necessary condition for it to be inhabited by what "can be called Spirit and which animates the Jewish tradition."[79] But the desacralization is not total. The sacred does not disappear from the desacralized world: it degenerates, and "[t]he sacred which degenerates is worse than the sacred which disappears. That is why the sacred is not sacred, why the sacred is not holiness."[81] The world in which these remainders subsist is a "bewitched world, that is, [a world] with no exit."[82]

But Lévinas, in a deeply dialectical way, uses the distinction made by Rabbi Eliezer in our text between effective magic and the magic of an illusionist, that only plays on appearances. In fact, he sees in sorcery "the mistress of appearance," and that is also where possible salvation is to be found: "Real desacralization would attempt positively to separate the true from appearance, maybe even to separate the true from the appearance *essentially* mixed with the true."[83] This is what the spirit that animates the pharisaic will would make possible, as Lévinas suggests in a paragraph that he calls, perhaps with a certain irony, "The Scent of Holiness":

> [W]hat animates the Pharisaic will . . . is separation from a world in which *appearance* falsifies *that which appears*, from the very dawn of its manifestation . . . the *separation* of the Pharisees [let us recall here that in Hebrew, "Pharisee" used adjectivally means "separate"—HA] . . . is an absence from the immediacy of possessing by means of prohibitions and rules, a hope of *holiness* in the face of a *sacred* that cannot be purified, *Judaism as an irreducible modality of being present to the world.*[84]

As is his habit, Lévinas brings to light and renews the depths that attentive study of the talmudic text can reveal. To "separate the true from the appearance *essentially* mixed with the true" is a message that one understands all the more clearly when one realizes at the other extreme, as we will see in the next chapter, the degree to which what we have called the diluted sacred and its dissolution establish widespread, systemic verbal fraud, *ona'ah* beyond all bounds. From this point of view, there is nothing to be added to his description of the modern world:

> That is what sorcery is: the modern world; nothing is identical to itself; no one is identical to himself; nothing gets said for no word has its own meaning; all speech is a magical whisper; no one listens to what you say; everyone suspects behind your words a not-said, a conditioning, an ideology.[85]

Financial fraud, which has become normal, is not forgotten either. In the conjuring up of sorcery through the intervention of demons, which the Talmud distinguishes from sorcery without intermediaries, Lévinas sees the utilization of technology in the service of the degenerated sacred:

> Beside a rational technique, at the service of human ends, there is a technique that is the source of illusion, a technique which allows the production and sale of cucumbers: the technique displayed by the beneficiaries of stock exchange speculations.[86]

But in reading Lévinas's text, one cannot avoid a certain discomfort faced with the possible misunderstandings about this contrast between holiness and the sacred, since one must understand the *essential* admixture of appearance to the true to be *internal* to experiences of the sacred itself and of its majesty, of its "prestige of prestiges." And the distinction between "holy" and "sacred" is not essential but internal to the sacred, having more to do with the way one engages with it than with its nature. This, incidentally, is also what is suggested by the position mentioned earlier,[87] the position of those, among the pharisaic teachers no less, for whom magic in itself was not prohibited and that was also the position of Rabbi Hanina, on which Lévinas comments in the section "There is no sorcery—."[88] In the same way, the distinction between effective magic and illusion is secondary to the initial biblical prohibition; it is introduced by talmudic interpretation.

We thus have to take another critical look at the emphasis Lévinas places on the opposition between sacred and holy, which seems so essential to him that it inspires the title of the entire collection. Allow me to make two remarks on this, one on the form, the other on the content.

My first remark is this: nowhere does the talmudic discussion that is the topic of this lesson explicitly speak of the question of the sacred. Lévinas does mention this at the opening of his commentary. He apologizes for it but asks us to allow the content of the commentary to be its justification,[89] which is how the talmudic commentaries themselves often proceed.

The second remark I would like to make is this: the distinction between sacred and holy raises a delicate problem of translation and interpretation because one and the same Hebrew adjective, *kadosh*, is sometimes translated by one of these words and sometimes by the other. There certainly are two Hebrew nouns for the substantive "the sacred," one masculine, *kodesh*, and the other feminine, *kedusha*. Hence perhaps the temptation to translate the first as "the sacred" and the second as "holiness," playing on the similarity between the genders that is obviously not found in other languages. But this translation problem in fact raises a basic problem. Lévinas's French introduces a distinction that is far from innocuous. As indicated by the different etymologies of the two words, *sacer* for "the sacred" and *sanctus* for holiness (in French *le sacré* and *sainteté*, respectively), we are dealing here with two very different semantic fields. Unlike *sanctus*, *sacer* simply means "consecrated to" anyone or anything, a god or a devil, a good cause or a mission of destruction, blessed or cursed. This is the distinction that Lévinas takes up, in a way, but he projects it onto the Hebrew world in which only the notion of *kadosh* is a priori pertinent, and that is what is problematic. The distinction that Lévinas is making is original and essential to the Latin terms, but it does not apply to the Hebrew term. A notion that is conveyed by one root, *kadosh*, expresses both sides of the distinction; it carries the meanings of both *sacer* and *sanctus*. As I have mentioned, men and women who were consecrated to pagan prostitution cults were called *kadesh* and *kadesha* in Hebrew. Sorcery, however, is not a specifically pagan perversion, at least not in the eyes of Rabbi Akiba, according to Lévinas's own interpretation:

> It is a perversion of the holy people itself. . . . [I]t is the excess of knowledge itself, that which is beyond what can be borne in truth, the illusion which derives from the unbearable truth and which tempts from the very depths of the truth; a Jewish perversion, that is to say, the perversion of all those able to rise to the true, of all those who assemble at the foot of Mount Sinai.[90]

It would appear, then, that the same potential opposition that runs through *sacer* also runs through *sanctus* and that what Lévinas is discovering here is the unique, though potentially divided, semantic field of *kadosh*. But the insistence in the rest of the text on what he defines from the outset as "holiness, that is, separation or purity, the essence without admixture that can be called Spirit,"[91] is at the very least a source of misunderstanding, if not a contradiction of what Lévinas says in other parts of his commentary. The appeal to holiness, here distinguished from and opposed to the sacred, misleads by evoking the otherworldliness of pure spirits separated from the life of the body and the constraints of its materiality.

Yet that is precisely what Lévinas is opposing when he emphasizes a concern for the concrete in "the minutiae of the law" such as the details of the rules of purity and impurity, that is to say, of life and death, which are also discussed in this Talmud passage—as in the story of the oven. Before addressing a formal analogy established by this text between certain rules concerning *shabbat* and sorcery, he even goes so far as to wonder whether "spiritualization" is not another form of sorcery,

> [t]he one which does without instruments, the one of the mere murmur, of sheer breath . . . , [of the] magic . . . of interiorization . . . , [of the] appeal to good intentions. . . . An interior magic with infinite resources: all is allowed in the inner life, all is allowed, including crime. The abolition of laws in the name of love. . . .[92]

We see therefore that the opposition between the holy and the sacred, instead of being an opposition that is internal to the sacred itself, does a disservice to the text, and that is true of how it is expressed from the point of view of Emmanuel Lévinas's thinking, in this commentary as in other works of his.

The desacralization of the modern world opens up a domain that is neither sacred nor holy, in which it is still possible, according to his lovely expression, to "positively separate the true from appearance" and to thereby render it *kadosh*, that is to say, to "consecrate" it in some sense. This is the goal of the rites and practices of separation, which do not imply an exit from the world and obviously do not suppress the *'hol*, the "sand" of everyday existence (often translated as "profane"!). This domain is the domain of the Law that separates spaces, as the Pharisees themselves were separated: spaces in which the sacred can be consecrated by its own separation, the limitation of its overflow. The paradigm of this is the separation-limitation concerning Eros.

This, in fact, is the separation to which the Bible, according to the rabbinical reading, exhorts us in the famous text of the nineteenth chapter of Leviticus, which introduces an entire series of laws both ritual and moral, "all the 'bodies' of Torah," as Rashi puts it, including the laws about loving one's neighbor and keeping *shabbat*. The biblical expression *Kedoshim tihiyu ki kadosh ani*—most often translated as "be holy because I am holy" but which can just as well be translated "be sacred because I am sacred"—is in fact a curious expression that demands some explanation. Rashi invites us to read it as "be separated because I am separated" or "distinguished because I am distinguished," with the laws about sexuality discussed in the previous chapter of Leviticus (chapter 18) serving as the paradigm of this separation.[93]

What is implied here is not an allusion to the divine transcendence of theologians but rather an allusion to an immanence and a presence in the world with some behaviors set apart, behaviors that are distinguished among other behaviors in the image of the distinguished presence[94] of the god of Israel within the world of which those behaviors, along with that presence, are a part.

Rules, rites, and practices are exactly what is at stake in the discussions, ruptures, and dramatic reconciliations among the Pharisees, with Rabbi Eliezer on one side and his disciples and colleagues on the other, all of them in agreement, in the end, as far as sorcery is concerned, about the need to study and experiment with the sole purpose of acquiring the knowledge that undergirds all these magical techniques (let us recall that until the Renaissance, science was not distinct from so-called natural magic). But the fundamental disagreement between the two groups, as we saw in the story of the oven, has to do with the source of these rules of separation. Do they have their source in the crystallized sacred of divine revelation or, rather, in the wisdom of men on earth, themselves virtuous because separated—"pharisaic"—in their way of life?

Under these circumstances, Rabbi Eliezer's severity and obstinacy in defending his theses are understandable. Whether he received his Torah from his teachers or from quasi-prophetic revelations, he cannot be anything other than convinced that he possesses the indisputable Truth, which has truly fallen "from heaven." Any attempt at modifying the application of that truth and, even more so, at defending opposing theses, cannot therefore be anything for him but a sign of inadmissible relativism or of a compromise with the demands of existence "on earth," like a kind of *Realpolitik*.

But in the talmudic era the age of prophets is already no more. It is thus the age of Rabbi Eliezer's opponents, even if at his death those opponents pay tribute to him as well as to the knowledge that dies with him.

8

Dissolution

The two examples we looked at in chapter 7, of Plutarch and Rabbi Eliezer ben Hyrcanus, show how, at the beginning of the second century CE, revealed Truth was forced to undergo a change in status when revelations ceased. This general phenomenon constituted by the progressive disappearance of prophecy in antiquity was experienced differently by the different schools and traditions present in the Greco-Roman world. The birth of Christianity was one such response, parallel to and in competition with the transformations of the pagan philosophical schools and cults to which Plutarch is an exemplary witness. For their part, the pharisaic schools, whose teachings are collected in the Talmud, reacted to the same phenomenon by constructing a continuity, across the rupture, with the ethical and legal context of the ancient Law of Moses. Despite dispersion and the destruction, on two occasions, of the Temple in Jerusalem, the site of the Hebrew sovereignty to which, in fact, the ancient Law had been tailored, the Law was instituted as the "written Torah," the scripture of reference around which the renewals of the "oral Torah" developed. While Rabbi Eliezer, like his teachers, colleagues, and disciples, was concerned with jealously preserving the heritage of that Law against its dilution in the Babylonian world, and later the Greco-Roman world, that surrounded it, he faced, as we have seen, the same challenge that was posed for everyone by the end of prophecy. In a parallel development, Saint Paul facilitated the reception of Christianity in the pagan world precisely by lifting the obligations of the Law. But whatever the various responses were that different groups gave to this challenge, this was the end of pure and absolute truths fallen from heaven and the beginning of what could already be seen as a relativism of truths built "from the earth," step by step. A powerful image from the Midrash has the angels opposing the creation of human beings in the name of Truth because they see in this creation, and rightly so, the danger that falsehood will break out in the world. We know, of course, that in the legend the Creator does not go along with them and responds instead by simply throwing the Truth to the ground and assigning it a new destiny: to "sprout from earth."[1] This is the program that was then taken up against Rabbi Eliezer by his colleagues. But the angels were not completely wrong, except in judging creation according to their own standards. As predicted, lying and fraud accompany human existence. There is no more room for a pure Truth, "totally naked," once it has to pass through the language of real men, women, and children. We saw in chapter 1 that Vladimir Jankélévitch distances himself from what he calls a moral purism by propounding values, from the start, that prevail over the value of truth: values such as that of "pious lies." This is a relative moral relativism that takes the limited nature of human virtue into account, just as epistemological relativism, which is also relative, takes the limited and partial nature of knowledge into account. Truth in an established and crystalline form, like the legendary city named Truth, which instantly killed anyone who pronounced the slightest lie,[2] is a deadly utopia for a human existence in which a certain modesty is necessary to preserve the private sphere of each and all. For it is truth itself, thus veiled, that is thereby preserved from the mendacious glare of its brutal unveiling. The only remaining possibility is to search for truth by hunting down unjustifiable errors and lies, an interminable quest with no guarantee of success; this is a casuistical process in which the sincerity and disinterestedness of those who dedicate themselves to it are its only guarantee, and that is obviously relative. In our legend, these people are the only ones capable of judging the situations in which it is recommended that good lies be used to cover the truth with the necessary veils.[3]

The world of *ona'ah* thus necessarily establishes itself once *measure*, *weight* and *number* come down from the heaven of the absolute to regulate the exchanges between human beings. For with this new status acquired by truth, the danger of too much lying emerges and an intermediate space must be established between the two extremes. The first extreme is what

I have called the crystallized sacred, the source of the truths revealed by oracles and prophecy, as continues to be the case for transitional figures like Plutarch and Rabbi Eliezer. Crystal balls of all kinds, which are believed to transparently reflect absolute truths, are the degenerate remainders of this crystallized sacred and give rise to nostalgia for it. The other extreme is its dissolution into systemic falsehood.

Propaganda: Half-truths and total falsehood

At the other extreme from the crystallized sacred, which is supposed to be the source of absolute truth, its progressive dilution (and the resulting desacralization of the social bond) has produced another extreme, the extreme of the dissolution of truth into systemic falsehood.

The desacralization of oracular language, of money, and of signs of power in general has obviously allowed for a liberation of the masses from the stranglehold in which, in ancient societies, those who possessed these signs of power held the public. Modern democracy, which extended the finally rather limited field of Athenian democracy, was able to be invented in Europe a few centuries ago because it benefited from this desacralization, and in turn, encouraged the freedom of thought and expression that that desacralization had made possible. To judge from the appeal that the model of Western democracy has held for increasing numbers of nations in the two centuries since the American and French revolutions, this is a fortunate evolution. The model continues to have a magnetic pull, along with the material and intellectual development that has accompanied it, even in the countries that have not adopted it and whose peoples are subjected to more or less totalitarian or violent dictatorships.

In the eyes of any objective observer, if there is such a thing, there can be no doubt that there has been a certain progress in the history of humanity, not only material progress (in the accumulation of goods and of means of avoiding pain) but also intellectual progress (in the accumulation of knowledge) and even moral progress, whatever people may say. It is fashionable to contrast technical and scientific progress with the moral stagnation of humanity or "of man," as they say, as if we were talking about a particular person. Yet most people today have rejected, as abominations, behaviors that only a few centuries ago were considered perfectly normal by everyone, including the highest moral and religious authorities. Think of torture in all its forms, especially as a way of meting out punishment, including the death penalty; of slavery; of forced labor by children; of famines inflicted by one society on another. Even if these abominations continue to be perpetrated in many countries, they are carried out in violation of national and international rules and laws, which makes it very different. War itself now has a different status in the minds of most people. Once considered to be the normal means for settling conflicts between peoples, it was an occasion to witness the highest virtues, such as bravery, brotherhood in arms, a chivalrous spirit, and patriotism. But after two world wars and their atrocities, war is now seen as a last resort to be avoided at all costs and even, for some, a crime under any circumstances, as if the notion of war crimes, invented after World War II to characterize certain forms of waging war, were now extended to all war, in the sense that there could then be no war, even a defensive one, without crimes.

This attitude obviously does not prevent wars, but it does mean that they must be constantly justified by the governments that conduct them, justified to public opinion in their own country and to international institutions that undertake to stop them, sometimes successfully. There has, therefore, in spite of everything, been moral and legal progress.

We must also stress that dictatorships do not have to respond to this progress in the same way that democracies do. In democracies, the free expression of public opinion and of criticism of the elected government allow this progress to be felt, even if it is relative. One spectacular result is that there are practically no more wars between democracies. Only dictatorships are still at war, among themselves or against democracies. Then there are still civil wars, with interference from great and medium-sized interested powers, even democracies! In short, things are far from perfect, but the greater number and higher quality of exchanges and transactions, what we now call "globalization," is both the cause and the effect of the transformation of humanity that we are witnessing: a process that certainly involves threats, to be sure, but also hopes. It is not hard to see that the more the future is open to creative imagination in political regimes where it is possible to think freely and to express one's thoughts critically, the greater the hopes for better lives and for the prevention of new catastrophes.

Nonetheless, the multiplication of commercial, technical, and cultural exchanges, independent of any reference to a crystallized sacred imposed on everyone, is accompanied by a perverse *worm-in-the-apple* effect that is at the root of reactive, reactionary, and to some degree obscurantist regressions towards a return to the protector-sacred of different traditions. Indeed, like a worm in the apple of trades or exchanges, the distension of the ancient bond between the words of the oracle and the hidden truth that they are said to express, between money and the real value of material goods, between the monetary or linguistic sign and what it signifies, creates an area—and an era—of systemic falsehood. The era of accurate information is diluted in false information; truth is diluted and dissolved in falsehood (voluntary or not) to the point that they become indistinguishable from each other.

And yet this is an old story. We saw in chapter 3 how the perversion of language that was connected with the corruption of democracy of which it was both a cause and an effect had already been described in ancient Greece by Thucydides. Over the centuries, numerous authors have taken up this description of what Thomas Gustafson calls the "Thucydidean moment" as they, too, encountered and studied the same phenomenon. But as in many other domains, the twentieth century, thanks to a double explosion, both demographic and technological, witnessed an amplification and an acceleration of this phenomenon.

Information, transformed into propaganda and an intoxication that manipulates public opinion, spread brutally in the two great totalitarian dictatorships, the Nazi and Fascist regimes and, in a different way, the Communist regimes, that in the twentieth century gained power, imposed their terror, and fortunately crumbled and fell apart, having caused millions of deaths in just a few decades. There one could see the power of words in the falsification of the facts they are supposed to describe. For this purpose, the Nazis created Goebbels's notorious Propaganda Department, while the Communists relied on a perverse rhetorical use of Marxist ideology. In the first case, socialism, turned into national socialism, masked the dictatorship of the *Führer* and the SS, the spearhead of his party. In the second case, socialism was expected to come about later thanks to the "dictatorship of the proletariat," that is to say, again, the dictatorship of the Party and its *nomenklatura*. From that point on, all words were perverted. The democracies tried, weakly at first because they did not really believe in it, to resist, in the name of freedoms, the hegemonic programs of these regimes. They thus became regimes "corrupted at the hands of the powers of money," destined for decay and death, for replacement by or submission to the rule of Superman and the Superior Race or to the rule of the dictatorship of the proletariat marching towards the New Man.

The first thing to be done was obviously to demonize the enemy—that is to say, everyone else—by dehumanizing him with the vocabulary that was allegedly being used to describe reality. The Communists invented the charming labels of "viscous rats" and "lecherous vipers" for those the Party sought to get rid of. For Goebbels, following Hitler, Jews were the subhumans par excellence, associated with Gypsies and blacks among the degenerate "races" but even more dangerous because they had been integrated and assimilated, thus "hidden," and schemed to dominate the planet. This discourse went over all the better because it was not radically new. It was rooted in old Christian anti-Semitism and had already been shaped in czarist Russia at the beginning of the century by the infamous forgery *The Protocols of the Elders of Zion*. The two dictatorships opposed and demonized each other—except during the two years of the German-Soviet pact when their leaders found it useful to enter into an alliance against the democracies—by using the bizarre terms "Jewish Bolshevism" and "Judeo-Capitalism" against each other; in both cases, the Jews were identified with the "international plutocracy."

One could make a list of all the words that were diverted from their meaning to designate exactly the opposite of what they said. The countries conquered by the Red Army, in which Communist dictatorships were imposed, were called "people's democracies" (a tautological phrase intended to reinforce their character as "true" democracies?), which was evidently supposed to distinguish them from so-called "bourgeois" democracies. But the same kind of expedited "justice" was apparently done there as was applied by the "popular tribunals" of the French Revolution during the Terror. "World Youth Festivals for Peace" were organized that were vehicles of propaganda for extending the hegemony of the Communist International, that is to say the Soviet Union, whose methods were in no way peaceful. The Western democracies, on the other hand, whose freedoms were devalued in Communist jargon under the name of "formal freedoms," evidently constituted the camp of "imperialism," of America and its "lackeys." Similar perversions of language, transposed into Chinese, could also be found in the Maoist form of Communist dictatorship.

But this is all well known and documented, and the only reason I mention it briefly here is to stress what is less known: the perversion of language by propaganda was not, contrary to what is commonly believed, invented and initially developed by the dictatorships. Dictatorships did use propaganda, systematically developing it as a unidirectional weapon. But propaganda had already been produced by the new means of communication that had begun to be used in a massive way in the democracies and in particular in the largest of them, the United States of America.

This is why I spoke of the worm in the apple in the context of the progress of humanity that accompanies the progress of democracy. This obviously does not mean that dictatorship is better than or even as good as democracy; it only means that democracy, always threatened from the inside, is particularly vulnerable to systemic falsehood, which can lead to the destruction of the democracy itself.

From this point of view, the history of propaganda and of its development in the twentieth century, running parallel to the development of mass media, is very instructive. Dictatorships used propaganda and the mass media brutally, silencing everything that did not follow the party line. But democracies began to use them in a gentler way and continue to do so, ever more effectively, as the techniques of mass communications evolve. Aristotle was already aware of the role of rhetoric, that is to say, of the form of discourse rather than its content, in the workings of democracy in the marketplace. As a remedy, he suggested that all citizens study rhetoric so that there would be a somewhat even playing field. Democracy, supposed to be the government of the people, is in fact the government of "opinion," which is manipulated and manipulates itself, with no way out but to forge ahead with its own critique, a critique that is itself manipulated and manipulating.

This, once again, is better than the linear and brutal form of totalitarian propaganda. But this gentle and self-manipulating form is at the same time a dangerous weakness when a democratic regime marked by freedom of opinion is threatened by a totalitarian regime of censorship and controlled opinion. During the Cold War, François Mitterrand used to say that the pacifists were in the West and the missiles were in the East. This was already the case between the World Wars, when the pacifists, who never wanted to see the horrors of the First World War repeated, reacted to Hitler's threats by justifying them through the mistakes of the Treaty of Versailles and the humiliation of defeated Germany, and recommending that Nazi Germany's massive rearmament not be taken seriously. This rearmament had plenty of time in which to be implemented, sheltered by Goebbels's propaganda from any check that public opinion might have placed on it, whereas the Western democracies, especially France, were subject to criticism from all sides, some of it justified, that only reinforced the accusations of decay and corruption.

It might appear that all of this is behind us. The Nazi dictatorship was defeated militarily and politically. The Communist dictatorship was defeated economically and politically. But the worm is still in the apple.

Let us, therefore, recall propaganda's democratic origins, long predating Goebbels's diversion of propaganda to his own advantage and transformation of it into a machine of hatred. These origins are brilliantly laid out in Edward Bernays's book *Propaganda*,[4] a doubly foundational work: foundational for propaganda itself and for the theory of propaganda. Bernays published the book in the United States in 1928 after having witnessed the government's first great manipulation of public opinion after it had decided to enter the war in 1917 although the population generally opposed it.

President Wilson created a Committee on Public Information with the goal of manipulating public opinion, and it fulfilled that mission very effectively. The members of the committee, journalists and specialists in public relations, invented most of the techniques that were later used for "soft sells" to the public to get them to "buy" something, be it a commercial industrial product or an idea, a political program, the election of a governor or of the president, etc. Bernays himself, as a journalist and public relations agent, was associated with the work of the committee. A nephew of Sigmund Freud's, he was brought to the United States as a one-year-old, in 1892, when his family emigrated there. He quickly understood the resources that advertising could provide for getting the public to approve of what one wants to "sell," first in the literal sense and then in the figurative sense, especially when the task is to change public opinion on a question of politics.

Very quickly, Bernays the student became the expert, putting into practice and theorizing what he had learned by creating one of the first public relations agencies, if not the very first one. It was not just a matter of advertising but of selling a newly created service to his "clients"—companies, entertainment producers, ideological movements, politicians, and others. The function of this new profession was to help those clients get public opinion to accept whatever would help the clients' interests, by playing the role of the professional and "scientific" middleman between the clients and the opinions of the clients' potential clients. Obviously, all available means of mass communication, what would later be called mass media, were mobilized: all the resources of journalism, advertising, sociology, and the psychology of emotions, including the psychology of the unconscious discovered by Bernays's uncle, Freud. In his book, Bernays very openly lays out his methods with a mixture of cynicism and a clear conscience, constantly recommending using them in the service of good causes and honest undertakings. Bernays's success was not long in coming, even if his first disciples very soon turned out to be the propaganda machines of the dictatorships of the extreme right and left. But public relations agencies quickly became, first in the United States and then in Europe, indispensable to the functioning of democracy and of industrial and financial capitalism. Today, their professional methods of manipulating public opinion are applied in all fields: fashion, politics, the economy, the social, religion, the arts and sciences. Bernays already explains how "[i]n some departments of our daily life, in which we imagine ourselves free agents, we are ruled by dictators exercising great power" that constitute an "invisible government" of specialists in propaganda operations.[5] We will see how over time this invisible character has acquired the status of Edgar Allan Poe's purloined letter, all the better hidden for how it displays itself in front of everyone. These methods have been adopted and developed by all regimes and ideologies, democratic and totalitarian, capitalist and anticapitalist, socialist, environmentalist, internationalist, etc.

The American linguist and human rights activist Noam Chomsky, who has written extensively on language and politics and on the mechanisms by which information is placed at the service of political and financial power in democracies,[6] sums up the state of affairs in a succinct formula: "propaganda is to a democracy what the bludgeon is to a totalitarian state."[7] This diagnosis, which is meant to be a denunciation of the American government's manipulations of public opinion, also points out and emphasizes, in a way that is perhaps unintended on the part of its author, the difference between democracy and totalitarian states, which is, finally, irreducible. For the totalitarian state uses both violence and propaganda. Furthermore, insofar as democratic freedoms, especially the freedom of expression, are respected, any propaganda can lead to counter-propaganda.

This counter-propaganda may be just as mendacious and manipulative (which counts for nothing in the search for truth) as the original propaganda, but it contributes to the creation of counter-powers, of varying degrees of effectiveness, to the kind of one-way manipulations that are found in totalitarian regimes, in which all counter-power is suppressed by violence. One spectacular example: in the nineteen fifties, this worm in the apple of democracy was denounced by the American government itself, when President Eisenhower famously warned against the invisible influence of the "military-industrial complex" on the politics of his country! That did not prevent Bernays from participating, also in the nineteen fifties, in campaigns of political destabilization organized by the CIA in Latin America to overthrow democratic governments that opposed this notorious military-industrial complex.[8]

For several decades now, manipulations of all kinds have been able to light some counter-fires by virtue of the very fact of the preservation and progress of democratic freedoms. One of the cult books of the American youth protest movements of the nineteen sixties, Herbert Marcuse's *One-Dimensional Man*,[9] denounced the one-dimensional nature of these manipulations, which had led to the uniformization of a society captive within its own conformity. But this very denunciation, along with many others, finally led to the explosion of this captivity and helped the progress of movements such as those of the Beat Generation and the California hippies, which hastened the end of the Vietnam War, and of movements such as the Civil Rights Movement, which transformed the condition of Black Americans in ways that were unimaginable at the time.

In the dictatorships, on the other hand—whether Communist, as in the Soviet Union, its satellite regimes, and Maoist China, or Fascist, as in Franco's Spain and in Portugal—they used their totalitarian violence to impose their propaganda as the only legitimate truth for decades. It took the collapse of these regimes, under the pressure of external and internal opposition, for their "one-dimensionality," imposed by brute force, to come to an end.

These evolutions in propaganda and counter-propaganda over the course of the twentieth century and at the beginning of the twenty-first obviously render some of the points that Bernays makes obsolete, though some of the other points remain valid. An entire series of practices that seemed very new in the nineteen twenties have now become standard methods of conducting human business. It has become a commonplace for every company to carry out market research before launching any product whatsoever, along with implementing the greatest variety of sociological analyses, analyses of the psychological profiles of potential buyers and of the possible efficacy of advertising and media, etc. Public relations agencies have extended their fields of activity to become marketing and communications consultants and finally just plain communications consultants. The election campaigns of candidates for political office are no longer imaginable without the investment of huge sums in order to finance the implementation of their propaganda according to the methods developed by their communications consultants. Just as in games of chess, the invention of new "moves" always confers an advantage, but nothing can be done in the competition between communications consultants working for rival clients without mobilizing insane sums. As Bernays mentions, the first politician whose election was due to fundraising by an industrialist with an interest in his party's victory was William McKinley, first elected to the governorship of Ohio in 1891 and then to the presidency of the United States in 1896. Bernays later uses McKinley's story as an inspiration in developing the technique and the associated methods of shaping public opinion.[10]

The [first—trans.] presidential campaign of the latest president to be elected in the United States, Barack Obama, raised funds that went beyond anything ever seen before, and especially beyond what his unfortunate competitors had been able to raise. But this is considered to be perfectly normal and has not prevented his election from being perceived as a blessing by the majority of public opinion not only in the United States but pretty much all over the world. His inauguration in January of 2009, widely televised, really seemed like the consecration of a potential savior. The role of money in this victory was barely mentioned, and when it was, it was mostly in the context of emphasizing that the main sources of funding for his campaign had been modest contributions by small donors, the actual number of which was multiplied many times over by the campaign for public opinion—that is to say, the propaganda—waged on the Internet. Edward Bernays would have been proud of his disciples' good work, even more so because this time the propaganda, at least in the eyes of public opinion (!), worked in the service of the good and of honesty. For, in the context of American democracy and its ideals, the question of the morality of these practices arose from the start. The inventors of public relations and mass communications were no fools. Even though the word "propaganda," invented based on the Latin *propagere* ("to propagate") by the *Congregatio de propaganda fide* ("Congregation for the Propagation of the Faith") and then taken up during the French Revolution as the simple act of propagating doctrines or opinions, had no pejorative connotation whatsoever before then, in the twentieth century it rapidly acquired what Bernays calls an "unpleasant connotation."[11] Increasingly, the word evoked manipulation by any and all means, including falsehood and deception in all their forms. That is why Bernays's book, like the practices of his disciples and successors, seems like a mixture of cynicism and moral preoccupation! "Yet whether, in any instance, propaganda is good or bad depends upon the merit of the cause urged, and the correctness of the information published."[12] Two virtuous criteria, to be sure, but very difficult to apply.

For the methods of propaganda are intrinsically perverse, whatever cause they serve and however accurate the information. We can already see this in Bernays's descriptions and even more so in propaganda's later developments:

> The conscious and intelligent manipulation of the organized habits and opinions of the masses is an important element in democratic society. Those who manipulate this unseen mechanism of society constitute an invisible government which is the true ruling power of our country.[13]

These are the words with which Bernays begins his book. And he cites at length from an article from *Scientific American* pleading for the restitution of respectability to the good old word *propaganda*, invented in the seventeenth century in Rome by a congregation of cardinals for the *propaganda fide*, the "propagation of the faith."

> [W]e can see that in its true sense propaganda is a perfectly legitimate form of human activity. Any society, whether it be social, religious or political, which is possessed of certain beliefs, and sets out to make them known, either by the spoken or written words, is practicing propaganda. *Truth* is mighty and must prevail. . . .[14]

In other words, propaganda and public relations consultants exist to allow an intelligent but invisible minority to cause truth to triumph over error, light over darkness, and order over chaos, in accordance with the title of the first chapter of *Propaganda*, "Organizing Chaos." Bernays keeps returning to the idea of an "invisible government," which is obviously not invisible to everyone and certainly not to his consultants. Hence a form of ethical preoccupation with the justification of this activity in the article from which he goes on to cite:

> If any body of men believe that they have discovered a valuable truth, it is not merely their privilege but their duty to disseminate that truth. If they realize, as they quickly must, that this spreading of the truth can be done upon a large scale and effectively only by organized effort, they will make use of the press and the platform as the best means to give it wide circulation. Propaganda becomes vicious and reprehensive only when its authors consciously and deliberately disseminate what they know to be lies, or when they aim at effects which they know to be prejudicial to the common good.[15]

But Bernays himself is not naïve. He knows that propaganda serves everyone, the Ku Klux Klan as well as charitable organizations.[16] As a professional, he exposes the motors of manipulation. And in the different ways of using those motors, deception cannot be avoided, even if it is "for the public good," which is far from always being the case. This is easily shown by the numerous examples, drawn from all fields of human activity, that Bernays analyzes in detail in his book.

> There is no means of human communication which may not also be a means of deliberate propaganda, because propaganda is simply the establishing of reciprocal understanding between an individual and a group.[17]

And yet, for

> the successful propagandist . . . it is not sufficient to understand only the mechanical structure of society, the groupings and cleavages and loyalties. An engineer may know all about the cylinders and pistons of a locomotive, but unless he knows how steam behaves under pressure he cannot make his engine run. *Human desires are the steam which makes the social machine work.*[18]

This is why it is necessary for the specialist to know and make use of all the levers that the human sciences, including the sciences of the unconscious, can place at his disposal. In particular, instead of trying to convince his target audience directly of the value of what his client has to offer,

> [t]he new salesmanship has found it possible, by dealing with men in the mass through their group formations, to set up psychological and emotional currents which will work for him. Instead of assaulting sales resistance by direct attack, he is interested in removing sales resistance. *He creates circumstances which will swing emotional currents so as to make for purchaser demand.*[19]

It is not only businesspeople, but all communications consultants, who know very well that manipulating opinion means manipulating emotions. But today, thanks to television and the Internet, global emotion, which can spread instantly without leaving time for reflection, has become one of the most effective ingredients of the self-manipulation of national and international public opinion, using the half-truths that are the effect of what I have elsewhere called a "morality of indignation."[20] This is what Bernays did not foresee. Trying to predict what the future of propaganda will become as the public at large comes to be aware of its methods, he concludes his book with these sentences: "Propaganda will never die out. Intelligent men must realize that propaganda is the modern instrument by which they can fight for productive ends and help to bring order out of chaos."[21]

And yet, since 1928, matters have not stood still. What was new then has become commonplace and fuels a veritable communications industry, what a study published in 2004 called simply "the industry of lies."[22] The motor of this industry is what we now call lobbying, whose practices, institutionalized in the United States, have also developed in Europe, where lobbying firms and networks have multiplied. Yet even the authors of this study seem naïve in that, like Bernays, they still suppose that the effectiveness of these practices lies in their "invisibility" and that one has only to unmask them in order for them to be neutralized. But the lobbyists in the United States Congress are very visible. They set up storefronts, and this practice has spread to Europe and especially, but not exclusively, to Brussels, where they lobby the European Commission. The public activity of one lobby only triggers activity by a lobby on the other side, which will mobilize as many resources as possible in order to use the exact same methods against the first group. Sometimes the counter-propaganda even uses exactly the same arguments as its adversary, simply turning them around. The authors of *L'Industrie du mensonge* themselves give the example of environmental and antienvironmental lobbyists who ended up joining forces when it became clear that there were profits to be made from environmentalism.

This example, along with others having to do, especially, with the management of food scares and public health problems, make clear the extent to which unmasking lobbying activities is far from sufficient to disqualify them. Later on, we will see how these areas are, in a way, "privileged" as sites of manipulation in that they have to do with *scientific* information, which is supposed to have more truth value than others. It is not the case that public opinion can only be successfully manipulated when the manipulation remains invisible.

Professional lobbying, which labels itself as such, tends to find itself in the same position as advertising, which is incidentally one of lobbying's tools. Advertisers are required to signal that their messages *are* advertising so that they will not be confused with editorial content, for example. Lobbying is obviously more sophisticated in that it also uses the media in every possible way to influence opinion. But the effect of its having been institutionalized is that it is placed under similar constraints: it must issue a public message that its activity is unilaterally in the service of one particular cause, product, company, etc. As a result, a kind of framing and of regulation of its practices can be set up and attenuate its deceptive character, as is done with advertising. Not everything is possible in advertising, especially not "false advertising." In the same way, all lobbying worthy of the name seeks to avoid accusations of influence peddling or of corruption, which would be likely to damage its respectable status. But that is only possible in a democracy. As in the case of propaganda, when it is a totalitarian regime in which the "industry of lies" is at work, that fact profoundly modifies the effects of lobbying at the same time as it weakens the democracies that are in conflict with such dictatorships even further.

In fact, the very notion of an "invisible government" of the most intelligent, a key notion in Bernays's analyses, must be heavily modified. First of all, when dictatorships take hold of propaganda, the propaganda is then in the service of a government that is completely visible to everyone and it does not in fact replace violence, as Chomsky's formula would lead one to expect, but superimposes itself on it. And in the conflicts that set dictatorships against democracies, the dictatorships are at an advantage in that their propaganda benefits from the freedom of expression that prevails among their adversaries. The dictatorships can make use of all the communication techniques at their disposal to praise the supposed merits of their ideology as compared to the actual weaknesses of the democratic regimes, thus profiting from the fact that exposing and denouncing these weaknesses is part of the normal functioning of democracy.

But in democracies, too, the nature of "invisible government" as a manipulation of public opinion has changed and been replaced by the self-government of a public opinion that manipulates itself. In fact, propaganda, along with advertising and with greatly increased access to media, has become commonplace and is available to just about every group that is competing with others to gain market shares or a share of power. Communication, driven by the activities of a whole range of professions, has become a goal in itself.[23] Just as Marshall McLuhan announced in his famous message about the working of mass media: "the medium is the message."

The result is that the content of any propaganda put in place by a public relations or lobbying agency necessarily triggers counter-propaganda, at a speed and level of efficiency that depends on the talent and the financial resources of another such agency at the service of a competing pressure group. In other words, the democracy of public opinion has become a war of each against all. Instead of oratorical jousts in the marketplace of Athens or in parliamentary halls, where everyone can see the speakers' faces and the weapons of rhetoric are used, a multitude of "invisible governments" now wage war on one another to win over public opinion. And thanks to the anonymity that is granted by the virtual nature of the Internet, it is now all the more so: a global marketplace filled with even more dangerous fraudulent speech. A war of each against all, fortunately limited to verbal and nonverbal communication, but a war that does not always avoid violence, the violence of the passions that are stirred up by propaganda.

In this widespread competition over the mastery of information, a new practice has appeared, complete with its own experts: spin and its spin doctors. Bernays is credited with the invention of this practice as well, rightly or wrongly ("for to those who have, more will be given").[24] It is true that he lived to be 103 years old and was alive until 1995, and that he lived long enough to see the procedures that he had applied develop and become widespread. There are so many beliefs and behaviors that he shaped, whether convincing women to smoke for the greater profit of the tobacco industry or getting politicians elected thanks to manipulations of their public image, using, in particular, tools such as opinion polls and the well-organized deployment of entertainment celebrities.

The English word *spin*, originally from "to spin a textile fiber" or "make a whirligig turn," first entered the French language by way of quantum physics, where it is used to designate the kinetic momentum of an elementary particle turning on itself. But it is now commonly recognized in its new meaning as a fabricated story, the hijacking of information, a dirty trick, turning propaganda back against itself—in other words, as manipulation of the media and the public opinion that they influence. With spin, the meaning of a news item or an event is transformed by tendentious interpretation, bound up with partial presentation. Some public relations experts have acquired the title of "spin doctors," a title they are quick to employ to accuse their adversaries of the same practices.

One of the results of these practices is the growing number of self-fulfilling prophecies when the information into which promotion and advertising have filtered has to do with the future. Once the public has been convinced of the near-certainty of a prediction that is not catastrophic, as long as there is no obvious reason for wanting to prevent its being carried out, everything falls into place in such a way that agents determine their activities in accordance with the prediction and for that very reason, the prediction is then fulfilled. The beliefs of the public are thus reinforced by those whose function it is supposed to be to report on those beliefs. The journalists who are supposed to describe the state of public opinion and to choose the information and the news they think should interest the public in fact *make* public opinion and determine what the public's main interests are.

In this way, of the two moral criteria that Bernays assigned to propaganda, "the merit of the cause urged" and "the correctness of the information published," the second criterion is the more difficult to establish: a piece of information that starts out as neutral because it concerns a future that is still uncertain is then proved to be true after the fact when it satisfies the wishful thinking of public opinion, which is shaped at the same time as it becomes aware of itself.

The global result of this state of affairs is the reign of the appearance of systemic falsehood, in which it becomes ever more difficult to distinguish between truthful and deceitful discourse. This is also the reign of conspiracy theories, of the kind of "they're not telling us everything" beliefs that are popularized in the scathing humor of comics like Anne Roumanoff.[25] Many intellectuals, who really ought to be less vulnerable to such trends, also fall into this trap, learnedly explaining to us what is "truly" to be found behind what "they" hide from us. For in the middle of the interlinking chains of cause and effect, of self-fulfilling prophecies and spins of all kinds, it is always easy to isolate one particular factor or causal chain and to present it as the true cause of what ails us, that is being hidden from us by "them" to deceive us.

And finally, the Internet has only amplified the great mixture of true and false, of fiction and reality, of game and manipulation. For on the Internet, arbitrary information and anonymous sources reign supreme. It is like an ocean of rumors, where those whose spokespeople shout the loudest are the ones who stay afloat—for a while. The Internet has also added speed to the array of communication tools, or should we say weapons. One public relations expert, who succeeded in making his company prosper in only a few years, outlines the changes produced in his profession by the entrance of this higher speed. His credo seems to be almost verbatim the same as Bernays's, but boasting, in addition, of how important the speed of response is for him as a professed spin doctor:

The world has changed drastically. Public relations is the fastest way to build a brand. Look at the presidential race, hit movies or the best video games on the market. Public relations is the best way to shape people's minds and opinions.

The innovation comes from his use of blogs, MySpace, and Facebook. Good publicists post the most striking elements of their campaigns on these platforms rather than via classical media: "Because if you call me and tell me that tomorrow you'll publish a negative story about my client, I'll create a spin on the story and an hour later it'll be up on all the competing websites."[26]

But things are even more complicated because systemic falsehood is obviously not simply the pervasiveness of the opposite of the truth. That would be too simple: then it would be enough just to systematically take the opposite side. But it is in fact the total *dissolution* of the true into the false, of the sacred into dogmatic caricatures of itself. Systemic falsehood, in fact, involves the liar's *paradox* as a general condition. It is as though, carried off in the apparently unlimited stream of information, we kept being confronted with the undecidable by someone saying to us, "I am a liar." *How can we believe it and how can we not believe it?*

Recent events to which we have already referred provide a spectacular example of this state of affairs. As in the return of the sacred, it would appear that the true and the good—Bernays's two criteria—reemerged after all at the installation of Barack Obama as president of the United States. Presumed to be "the most powerful man in the world," he was welcomed by public opinion almost everywhere in the world with enthusiasm and the hope accorded a savior. The ceremonies involved in his taking office, broadcast at length on television channels everywhere and on the Internet, were the rituals of a true *enthronement*, with the sacred character of an installation on the throne.

As we have seen, the propaganda in this case, including the massive deployment of the Internet, which constituted the crossing of a new threshold in communication technology, seems to have worked "for the public good," according to the moralizing mission that Bernays wanted to assign to propaganda in spite of everything. Hence the "consecration" or "coronation," which is also in fact the coronation of Truth, or rather of what remains of it, perhaps, in the world of systemic falsehood. For the hope is always there that we may *truly* be able to believe, despite everything, either in what we see and hear or else in its opposite. And to satisfy this hope, a *relative* truth, as compared to lies that are decidedly too big, can be enough. Compared to the saturation of public opinion that had been produced by the Bush administration, involving an accumulation of errors of judgment, voluntary or involuntary lies, and manipulations of power by the infamous military-industrial complex already denounced by Eisenhower, with the whole having been cleverly exploited on the international scene by the anti-American propaganda of new dictatorships, Obama's discourse, in connection with his personality, suddenly appeared as the discourse of Truth. This is the same effect, albeit greatly increased through the amplification of the media, as the "truthful talk" [*parler vrai*] that was once seen in France, first with Pierre Mendès France and, later, Michel Rocard.

But the problem still remains of knowing whether the confidence that has thus been regained is just producing a little "bubble" that has some chance, at least for a time, of succeeding, or whether, by some accident along the way, it will appear after the fact to have been the effect of an even cleverer spin than the ones that preceded it.

International public opinion: Systemic falsehood in current affairs

The international arena is a privileged place for observing the multiplied effects of systemic falsehood. For it is here that totalitarian regimes and democracies encounter each other, with the asymmetry produced by the unequal effects of propaganda in their different contexts, as I have already described. At stake in such confrontations is what has come to be called "international public opinion" as a way to justify the recourse to military force, whether beforehand or after the fact. For in democracies, as we have seen, war is no longer considered to be the normal way to resolve a conflict. In democracies, unprompted, spontaneous public opinion tends to be pacifist and to underestimate the danger of aggression from expansionist totalitarian regimes, as it did with the Nazi and Soviet dictatorships.

This is currently the case with the conflicts that are sharpened by the economic stakes of control over energy resources, conflicts that today pit the Western democracies of the North against two kinds of dictatorships: military dictatorships on the model of the former Soviet Union, such as North Korea and certain populist regimes in Latin America, and radical Islamist dictatorships in certain Arab or Muslim countries.

It is, moreover, remarkable that in some cases, a certain continuity can be seen between the totalitarianisms of the twentieth century and those of the twenty-first. In the nineteen fifties, Nasser's Egypt, Hafez al-Assad's Syria, and the military dictatorships in Argentina and Guatemala were the most welcoming places for Nazi leaders on the run. Arab nationalism, which developed parallel and in opposition to Jewish nationalism in Palestine, first sought the support of Nazi Germany, during the war, through agreements between Hitler and the Grand Mufti of Jerusalem. At the same time, one of the Zionist parties that had the most influence among the Jewish population in Palestine, from which the state of Israel was to arise, was a Marxist party that celebrated, as Communist parties then did, the virtues of the "great Stalin, Little Father of the Peoples." A little later, and up until the end of the Cold War and the fall of the Berlin wall, nationalist movements of independence turned towards Soviet Russia when decolonization had been unable to result in sufficiently democratic regimes. This was the case in several African countries as well as for the initially secular nationalist movements in Egypt, Syria, and Iraq, as well as for Yasser Arafat's Palestine Liberation Organization. It was only after the Soviet Union collapsed, along with the Soviet illusions that were harbored both internally, by the peoples subjected to the Communist regimes, and externally, by those who had seen in those regimes their hopes of emancipation, that these movements were gradually infused with a new Islamist ideology, first in the search for identity and then drifting down the slippery slope of the religious fanaticism of radical Islam. A new totalitarianism with hegemonic aims was thus constituted in which we find once more the ingredients of the totalitarianisms of the twentieth century.

Equally remarkable is the fact that this totalitarianism finds allies, or "fellow travelers" (as the Stalinist Communist Parties used to call them), among environmentalist antiglobalization progressives in their shared opposition to globalization and colonialism, even though the aim of these totalitarian regimes is to establish a reign of religious fundamentalists while the aim of the ecologists is to establish a "green," anticapitalist world of peace and social justice. Caroline Fourest's richly documented book on this topic shows how these networks and their propagandas intermingle and permeate each other at large conferences and forums such as the Durban Conference in 2001, the World Social Forum in Porto Alegre in 2002, the European Social Forum in London in 2004, and others,[27] producing an interpenetration between new post-Cold War progressive ideologies and the resurgence of the Muslim Brotherhood's program of Islamist renewal from the nineteen thirties. It would seem that a visceral resentment of the American and global capitalism that emerged victorious from the Cold War is being fueled by a nostalgia for revolutionary ideals of any kind among leftist intellectuals, some of whom even go so far as to identify military and religious fanaticism as "liberation theology."[28] This only exacerbates the manipulation of words, as for example when so-called "antiracist" movements call anyone who opposes fundamentalist Islam a racist, or when "anticolonialist" is used to imply an opposition to the values and the culture of the West, seeing it as necessarily colonialist *in its very essence* even in the absence of colonization, including and maybe most of all where the status of women is concerned.

Opposition to the Western democracies, that is to say, to North America and Europe, has once again become a head-on confrontation; as in the past, it is fueled by economic inequalities, the frustrations of impoverished peoples of the South faced with these inequalities, and the exploitation of their riches by the peoples of the North. In the twentieth century, the barrier was not so much a barrier between North and South, but it did already separate the democracies, which were relatively rich, from the dictatorships, in which those in power drew their strength from their countries' economic inferiority (post-Weimar Nazi Germany, Soviet Russia). As is the case today, the explosive combination of humiliation and frustration fueled what Nietzsche considered the most dangerous of evils for the humanity of a human being: resentment.

The content of the religious ideology of radical Islam is obviously different from the content of National Socialism or that of Marxism-Leninism in its Stalinist or Maoist forms. But we can see that there is still a barrier that runs between developed democracies and totalitarianisms that seek to compensate for their underdevelopment by charging ahead into confrontations. It is not only Islam that has seen the return of religion, including its fundamentalist and fanaticist forms. It can also be observed in the other monotheistic religions and among Hindus and Buddhists. Gilles Kepel's *The Revenge of God*,[29] already a few years old, lays out the mechanisms by means of which modernity, believed to have ejected religion from its position as the chief authority, in fact engendered the renewal of religious movements that were even stronger for being able to claim that they were returning to an ancient tradition. These analyses are still relevant, and have been brought pretty much up to date now by John Micklethwait and Adrian Wooldridge's analyses of how "God is back" and "how the global revival of faith is changing the world."[30]

But the effects of religious fundamentalism on the rest of society are very different depending on whether they can unfold under the protection of a totalitarian regime or whether they are restrained by a regime in which the freedom of expression and the freedom to criticize different beliefs is guaranteed by law and exists in practice. As Micklethwait and Wooldridge write in the conclusion of their investigation into the role of religion in the local and civil wars that have torn and are tearing apart populations in Africa and Asia, it is "the union of religion and power" that can be the "fatal poison" denounced by radical Enlightenment. The effective separation of church and state in a way that guarantees both the independence of government and the freedom of thought and expression, both philosophical and religious, along the lines proposed by Spinoza in his *Theological-Political Treatise* and taken up by the founding fathers of American democracy, remains a necessity today.

This is the context in which the systemic falsehood of propaganda can spread even more, considerably amplified by the increase in communication technologies, always with the same inevitable asymmetry between democracies and dictatorships.

On the diplomatic stage, and on the stage of international opinion, there is no regulation that limits falsehood, the manipulations of language, and the inequality of exchanges. The international organizations that were created, along with the United Nations, to fulfill this role (the World Trade Organization, the Group of Eight, the Group of Twenty, and others) are themselves constrained to respect the sovereignty of states in a kind of makeshift international democracy, one vote per state, whatever its political regime, the number of its inhabitants, or the conditions under which they live.[31] This is just a very basic level of democracy compared to the ideals of the Universal Declaration of Human Rights, and yet it is preferable to a naked violence with no attenuation even by a minimum of exchanges, even mendacious exchanges, in the marketplace of national and international public opinion. Let us recall, however, among other examples of this diplomatic democracy between states, that it was a vote of this sort by the General Assembly of the United Nations that once decided to define Zionism as "racism," until another vote later contradicted that decision.

On this stage, the rhetoric of propaganda can make use of all of its resources. One of the most effective means already proved itself in the twentieth century, the perverse manipulation of language that manages to twist the use of words to designate the opposite of what they mean. Following the "popular democracies" of Communist dictatorships, the Maoist "Cultural Revolution" was the phrase used to cover the abuses of the Red Guards under the control of the dictatorial power surrounding Mao, and "the defense of freedom" justified the military coups supported by the CIA that established bloody dictatorships in Latin America. But the twenty-first century has reached new heights with the United Nation's "Commission on Human Rights" and its infamous 2001 Durban "World Conference Against Racism." This commission was dominated by states where the rights of men and women have been and are today openly trampled, supported by NGOs that openly spread the most clichéd anti-Semitic slogans . . . always in the name of "antiracism." In these countries, religious and ethnic minorities are regularly persecuted under the pretext of protecting the official religion. As far as "antiracism" was concerned at the conference, the same reversal of the meaning of words took place as when a pyromaniac claims to extinguish a fire or a burglar shouts "stop, thief!"

As during the heyday of Soviet "anti-imperialist" propaganda, which claimed to be defending world peace and popular liberation, the "World Conference Against Racism" served, on the contrary, to draw people's attention away from the growing problems of underdevelopment and of the curtailment of freedoms in the participating countries. With this goal in mind, the reality of the Arab-Israeli conflict provided a readily available target against which to turn public opinion by condemning the worst crimes committed there—crimes of which those countries were themselves guilty—using time-tested "anti-Zionist" rhetoric and calls for the destruction of Israel.

This episode is interesting for its partially counterproductive effect: people could see that a threshold had been crossed; the lie was too big. The United Nations Commission was replaced by a "Human Rights Council" that was supposed to work differently, but that did not prevent the Council from holding a second conference "against racism" in Geneva, in 2009, "Durban II," organized again by the same countries. The most flagrant excesses of Durban were avoided, with some difficulty, thanks to threatened boycotts (some of them carried out) by the democracies, which did not want to fall into the same trap again. Had lying then been brought back down to an acceptable level?

As Guy Debord says: "In a world that is *really upside down*, the true is a moment of the false."[32] For all is not false, of course, in the condemnations of democracies for their manipulative and freedom-killing excesses that contradict their own foundations, especially when they come in response to aggressions from the enemies of freedom. But it so happens that totalitarian regimes also have their industrial-military complexes and their systems of propaganda, but with the addition of violence and the suffocation of all opposition and criticism. And the democracies are most often at a disadvantage in the use of public relations because the plurality of possibly conflicting opinions and propagandas that express themselves in democracies lays them open to the propaganda that comes from dictatorships. Dictatorships profit from accusations that come from inside, from members of the democracy themselves, accusations of failures, flaws, and crimes to which democracies are far from immune, and all the more so when they are themselves in conflict. Now as in the twentieth century, current affairs provide us with new examples of this phenomenon. Just as in the past, the most effective propaganda imposes its choice of ready-made words or, as they are called, "talking points," circulated by lobbying firms. These phrases are then used and taken for granted, without much reflection. And their weight is such that if one does want to reflect on them, one needs a dictionary of misleading words, words that designate something other than what they say, but without saying so, depending on the place and geopolitical context—not to mention the perverted invocation of moral values such as freedom, human rights, justice, and respect.

Now that war is tending to become illegal, one of the most-used weapons of propaganda is the claim of *victimhood* for one's own camp. Starting in the nineteen seventies, Israel, which had until then tended to obscure the genocide-survivor status of a part of its population, began to fall into the trap of victimhood, increasingly invoking the persecutions as a way to respond to the challenge to its legitimacy from Arab-Muslim nationalisms. Historically, this justification is a half-truth, since the Zionist movement itself developed as a nationalism of the Jewish people defending its right to self-determination on the same land, in Palestine, long before the Second World War. But this move triggered a one-upmanship of victimhood. Another half-truth: Palestinian Arabs were said to be nothing *but* victims unjustly paying the price, in the Europeans' stead, for the Jewish genocide at the hands of the Nazis, as though the history of the conflict came down to that and had begun in 1948 with the creation of the state of Israel and the Palestinian *nakba*, ignoring the Arab states' share of responsibility and especially the series of opportunities that were missed because of their repeated refusals of a division into two states. At that point, it was much more effective to respond to Jewish victimhood with Palestinian victimhood and to claim the status of "innocent" victims rather than that of combatants defeated in a conflict between nationalities.

Another example of victimhood as a tool of propaganda: terrorism has always justified itself as the weapon of the weak and of the victims of oppression; the "war on terror," meanwhile—a curious and absurd expression, as if one were waging war against a weapon—justifies itself as protecting future innocent victims.

A third example is that of the victims of slavery. The slave trade and the denial of humanity to slaves were obviously very real. But for some years now that slave or victim status has been claimed as an essential component of the identity of peoples descended from slaves, after several generations in the Americas. It is as victims that some of these descendants expect contrition and reparations from the Western democracies of today that are the heirs to the colonial empires. And these democracies, by the way, often respond to this expectation through public opinions shaped by a guilty conscience.

Yet in all of this, it is as though slavery had only ever been practiced in this part of the world, by Europeans or the descendants of Europeans; as if the trade in black slaves had only been practiced across the Atlantic and as if slave trade across the Indian Ocean and even within Africa had not existed. And as a result, requests for forgiveness only come from Western democratic regimes. One never hears of them in countries in which an authoritarian power reigns, sometimes in conflict with the West, but with just as great a weight of slave-trading and slave-holding history and where, in some cases, slavery still exists today. This does not prevent them from joining the chorus of condemnations of the slave-holding and slave-trading past of others.

Despite the obvious differences among these situations, the complexity of which obviously does not just come down to the simple one-upmanship of victimhood, these examples also highlight the asymmetry of propagandas.

In a general way, the advantage that totalitarian regimes have over democracies in the strategy of deception leads to the classic defensive reaction expressed in the infamous slogan "No freedom for the enemies of freedom." But pushed to the extreme, this reaction endangers democracy itself, as a good number of democratic intellectuals in the United States quickly sensed when antiterrorist measures were enacted by the Bush administration after September 11, 2001. Hence the opposite position: "fighting to guarantee the freedom of expression of one's worst enemies"—at the risk of seeing a democracy of opinion destroy itself, which can happen when skillful propaganda is able to profit from democratic freedoms to the point that it brings a totalitarian ideology to power, possibly even by free elections, and the first effects of that are then to suppress those very freedoms.

But all of this, however you take it, obviously has nothing to do with truthfulness, to say nothing of truth itself.

When the President of the United States spoke of an "axis of evil" to designate al-Qaeda and its real or supposed allies in countries suspected of supporting Islamist terrorism, a large proportion of American public opinion and almost all of global public opinion ridiculed this strange intrusion of moral and religious vocabulary into politics, which is governed by economic and geopolitical interests. But when totalitarian governments mobilize millions of people, in the name of Islam, against "the great and the little Satan" (the United States and Israel), public opinion in those countries is forced to adopt that vocabulary, while a large proportion of the public opinion in democratic countries, with a certain amount of paternalism, accepts the use of these expressions by the masses and their governments and even picks them up themselves, translating them into more "civilized" expressions such as "American imperialism," "Israeli aggression," etc. Meanwhile, almost half of the population of those countries is convinced that the genocide of millions of Jews in Europe never took place and, on a completely different topic, that Americans never landed on the moon. The unilateral propaganda of totalitarian power is able to persuade public opinion in the area under its control that these realities are themselves lies produced by, respectively, "Zionist" and "imperialist" propaganda.

Since the attacks of September 11, 2001, academic circles, especially in America, have debated the pros and cons of the thesis of the clash of civilizations.[33] This brings up the issue, for those who support the thesis of a return of the dangers of totalitarianism by way of radical Islam, of a new challenge to democracy in the twenty-first century. And in fact, the ideology that some people call "Islamofascism" is associated with the power of totalitarian governments and serves the al-Qaeda movement as an ideology for the conquest of power.

And in Western public opinion, among those who do not support this thesis, one can find the same condemnations of democratic regimes, and of the United States in particular, in the name of the values of democracy itself, condemnations for the "disproportionate" responses of these regimes to the war "against the Jews and the Crusaders" that has been declared against them. For, in fact, it is the case that the total number of victims of these responses has been much greater than the number of victims of this war itself. Forgetting that the victims of responses to a war are also victims of the war itself, critics of this kind of response *within* the democracies that pursue it, essentially the United States and its allies, then make accusations of war crimes on the basis of this arithmetic.

Such critiques often reuse the words of the old "anticapitalist" and "anti-imperialist" ideology to explain, if not to justify, wars that are explicitly declared in the name of religious fanaticisms, thus overlaying them with more respectable "causes," which are real but only partial, and seeing in these wars nothing more than the effect of the North/South conflict of the rich against the poor.

What is new to our vocabulary, compared to the vocabulary of the first half of the twentieth century, is the reference to *absolute evil*, the Nazi extermination whose Hebrew name, *shoah*, is now part of the international vocabulary. In conjunction with the claim to victimhood, it is easy to call the adversary a "Nazi" and designate his behaviors as perpetrating a genocide; the issue is always determining the extent to which it does or does not partake of the absolute evil for which the *shoah* has become the standard.

And the beginnings of an establishment of international tribunals are not immune from the effects of propaganda and counter-propaganda. There, too, the use of phrases such as "war crimes" and "crimes against humanity," which were assumed to be unequivocal, turns out to be more and more ambiguous. The Nuremberg trials, where those phrases were used at the end of World War II, is sometimes stigmatized as the site of a victors' justice enacted over a defeated Nazi Germany. And as a matter of fact, one cannot but see that the Allied leaders could also have been condemned for war crimes (although not for crimes against humanity) if one judges by the enormous number of civilian victims of their massive bombardments, including in the countries that they were liberating from Nazi occupation. But it is not enough to explain this "double standard" as an effect of victors' justice. The condemnation is also a condemnation of the regime that committed these destructions and of its goals in the war. Transposed into the contemporary world, this would mean that it is not enough to count what is euphemistically called "collateral damage": killed, injured, and displaced civilians. Going against a principle of classical penal law, according to which a tribunal can condemn an individual only for what he has done (or has caused others to do), international penal law tends to condemn countries not only for what they do, but also for what they are. But this kind of law, like the law of humanitarian interventions, is obviously contrary to the principle of respect for states' sovereignty. These contradictions leave room for all the manipulations of propaganda and counter-propaganda with, here too, the same asymmetry between democracies and dictatorships: the balance of power in the war of information and public relations always favors the dictatorships even if they are economically and militarily weaker.

The clash of civilizations is probably not inevitable, but the clash between totalitarian propagandas and the propagandas of the regimes of freedom most certainly is. Lying is tolerated in a democracy, as in rhetoric, but only up to a certain point. As in the world of *ona'ah*, which renounces absolute purity but establishes a threshold above which deception is not tolerated, the limits of lobbying and advertising practices are relatively well defined, all the more so because they are identified as such and because they contradict one another. The lies that are used in the service of dictatorship, on the other hand, observe no boundaries; they are both cynical in their perversion of vocabulary and unbridled, in that there are no checks to the regime's power to manipulate the opinion of its own people and the public opinions of the states with which it is in conflict.

The clash of propagandas is perfectly summed up by Arthur Koestler, who said about the democratic responses to Communist propaganda in his time: "[W]e are fighting against a total lie in the name of a half-truth."[34]

Contaminated science
The complexity of the real
and the underdetermination of scientific theory

Science, with its ethos of disinterested research, of knowledge for knowledge's sake, has seemed as though it had to be the last refuge of truth. It replaced the oracle as the source of inescapable truth, and the adjective "scientific" is still often used as a guarantee of truth. The instrumental rationality of science and technology has contributed significantly to the loss of credibility that religious dogmas have suffered and to the disenchantment of the world in the societies in which modern science developed. The expression "science says . . . " is generally used as the equivalent of "it's objectively and undebatably true." And yet, there are several reasons that come together to strongly relativize this blind confidence. First of all, scientific truth is only ever established locally, in a well-defined domain of validity, and extrapolation from that is always dangerous. In Spinoza's treatise *On the Improvement of the Understanding*, the "given true idea" is the starting point for a step-by-step process for producing truths, a procedure that is similar to the use of primary tools to help make more sophisticated tools.[35] The next step is for theories to be established in the context of a history of science that develops over time. They are always subject to refutation in the short or longer term, or at the very least to modification by new discoveries. Furthermore, the *underdetermination of scientific theory by the available evidence*, already observed long ago in the case of the most general physical theories,[36] is still inevitable when it comes to the models that are being developed today to account for complex phenomena. This underdetermination consists in several different models' seeming to be "true" because they account for the same available observations.[37] Or, to put it another way, the system being studied is such that the number of available observations is limited in relation to the number of models that account for it. The problem here is not a deficit of good models but, on the contrary, *too many "good" models* such that the empirical observations available are not sufficient for discriminating among them and, ideally, making it possible to refute all of them but one. This phenomenon is of particular importance today because of the level of computer performance that makes it possible to model very complex systems, not only in biology and the cognitive sciences, neurology and neuropsychology, or economics, but also in scientific ecology and the climate sciences. The result of this underdetermination of models by the observed evidence is that the models that are retained and accepted by the community of experts are bearers of a new species of truth, a "complex truth," if we may call it that, that is in fact a likelihood whose opposite is not only error or falsehood but also other likelihoods.

Big science: Scientific information and public relations

We will return to all these reasons, especially in the context of the mutual entanglement of scientific ecology and environmental ideologies, but in the meantime we must add one more to the list, namely the infiltration of science and technology by propaganda and the demands of public relations, with the excesses that follow from that. Scientific research in the twentieth century underwent an accelerated evolution that went beyond anything that had been seen before, not only in its results but also in its practices and its relations with society. Nuclear energy, electronics, information technology, biology, and pharmacological chemistry have produced profound modifications of the human condition in our bodies as well as in our minds and in the models we make and imagine. In turn, scientific research has left the artisanal laboratory and the ivory tower in which experts remained separated from the societies in which they lived. With the emergence of big science and its huge budgets, for which the large accelerators and the exploration of space were the prototype, soon extended to biology and computer science, science has become a social, economic, and political affair.

The autobiography of one of the most brilliant scientists of the last century, Erwin Chargaff, whose work covers most of the century, bears poignant witness to this evolution. Chargaff was born in Vienna in 1905 and died in New York in 2002. He began his career as a chemist in Berlin in the nineteen thirties and immigrated to the United States in 1940, where he kept working into the nineteen seventies. He was one of the most original and prolific pioneers of the molecular biology revolution that began in the nineteen forties and is still not over. One of the first scientists to be interested in the biochemistry of DNA, Chargaff discovered the structures of invariance that are characteristic of all DNAs. Known as "Chargaff's rules," they are at the basis of one of the most astonishing discoveries of molecular biology: the existence and structure of a universal genetic code that is the same for the DNAs of all known living beings. In the autobiography that Chargaff published in 1978,[38] he describes the evolution of science as he experienced it and the catastrophic predictions this evolution leads him to make for the century to come, with a sad humor that is ferocious toward some of his colleagues and tinged with self-deprecation. Although he remained fascinated to the end by the intellectual adventure of science in the making, two events profoundly disappointed him in his hopes for this very science. The first was the discovery, with the explosions in Hiroshima and Nagasaki in 1945, that nuclear physics had released the thousand fires of a science of death. The second event made an even deeper impact on him because it concerned the science to which his own work had decisively contributed. From the outset, he saw and vehemently denounced the excesses, both theoretical and technical, of molecular biology. He had immediately identified and mocked the very real theoretical excesses of the "dogma" of molecular biology that made a fetish out of DNA and its double helix, which he described as "the mighty symbol that has replaced the cross as the signature of the biological analphabet."[39] But he never stopped announcing, Cassandra-like, the future catastrophes that biotechnologies, as manipulations of the living, would produce. Nonetheless, his own clear-sightedness prevented him from being certain about this catastrophic evolution because, as he says in conclusion, "it will be a long time before it appears whether I was right or wrong."[40]

It is possible not to share Chargaff's dark pessimism,[41] the personal elements of which he readily acknowledges, but we cannot deny the clarity of his analyses of the practice of scientific research as it evolved over the twentieth century. Once made up of the contemplation of the wonders of nature by isolated individuals or small teams, progressing slowly and without fanfare, it has increasingly been replaced by the collective activity of large specialized laboratories. They work towards mastery and transformation in an ever-accelerating rhythm, and their work is increasingly subordinated to the publicity that is required to justify the ever-greater funds they need.

In fact, as Bernays already saw, the methods of promotional propaganda and public relations have increasingly infiltrated the practice of the sciences at the same time as science has become a collective undertaking that is engaged in the channels of economic productivity. That is to say that science today is partially contaminated by the industry of lies.

Up through about the nineteen sixties, it was frowned upon for scientists to talk to journalists about their work and its expected effects, no matter how spectacular. The public image of contemporary science in public opinion was conveyed by popularizers of science, with a few mythical figures such as Louis Pasteur, Albert Einstein, and Marie Curie being held up for particular adulation. Actual scientific information was only supposed to circulate within closed channels, within communities of specialists working on the same subjects and therefore able to understand it directly, without needing extra explanations. Several factors caused things to change. The new discoveries in the biochemistry of DNA had specialists themselves worried about the possibility of applications they would later regret, as was the case, in part, for nuclear physicists and the atomic bomb. Those worries led to the Asilomar conference and moratorium on the limits of research in molecular genetics, which followed one of the first discussions ever that was public and open to the press about an ongoing research project. At the same time, scientific research in all disciplines was mobilizing an increasing number of professional researchers working in ever larger teams. Thus, it began to seem necessary to leave the ivory tower and to account for one's activities to society, first because of the possible social consequences of the applications of those activities, but also because of the increasing costs of research, which obviously had to be covered by society, whether through public or through private funds. The creation of the Universal Movement for Scientific Responsibility testifies to this sense of duty. The multiplying numbers of ethics committees that followed showed that scientific research, while it had become a specialized activity, had also become an activity whose social, political, and economic effects were growing more and more important. The same thing happened to scientists as had once happened to the army, when war was considered to be too serious a matter to be left to the military: science became too serious a matter to be left to the scientists. Hence the demand and the need to *communicate*, beyond the circles of specialists, about research in progress, the results obtained, and hopes for future results.

It is from this angle that the industry of lies gradually penetrated into the sciences and technology, which were soon pejoratively called "technoscience," even though this opening in communications first grew out of a perfectly justified sense of responsibility. For, as we have seen, public relations is itself a technology, with its own constraints. The connection between scientists and journalists, which has become essential, has turned out to be more difficult than anyone had imagined, creating dysfunction in this desired transmission of scientific information to a public of nonspecialists and to political decision makers.[42] The large laboratories and research institutes have created positions for press officers and public relations services, with all the advantages and inconveniences such a professionalization entails. The communication of scientific information has thus grown to be more and more like advertising, using journalistic scoops and public campaigns for or against certain projects. A variety of factors working together have gradually led these practices, which began with the best of intentions, into excesses that are sometimes not that different from just plain scams.

In the vast majority of cases, the issue is not a perversion that is particular to scientists or particular to journalists, but instead a real difficulty that is intrinsic to the constraints of their collaboration. Scientific research is committed to the long term. The significance of a discovery depends on its context within the history of a discipline, which is sometimes very long, and within which the questions, often complicated ones, arise that stimulate research. Communications to the larger public, on the other hand, involve the short term and simplicity, all the more because the media are now approaching instantaneous transmission. Information that is placed in context thus tends to be replaced by the news of the day, and it is scientific truth that is always the loser in that case. It is only over the long term that the "scientific" nature of an affirmation is even an approximate guarantee of its truth. The most recent "scientific" explanation of the day is very likely to be proven false by future discoveries. As we have known well since Popper, scientific theories are only very rarely positively "proven." They are accepted for their explanatory power until they are refuted by other theories with greater explanatory power. This progression from false theories to somewhat less false theories ought to make us consider any scientific explanation to be a candidate for being disproved, the more so the more recent the explanation is. This is already the case in the natural sciences, especially when one is dealing with complex objects, and it is even more so in the humanities.

This is why collaboration between the sciences and the media calls for great vigilance, which is very difficult to maintain when communication technologies are at the service of the transmission of scientific information. The fact that the two groups have opposite constraints ought to lead to reciprocal criticism and control. Otherwise, without anyone noticing, a kind of collusion takes hold, in which no-one knows who is manipulating whom, whether the journalist is using the scientist for a scoop or whether the researcher is using the journalist to promote herself and her search for grants. This often happens in good faith, particularly when the collaboration goes through the extra intermediary of a laboratory's or other research institute's public relations service.

There is no willed perversion here either, but only the effect of the constraints of the profession. Great were the surprise and the pain of public relations advisers of such institutes when they found themselves reproached, notably in the report of the French National Ethics Committee mentioned earlier,[43] for their professionalism in public relations technologies, so convinced were they that they had been acting for the good of science and of society.

But it is easy to see how these difficulties that are intrinsic to the transmission of scientific information can lead to excesses that come about all the more easily the larger the profits are that are at stake: profits for the laboratories, possibly helped by their public relations advisers, on the one hand, and profits for the media outlets that are indispensable to the relaying of this information, on the other hand. These excesses are all attacks on scientific integrity. The Anglo-American literature calls all forms of this kind of fraud "scientific misconduct." Scientific misconduct, or fraud, is not a novelty, but it has changed, in its nature as much as in its field of application. It used to be a matter of exceptions only, of rare individuals who were usually quickly found out and excluded by their colleagues in the scientific community. The nature of scientific misconduct was summed up in the formula "FFP": "fabrication [of data—AH], falsification, and plagiarism." This is how, in 2000, the United States Office of Science and Technology Policy defined misconduct in research. But another American institution, the Office of Research Integrity, soon contested this definition, judging it to be too narrow. And in fact, the results of a study published in 2005[44] show that the professional, social, and economic research environment created conditions for unethical behavior in research that extended far beyond the domain of FFP alone. In particular, far from being exceptional, scientific misconduct involved about one third of the three thousand scientists who had participated in the study if, in addition to FFP, one took into account such behaviors as modifying the methodology and the results of a study under pressure from a financing source, failing to report others' use of flawed data, or circumventing relatively minor aspects of the regulations on human subject research.

This indicates one of those changes in the nature of scientific research that Erwin Chargaff lamented. For the main reason for this state of affairs is the pressure that is exerted on every researcher. Publishing at all costs is a necessity not just for getting ahead, but often just in order to keep one's job, and the race for grants has now become an integral part of the researcher's profession.

Given this, it is not surprising that Bernays's disciples have had no trouble infiltrating the world of research, most often, as we have seen, entirely in good faith. But at the same time, lobbying has become increasingly effective as ever greater profits have come to be expected from science. The nuclear industry has become a battleground for both its supporters and its opponents. And the pro- and anti-GMO lobbies are still fighting, at the expense of any possibility of calm analysis of the risks and benefits for each case and each particular technology.

Lobbying in biomedicine

The pharmaceutical industry is not holding back: not only the drugs but also the diseases they are supposed to heal have become something to be promoted. The spectacular successes of scientific medicine over the course of the last century are in large part associated with developments by the laboratories of a series of effective drugs: antibiotics, hormones, painkillers, anesthetics, antipsychotics, chemotherapies against cancer, and more. Hence the image of pharmaceutical laboratories as in the service of public health. And yet, at the same time, the drug business has become a gigantic market where large companies invest millions in the research and development of new products and count on making huge profits in marketing those products whose therapeutic effects are then proven. This research is of course carried out properly, by conscientious scientists, following the ethical rules of biological and medical research. But here, too, there's a worm in the apple, because the pharmaceutical companies are both the judges and the judged, financing the research as well as the necessary procedures to ensure that the regulations are respected. Yet there can be hundreds of millions of dollars or euros at stake in whether public health authorities approve or reject a new drug being put on the market. And this is where public relations consultants have found an extraordinary new field of activity in the last few years, because large pharmaceutical companies are investing considerable sums not only in research and development but also in promotion and marketing. A series of studies have analyzed and denounced the "exploits" of the pharmaceutical lobbies and the techniques used to get people to buy this or that drug that has been put on the market with the help of heavy promotion.[45] The advertising world is not satisfied with simply picking up the scientific information that is being broadcast; instead, it superimposes itself in such a way that it is often difficult to draw the line between objective, nonpromotional information and advertising. All of these effects are amplified by self-medication and the direct sale of drugs to the public, which is now exploding thanks to distribution via the web. But even medical prescriptions are by no means safe from these excesses, precisely because of the scientific mantle around the new drugs when they appear on the market.

There have been several scandals in the news in which, after severe accidents had led to a particular drug being taken off the market, it later came out that toxic effects observed in the preliminary phases of clinical trials for that drug had been ignored or concealed. Let us note that this is not necessarily a result of negligence or incompetence—or, worse, of corruption—on the part of the regulatory agencies charged with overseeing the pharmaceutical industry. It is today's scientific medicine, known as evidence-based medicine, which brings risks with it that are sometimes difficult to evaluate. The novelty of twentieth-century drugs consists not only in their efficacy but also in the secondary effects, sometimes quite severe, that occasionally accompany them. The old principle *primum non nocere* ("first, do no harm") can thus not be applied in all circumstances.

Certain more or less painful secondary effects are considered acceptable risks in healing a grave pathology. Cancer-treating chemotherapies are a well-known example. In other words, the placement of a new drug on the market must involve not the certainty that there will be no toxic effect but a "risk management plan" based on relative estimates of the risks and benefits in as many imaginable situations as possible.

The scientific approach to complex phenomena—and disease is a complex phenomenon—only very rarely makes it possible to attain the kind of certain knowledge to which the classical physical and chemical sciences have accustomed us. It is easy to see how the advertising for a drug can profit from this context of relative uncertainty. But that is only the tip of the iceberg.

The pharmaceutical lobbies have invented a new form of verbal fraud by replicating the discourse of Dr. Knock [from the 1951 movie *Knock*, in which a charlatan doctor convinces an entire village population that they are ill.—*trans.*] on an industrial scale. In a first step, the public, including the medical public, is persuaded that a new disease has been discovered, even if sometimes it is just an old pathology rebaptized with a new name. In the wake of the disease's medical name having been "sold" to the public, it is easy to promote a drug that will heal it, either through direct advertising or via the physicians who prescribe it. And public sensibility is subjected to a kind of fashion of the day, with the duration of the fashion dependent on how long the drug's patent is valid.

The surreptitious use of biomedical science in these setups is an extraordinary example of the use of language in what it is hard to call anything other than verbal swindling, and the swindle is all the more effective because of the way that it mobilizes people acting in good faith. The field of functional disorders and of neuropsychiatry, although it is not the only field of medicine that has been taken over by these practices, is the most readily available one. It would appear that, because the limits between the normal and the pathological are not so clearly defined for behavioral and mood disorders, they lend themselves the best to such manipulations, to this "disease mongering," the term used by specialists in pharmaceutical lobbying, who, as engaged professionals (just like Bernays in his time), do not hesitate to publish articles on their work methods. One of them, the president of a New York agency that has worked for large pharmaceutical companies, explains: "No therapeutic category is more accepting of condition branding than the field of anxiety and depression, where illness is rarely based on measurable physical symptoms and, therefore, open to conceptual definition."[46] As one might expect, the words are important here. "Condition branding" is the attribution of a "brand" to a condition or state of potential patients, just as one attaches a brand image to a product to be promoted. And in order to do that, a new "conceptual definition" is necessary, that is to say, a new scientific name attached to the description of states that may in fact be normal but are, by the fact of receiving this new name, transformed into symptoms that *must be treated*. In this way, fatigue becomes "social anxiety" or "social phobia," the anxiety about the future felt by people in precarious emotional and material situations becomes "depression," and what used to be manic-depressive syndromes become "bipolar disorder." All of these, of course, are opportunities for marketing "mood-stabilizing" drugs, some of which are very powerful antipsychotics with serious side effects. "Attention deficit hyperactivity disorder" began to be widely diagnosed at the same time as Ritalin opportunely appeared on the market. As a result, thousands and thousands of rowdy children are now being medicated and "calmed down" by Ritalin, unless they, too, are diagnosed as "bipolar." But psychiatry is not the only sphere for verbal manipulation. What used to be masculine impotence has been rebaptized as "erectile dysfunction" to suit the needs of Viagra, which replicates, with very small improvements, the vasodilatory treatments that had been known for a long time but fell into disuse when it was fashionable to consider the causes of impotence to be essentially psychological. In the same way, overweight that is diagnosed as "obesity" and diffuse pain that is transformed, with no added biomedical information, into "fibromyalgia," merely by the magic of the name, are also all occasions for marketing drugs, each of which may bring in hundreds of millions for the laboratory that synthesizes, tests, and puts it on the market.

Since scientific pharmacology and medicine are fields in which one would expect to encounter the rigor and the objectivity that are supposed to characterize science, we might wonder how this verbal magic was able to penetrate there. There are several reasons for this, one of which is the disproportionate methodological importance granted to *statistics* as the scientific foundation for most of these "discoveries." Statistical information is a tool that is hard to use correctly, even when the users are scientists or physicians, and it thus allows for errors of interpretation, sometimes crude and sometimes subtle, that may explain the good faith of practitioners.[47] As the saying goes, "there are three kinds of lies: lies, damned lies, and statistics." But scientific medicine often relies—fortunately not always—only on measures of correlation that are too quickly interpreted as relations of cause and effect between symptoms and their supposed causes. In psychiatry, it sometimes happens that behavior or mood disorders are correlated with certain physical signs, bioassays, and/or brain imaging. This is sometimes the case with children who are therefore diagnosed as "hyperactive," although changes in these children's surroundings turn out to be just as effective as Ritalin, both for the hyperactivity and for the physical signs associated with it. This, along with other similar cases, shows that, contrary to what is implied by the opinion of the professional lobbyist cited earlier, the existence of physical symptoms correlated with the offending behaviors is not proof of an organic cause of these behaviors, nor is it a justification for immediate massive medication.

We know that statistical testing of the value of an interesting hypothesis for any reason, good or bad, can a priori only show the hypothesis to be false, but not to be true. If its falseness is not demonstrated, the value of the hypothesis remains undetermined, neither more true nor more false than other, untested hypotheses.

This is well known, and faulty interpretations are regularly denounced,[48] in the same way that interpretations that claim to have discovered the gene for a given specific behavior by measuring analogous correlations have also been debunked. But it doesn't make any difference. The desire to "scientize" medicine and psychiatry at all costs, in fields where the only quantitative methods available are statistical, wins out over critical thinking, all the more so because there is heavy pressure to publish and because the direct or indirect dependence of these fields on the pharmaceutical industry and its lobbies makes itself felt.

It is not just the truth of scientific discourse that is damaged by these practices. The resulting overmedication of the population in developed countries begins to worry people because it is accompanied by an increasing number of diseases caused by these drugs.[49] The verbal injuries that break into the scientific and medical world thus produce bodily injuries that can sometimes be fatal.

Will the denunciation of these excesses be sufficient to end them or will they just provide the occasion for new spins that divert them toward new profits, for example from parallel medicines that are deceptive, to various degrees, in their own way?

Political ecology and the uncertainties of scientific ecology

And finally, there is ecology, which is a new field that public relations agencies have discovered and become invested in more recently. The alarm has already been sounding for a long time now about the likely catastrophic consequences of the population explosion that has accompanied the explosion of technology.[50] The pollution of rivers, oceans, and the atmosphere became more and more obvious, as did the foreseeable depletion of oil reserves in the short or long term. At least since the Club of Rome's famous 1972 report,[51] the necessity of changing the dominant model of an indefinite pursuit of economic growth and the limitless exploitation of the environment has been recognized. But for a long time, the consequences drawn from these warnings were that in developed societies, people should rein in their consumption and their comfort and in developing societies, they should renounce that same comfort. For that reason, the environmentalist movement remained a minority movement, mostly made up of intellectuals. The goal was not very attractive for most people, since it seemed to be motivated by a guilty conscience, commonly associated with the unhappy passions of an overactive superego.

However, as soon as the market and the pursuit of profit were mobilized, encouraging the development of the production of new, so-called "environmentally friendly" or "green," consumer goods to replace the old polluting and environment-destroying ones, environmentalism began to become popular and, in a way, trivialized. This new concern with the environment now began to appear as a creator of value; of moral value, of course, but also of scientific and economic value. But in order to get to that point, Bernays's successors had to get to work. Joining the nuclear and pharmaceutical lobbies, often working against them but using the same methods, there were now environmental lobbies, for "organic farming" and the "green economy." The concept of "organic" [in French, *bio*—*trans.*] started out by taking advantage of the semantic confusion involved in the word "biological," which refers both to the "natural" in contrast to the artificial "chemical," and to the scientific through its association with the biological sciences. This confusion has led to the paradoxical situation in which "organic" agriculture rejects not only pesticides, herbicides, and other artificial chemical products, but also genetically modified organisms (GMOs), which could not, for their part, be more organic. But we all know that opinion does not always move according to consistent logic. The fear of the artificial "chemical" was enough to allow the "organic" label to benefit from a public relations campaign that integrated it into the environmental movement by combining moral and altruistic concerns about respect for the environment with the selfish concern with healthier food. The GMO label, in Europe, on the other hand, has mostly, among that same section of public opinion and without its meaning being much clearer, been the target of a negative campaign that associates it both with dangers to one's health and with the contamination of the "natural" environment—as if a cultivated field were natural—added to moral condemnation of the large food industry corporations. With the lobbies pitted against each other, at present it looks as though the anti-GMO lobbies have won in Europe, while the pro-GMO lobbies have managed to convince public opinion in other parts of the world of the utility of GMOs in the struggle against hunger.

In any case, the public relations war obviously activates all the available means of getting the public interested, appealing to a mix of science, medicine, and morality on behalf of the lobbies in question and their clients. The environmental lobbies have thus joined the industrial and political lobbies of all kinds, making possible the development of political ecology, whether in the form of new, independent parties or as part of the platforms of existing parties.

To achieve its success, environmental public relations has greened up practices that were successful in other fields. The Club of Rome's "limits to growth" were quickly replaced by "sustainable development" and more recently "green growth"; of course, the most effective means for accomplishing this kind of development appeared to be ever greater investments by companies of all kinds, small, medium, and very large, in the "green economy." Since these investments need to be profitable, it was and remains necessary to "educate," if not create, the consumers. And in order to do that, we find ourselves back at all the classical techniques of public relations, using just the right combinations of scientific reports and striking, imaginative images. As with all the major programs taken on by public relations agencies, either in the service of great moral or political causes or as promotional marketing campaigns for some particular product, the most visible stars of the entertainment world are mobilized, along with appropriate experts, to create the best conditions for propaganda in its original sense, the sense of "propagation" of the faith, as Bernays reminds us. In this case, though, the environmental message, both virtuous and true, takes the place of religion. Nonetheless, we still must beware of totalitarian excesses and of the oppression of peoples for their good and the good of future generations. Let us recall that in the last century, large numbers of scientists voluntarily mobilized in the name of what they believed to be the truth of their science to serve the propaganda of the Nazi and Soviet regimes.

We have not yet reached that point, but the mutual implication of public relations and science has reached new heights in the campaigns to sensitize people to "global warming." In this case, the hypothesis that human activity is responsible for a final catastrophe and the predicted destruction of the planet has served to transform public opinion from an indifferent stance to mobilization on all fronts. Fighting global warming became a moral, social, and political issue at the same time that the "green economy" showed that this fight could become profitable. Involved in the amplification of a virtuous circle, the sale of green products benefits from what one may call added moral, social, and environmental value. This creation of value was even crowned by a Nobel Peace Prize that was both political and scientific, shared by Al Gore, former unsuccessful candidate for the presidency of the United States, for his visual, filmic rendering of the coming climate apocalypse, and the IPCC (Intergovernmental Panel on Climate Change), an international group of climate specialists that authored a report providing scientific foundations for these predictions.

Yet it must be acknowledged that in order to get to this point, it was necessary, as in all good public relations, to engage in (a little bit of) false advertising. The Al Gore film passes conjectures off as certainties and extrapolates projections to an immediate future—the catastrophe is coming tomorrow—that are still hypothetical and, in any case, apply to a future that is a century or more away.

As for the scientific report, it, too, is influenced by the context of catastrophic thinking and finger pointing—which is all the more significant because scientists increasingly suffer from the public's mistrust of their activities, which are assumed to be the actions of irresponsible "sorcerer's apprentices." One of the ways in which this expresses itself is through a concern on the part of the specialists with communicating well with the politicians who commissioned the report and, through them, with the public at large. In order to do so in the IPCC document, however, it was necessary to simplify the recommendations in comparison with the contents of the body of the report, which was of necessity nuanced in its estimates (still only based on probability and sometimes contradictory) of the magnitude of the warming and its consequences as well as about its human origin. The all-too-well-known precautionary principle had done its work, and it was out of the question for a group of responsible scientists to risk being accused of underestimating a danger.

And yet, in this field, as in others, the precautionary principle can turn out to be counterproductive and thus to negate itself as a principle. The report's simplified recommendations stress reductions in the emissions of carbon dioxide, especially those linked to the human activities of the great industrialized cities, as if that would guarantee that the effects of climate changes could be prevented. Yet nothing is less certain. It is, in fact, a cheap assurance for the economies of the developed countries, but it can turn out to be dangerous for the poor populations of the developing countries, who are likely to be the main victims of these effects. Climate experts and urban development experts, meanwhile, take the minority position compared to the consensus reflected in the recommendations of the IPCC—but their position is not necessarily less justified for all that, as the history of science amply shows. In fact, they recommend making it a priority to invest in policies of *adapting* to climate change rather than investing everything in attempts to prevent it.[52] For measures that aim to adapt the living conditions of populations at risk (measures to do with urban infrastructure, possible relocations of populations away from areas exposed to flooding and landslides) would be much more effective than measures that are intended to fight the climate changes themselves, which we know, incidentally, to be largely inevitable. It has now become popular in developing countries to make the reduction of greenhouse gas emissions a priority, thereby conferring on them a virtuous image of responsibility "for the planet" and "for future generations," but it is much less popular in the countries where those poor populations actually live, and whose development, furthermore, will be slowed down if they have to apply these same measures.[53]

And finally, this is all happening in a methodological context that brings up a more fundamental and therefore more serious issue, in a way, in that the relative nature of scientific truth always seems to be ignored in this field even though this is one of the most difficult and problematic applications of the sciences of complexity currently being developed. In fact, an analysis of the mechanisms of climate changes as observed in the recent and distant past and then projected onto the future can only be carried out by using computer models of the interactions among numerous variables, which are the ideal tools for analyzing complex systems. And yet, as we have seen, *these models are largely underdetermined by the observed evidence*, to the extent that the amount of that evidence, which is not available at will as it is in an experimental setup in the lab, is very limited in quantity compared to the number of different models likely to be equally "good." The fact that a good model has been obtained, and then improved thanks to greater computing power—improved, for example, by taking supplementary variables into account that had been previously neglected or ignored—is in no way a guarantee that other models that are just as powerful but use different parameters might not be equally good at explaining the same observations, while the consequences of their predictions for the future would be very different. This kind of prudence in evaluating "good" models of climate change, which should be imposed by the inevitable underdetermination of scientific theory by the available evidence, is very rarely present in scientific communications intended for the general public. The modeling of complex systems is—at least as much as for statistics, if not more so—a site of partial and relative truths, mobilizing sophisticated calculations in the service of agreed-upon beliefs, often without the knowledge of the practitioners who are responsible for the calculations in the first place.

In this way, the entanglement of scientific ecology with political ecology favors the slippage of something that presents itself as an established truth into the realm of half-truths or half-lies, most often involuntary or manipulated to serve the needs of the cause, like little white lies.

And these slippages away from pure truths may in fact be justified—and the lies may be "white lies"—in that they are apparently part of the rules of the social game of the creation of values. As with the monetary exchanges that get the economy going and increase overall wealth, speculation about the future may be indispensable, based on taking some license with the truth of the values presented. It is only this kind of license, which produces new gains for some and losses for others, that can displace the static equilibrium, which rests, to be sure, on a truth that is established in the present moment because it is produced by the past, but which in a society in movement is synonymous with stagnation and death. Partial and provisional scientific truths are thus transformed into oracles. Like the ancient oracles, they provide an additional and apparently necessary guarantee of an apparent truth value—which is, however, false—to social and political movements, which are themselves the vehicles of moral values such as justice and solidarity. If the automobile industry decides to diversify, after all these years, into electric cars and thus diminish the pollution of cities, we can only be happy about that, whatever the good or bad reasons for doing so may be.

Is this to say that, as Chargaff feared, we are witnessing the end of the great adventure of modern science that was begun in the seventeenth century? Is science, too, doomed to be dissolved into systemic falsehood? Not necessarily, if we take the long view. We can always maintain the hope for a scientific truth that will emerge if it is given enough time. As in the past, unexpected fundamental discoveries may yet have many surprises in store.

Be that as it may, science and technology have contributed significantly to the desacralization of our world by replacing oracles and magicians; this is even truer today, when their limits in these oracular functions are increasingly recognized. But this desacralization is the disappearance of a pure and transparent crystallized sacred, the ultimate reference for the reality and the hidden nature of the things of this world. Yet this disappearance is in fact a dissolution. There is a sacred, somehow degenerated, that remains in solution, dissolved in modern societies, insidiously penetrating social life both in what remains of religion and in secularized existence.

Perhaps we need to learn to update the ancient separation-distinction between the world of the sacred, on the one hand, with its timeless origins charged with myths, with the social and individual imaginary, and with promises for the future; and the repetitive world of everyday life on the other, ruled by the anonymous and reproducible shared notions of instrumental reason. Games, the arts, and old rituals might then serve as the bonds, still indispensable, between these two worlds, both within individual subjectivity and in the field of social relations, without, however, the worlds becoming confused and dissolved into each other.

Conclusion

Between the crystallized sacred, the absolute source of revealed Truth, and its dissolution into systemic falsehood, there extends the entire field of half-truths and partial lies, white lies, venial lies, involuntary lies, and statistics. Note that the two extremes can meet. Confronted with what seems to be the defeat of any search for truth, skeptics and cynics sometimes favor an uncritical return to the dogmas of tradition.

The world of *ona'ah* establishes a realm of tolerance in the field of exchanges, a tolerance that is inevitable given the complexity with which the value of truth must be preserved, in spite of everything, in the networks of social relations. It is in these verbal exchanges that the entanglements between good and bad faith make the task more difficult, although these very exchanges can nonetheless inflict sometimes fatal injuries. It is here, too, that the *measurement* of a threshold of tolerance for verbal fraud and injury is practically impossible to establish quantitatively. In this realm, the ultimate objective beyond the search for truths is, instead, to avoid humiliation and to respect dignity.

Yet the crucial point in the notion of *ona'ah* lies in its establishing a profound identification, underneath the situational differences, between verbal injuries and the injuries produced by fraud in a commercial exchange. In every case, what is at issue is a divergence from the truth and an affront to its value, whether it involves the truth of prices in relation to the value of objects, the truth of words spoken in relations of confidence into which power struggles and conflicts of interest insinuate themselves, or the truth of statements of knowledge that have to some degree been perverted by subtle forms of rhetoric and the desire to persuade. Commercial fraud with respect to the truth of prices can be measured, at least approximately, and a threshold of tolerance can be established as a certain fraction above or below the market price.

The possibility of measurement is then extended, if not quantitatively then at least metaphorically, to other sorts of injuries. When we speak of half-truths, we are metaphorically quantifying lies as a fraction of truth (and of falsehood). In the same way, the measure of the injury done in an exchange is extended to *ona'ah* in general, to all forms of harm produced by verbal injuries, as a part of the being that suffers them. We have seen how these potentially fatal injuries can also, in the symbolism of the Kabbalah, reach a fraction of being, with a threshold of tolerance of one-sixth, on the model of the financial loss of a fraction of the value of an object in an unfair commercial exchange. In this case, the threshold of tolerance concerns a fraction of the being that is inevitably injured in the very process of its maturation into an adult individual and of its constitution as a social being inscribed in a generational chain.

This association between an injury suffered by a person in that person's being, an injury that may even be inevitable because of the evolving nature of a being in development, and an injury to what one has that is quantitatively measurable, seems to send us back to the *lex talionis*; we know that talmudic jurisprudence translated the biblical formula "an eye for an eye, a tooth for a tooth" into financial damages. All of this thus apparently recalls the pound of flesh demanded by Shylock in Shakespeare's *Merchant of Venice* to force his debtor to "pay in his person" instead of doing so in silver.[1]

But in fact this transposition does not consist in transforming people into merchandise. On the contrary, it is about making commercial exchanges personal, as far as possible; about introducing stakes that have to do with the nonmeasurable value of people into exchanges of money and merchandise.

And finally, we have seen that the chapter of the Talmud on *ona'ah* that states the laws concerning these types of exchanges of goods and words contains a fundamental principle about the origin of the words that are themselves statements of the Law, "on earth and not in heaven." This may not be entirely by chance, insofar as there is a radical innovation at issue in both cases, namely the introduction of the relative into what seems to have been posited by the biblical law as an absolute. Acceptable *ona'ah*, "less than one-sixth," creates an intermediate space between absolute prohibition and unbridled permissiveness. The law on earth is no longer in heaven because of a new reading of the divine written law. *Formally*, divine law certainly continues to be the absolute reference, even with respect to making the law descend from heaven; but it is in its form that it is the absolute reference, not in its content, which is subject to human interpretations. This holds for natural law as well as for moral law. For the human species is never done with its humanization. We and our descendants will have to learn to humanize technology and machines, in the same way as our ancestors humanized nature.

In other words, in the particular case of *ona'ah*, the question arises of the origins, at once heteronomous and autonomous, of the law, given that the law is originally social but, remaining law, retains its character of obligation and imposes itself as if it came from the outside. Natural law is binding and to acknowledge the law is to submit to the truth that is revealed in it. Moral law is binding by virtue of its establishment as such, whether it is acknowledged as social or divine, according to whether it is perceived as autonomous or heteronomous by the society that receives it and submits itself to it.

What we have learned, in fact, from the world of *ona'ah* is that the origin of the law cannot be perceived otherwise than as both autonomous and heteronomous: autonomous in its origins but heteronomous as a result of its status as obligation.

This heteronomy of the law, from which it draws its authority—as though the heteronomy provided a guarantee of truth—thus plays the role of a kind of transcendence, or self-transcendence, of nature by nature. This may be what Wittgenstein meant by the "transcendence of logic" and "of ethics," that the obligation received is transcendent even if its origin is natural, that there is an impersonal transcendence of one part of nature over the other, within the interior of human nature itself. The obligation of the rule of logic imposes itself on thought, while the obligation of law (moral, social, and religious) imposes itself on the passions. This transcendence of the law as obligation, or, rather, its transcendental nature, is quite different from the traditional transcendence of the God of theology, and also from that of the philosophies of the transcendental subject.

But the theological and political question of the sacred in the origins of the law is not resolved, for all that, in spite of appearances in the secularized societies. Despite the end of prophecy, the reflection on biblical prophecy has continued within the framework of the monotheistic theologies. The Word of God, revealed by the prophets and recorded in the sacred scriptures transmitted as such by the tradition, has replaced the oral oracles of the temples. The fact that these texts are now fixed in written form has encouraged a shift towards an increased emphasis on the absolute and unequivocal character of this word as unique and exclusive truth "fallen from heaven." Spinoza's project in his *Theological-Political Treatise* is remarkable in that it relativizes the explicit content of the sacred text while preserving the original biblical prophecy (whatever the mechanism by which the psyche of the prophet receives an image of revelation) as a vehicle, despite everything, of the Word of God—all this on the condition that we understand it to be the revelation not of a universal philosophical truth but of norms of social, moral, and legal organization. In Spinoza, this is not, as is often assumed, a tactical concession to the spirit of his times, dominated by the churches. It is not from a wish to avoid a clash with religion that he assigns to the ancient Hebrews' constitution of the biblical narrative the role of a paradigm of the prophetic revelation of the Law. Rather, it is because what we find there, as Leo Strauss saw, is the problem that has been posed since Plato's time and which remains a fundamental problem of political philosophy today: how to go from an individual human nature, assumed to be dominated by possibly destructive passions, to a relatively peaceful social existence. The fact that the state of society or culture is just as natural, given that the human species, like other species, seems always to have been social, from its beginnings, and animated by affects of solidarity and love as much as of envy and hatred, does not change anything. The question continues to be posed today: how to internalize the common law in the individual in the absence of heteronomy in the social law?

How does one believe in the value of the Law and submit to it as something that is acknowledged as true, "coming from heaven," when its origins no longer bear the evidence of any transcendence, when it is no longer stated in heaven? Leo Strauss's entire political philosophy seems to be steeped in this question and in the idea of returning to Plato and to what he calls the precritical rationality of Spinoza and of the Jewish and Muslim medieval philosophers. His prophetology, which is as Greek as it is biblical, implies an origin as opposed to a clean slate. We have seen that even among the ancient Greeks we find, at the origin of the "divine Law," a celestial truth revealed by divination; for Heraclitus, the content of this truth is unveiled by way of reason, which is also celestial, while for Plato, this truth is controlled by reason.

For we must account for the absolute character of obligation—its transcendence—even while its expression is inevitably submerged in the relativity of partial truths that "sprout from earth," as the Psalm says, carefully shedding the barks and weeds of error and lies.

In fact, the question of the heteronomy of the law is a flawed question as long as it continues to be asked in terms of transcendence. For things do not always play themselves out simply on the level of the beliefs of each isolated individual, whether that individual is a philosopher or a theologian, depending on whether the individual receives them from God or from society. In practice, these beliefs, imbued with the collective morals that are more or less shared in a given society, are themselves largely conditioned by the beliefs of other individuals, which are, in turn, conditioned by them. In other words, the reciprocal interactions between individuals and society are, in any event, at the origin of collective behaviors and of the more or less alienated ways that individuals can have of recognizing themselves in these behaviors.[2] In the context of the renewal of Spinoza studies in France,[3] this question has been asked by applying to relations between human beings notions derived from the ideas of *natura naturans* and *natura naturata*, of which human nature is an integral part. As the human being is not "an empire within an empire" in nature, each individual's *conatus* appears as a self-organizing force of affirming nature, a cause of itself in each of its modes. Each individual's regime of autonomy or heteronomy is thus nothing other than the degree of passivity or activity of each *conatus* in its relations with what is not itself, with what is different from itself, that is to say, as far as human societies are concerned, the adequation sof its self-consciousness: a greater or lesser degree of alienation depending on the level that individuals are able to attain, separately and together, in their progress toward wisdom.

Even though truth is no longer in heaven and does not fall from heaven, the search for truth on earth thus replaces prophetic revelation as the source of the law's obligations. The results of this search can thus impose themselves with a "moral certainty," in Spinoza's terms, in the same way that logical and mathematical "geometrical" certainty imposes itself on thought. Ideally, the "transcendence" of ethics tends to converge with the transcendence of logic. This is the way in which we can understand that "a wise man is superior even to a prophet." This is about the *search* for the truth by the sage who aspires to it and consecrates himself to it, rather than being about the Truth itself in a supernatural unveiling. This search proceeds in a pragmatic way, step by step. The tools it uses are: first, of course, reason, but then also experience and what remains of the heritage of ancient legal and religious traditions, because any attempt at a clean slate is illusory. In other words, the search for truth uses different tools in different geographic, linguistic, cultural, and social contexts; for that reason, the results of the search are also different and the universality of the moral law can only be constructed starting from these differences as well. But this is better than the cynical reign of public relations techniques and the spin doctors that go along with them.

We can of course comfort ourselves, as we have seen, with the thought that in a democracy, the reign of propaganda leads to the defense of half-truths against the total lie, exceeding all the limits of decency, that characterizes totalitarian regimes. For there is, after all, a difference between half-truths and a total lie. Even if it only happens some of the time, it is only in a democracy that the freedom of expression can make it clear that a lie is truly too big and expose it in the independent media or in the media that serve minoritary causes. In such cases, then, a scandal breaks out, sometimes with the perverse effect that people who later turn out to be innocent are condemned by public opinion without ever being charged.

But can we accept half-truths, that is to say, half-lies, with their implication of equal opportunities for the true and the false? Then any speech could be suspected of being half a lie, however one measures that half. Or put another way, this means that at any time, we have a probability of one-half, one chance in two, of encountering fraudulent speech that is as much an assault on the people it injures as on the truths that it tramples. Will blogs, Facebook, Twitter and other social media transform the half-lie into a total lie?

Should we not, instead, attempt to reduce that one-half fraction as far as we can—even if we know that it cannot be reduced to zero—by bringing it down, for example, to "less than one-sixth"?

List of Abbreviations Used in the Notes

References to Biblical texts follow the Jewish division of the text; the main sources, adapted according to Professor Atlan's own translations from Hebrew, are the Stone edition (*Tanach: the Torah, Prophets, Writings: The Twenty-four Books of the Bible, Newly Translated and Annotated*, ed. Nosson Scherman et al. [Brooklyn: Mesorah, 1996]) and the New Revised Standard Version (*The New Oxford Annotated Bible with the Apocryphal/Deuterocanonical Books*, ed. Michael D. Coogan, New Revised Standard Edition, augm. 3rd ed. [Oxford and New York: Oxford University Press, 2007]). References to the Babylonion Talmud (*BT*) are to the Soncino edition (ed. Isidore Epstein et al, London 1969–1990). In the notes, references are made to individual treatises and page numbers. References to Henri Atlan's works are abbreviated as follows:

ECF   *Entre le cristal et la fumée: Essai sur l'organisation du vivant* [*Between Crystal and Smoke: An Essay on the Organization of the Living*] (Paris: Éditions du Seuil, 1979).

EE   *Enlightenment to Enlightenment: Intercritique of Science and Myth*, trans. Lenn J. Schramm (Albany: SUNY Press, 1993).

SR1   *The Sparks of Randomness*, vol. 1, *Spermatic Knowledge*, trans. Lenn J. Schramm, vol. 1 (Stanford: Stanford University Press, 2010).

SR2   *The Sparks of Randomness*, vol. 2, *The Atheism of Scripture*, trans. Lenn J. Schramm, vol. 1 (Stanford: Stanford University Press, 2012).

SW   *Selected Writings*, ed. Stefanos Geroulanos and Todd Meyers (New York: Fordham University Press, 2011).

TNP   *Tout, non, peut-être: Éducation et vérité* [*Everything, No, Maybe: Education and Truth*] (Paris: Éditions du Seuil, 1991).

Notes

INTRODUCTION

1. BT, Baba Mezi'a, *Mishnah*, 58b.
2. Cf. Henri Atlan and Frans B. M. de Waal, *Les frontières de l'humain* [*The Frontiers of the Human*] (Paris: Éditions Le Pommier, 2007).
3. Cf. SR2, ch. 2.
4. BT, Baba Mezi'a, *Mishnah*, 58bff.
5. See Henri Atlan, "Knowledge, Glory, and 'On Human Dignity,'" trans. Colin Anderson, *Diogenes* 3 (2007), pp. 11–17, now ch. 13 in *Selected Writings*. See also Mireille Delmas-Marty in *Le clonage humain* [*Human Cloning*], ed. Henri Atlan, Marc Augé, Mireille Delmas-Marty, Roger-Pol Droit and Nadine Fresco (Paris: Éditions du Seuil, 1999), pp. 81–82 and 99–109. Compare below, ch. 2.

CHAPTER 1

1. Psalm 12:2–7.
2. Isaiah 57:4. [*zera' sheker* is imperfectly rendered "seed of the adulterer and the adulteress" in Stone 1053. Atlan explicitly criticizes Édouard Dhorme's translation of the phrase into French as "race of fraud."—*trans.*]
3. Spinoza, *Ethics* IV, prop. 72 and scholium, *The Essential Spinoza*, ed. Michael L. Morgan, trans. Samuel Shirley (Indianapolis: Hackett Publishing Company, 2006), p. 137.
4. Immanuel Kant, "On a Supposed Right to Lie from Philanthropy," *Practical Philosophy*, trans. and ed. Mary J. Gregor (Cambridge: Cambridge University Press, 1996), p. 613. Immanuel Kant, "Über ein vermeintes Recht aus Menschenliebe zu lügen," 1797, *Kants gesammelte Schriften* [*Akademie-Ausgabe*, hereafter abbreviated as AA], vol. VIII (Berlin: de Gruyter, 1917), pp. 425–431, quote 427 (http://www.korpora.org/Kant/aa08/). "Es ist also ein heiliges, unbedingt gebietendes, durch keine Convenienzen einzuschränkendes Vernunftgebot: in allen Erklärungen wahrhaft (ehrlich) zu sein."
5. Kant, *Practical Philosophy*, p. 611; AA VIII:425.
6. Kant, *Practical Philosophy*, p. 612; AA VIII:426.

7. Kant, *Metaphysics of Morals*, Doctrine of Virtue I.1.II.§9: Remark, in *Practical Philosophy*, p. 554 (AA VI:431); on the non-universalizable character of the maxim, cf. *Groundwork for the Metaphysics of Morals*, section 2 (AA IV).

8. Plato, *The Republic*, trans. G. M. A. Grube, rev. C. D. C. Reeve, *Complete Works*, ed. John M. Cooper and D. S. Hutchinson (Indianapolis: Hackett Publishing Company, 1997), bk. V, 459c, p. 1087.

9. Ibid., 459c–460a, p. 1087.

10. Spinoza, §1 of the *Treatise on the Emendation of the Intellect*, *The Essential Spinoza*, ed. Michael L. Morgan, trans. Samuel Shirley (Indianapolis: Hackett Publishing Company, 2006), p. 164.

11. Ibid., §33–42; *Ethics* II, props. 3 and 43.

12. For a Spinozist reader, these conflicts are nothing but the inevitable effects of the encounters between *conatus* through their passions of love and hatred, inevitable so long as the "guidance of Reason" over all human beings has not yet subsumed all these passions under "the intellectual love of God," that is to say of infinite Nature in its "naturing" power and its "natured" effectiveness. See especially Laurent Bove, *La Stratégie du conatus: Affirmation et résistance chez Spinoza* [*The Strategy of* conatus*: Affirmation and Resistance in Spinoza*] (Paris: Librairie Philosophique J. Vrin, 1996).

13. Vladimir Jankélévitch, *Traité des vertus* [*Treatise on the Virtues*], 1949 and 1968–1972 (Paris: Éditions Flammarion, 1986), vol. II, ch. III: "Sincerity," pp. 271–273. [*Our translation.*]

14. Ibid., pp. 275ff.

15. See *EE*, ch. 9: "Naked Truth."

16. Ibid., pp. 395–396; R. Judah Loew, *Netivot Olam* (Prague 1596), ch. 3, "The Path of Truth"; Midrash *Genesis Rabba* 8.

17. Psalm 85:12.

18. To name just a couple of works with evocative titles: in the United States, Richard Rorty's *Take Care of Freedom and Truth Will Take Care of Itself* (Stanford: Stanford University Press, 2006) and in Europe (in France and Portugal), Pierre De Roo's *Adieu vérité, ou, La ruse du philosophe* [*Farewell, Truth, or, The Philosopher's Ruse*] (Paris: Éditions Stock, 2007). De Roo develops a particularly interesting thesis in the form of a history of philosophy that purports to be the history of a ruse that passes off the truth of Being as something that it is not, or passes itself off as the Truth. De Roo presents this ruse as in fact inherent in human reason and intelligence, which draw their evolutionary roots from the ruse and from animal cognitive abilities. Rorty's book, meanwhile, is a recent exposé of the philosophical pragmatism that he developed and defended for some thirty years, to which we will return.

19. *EE*.

20. *SR2*, ch. 2.

21. Richard Rorty, *Philosophy and the Mirror of Nature* (Oxford: Blackwell, 1980).

22. Richard Rorty and Pascal Engel, *What's the Use of Truth?*, ed. Patrick Savidan, trans. William McCuaig (New York: Columbia University Press, 2007), p. 34.

23. Ibid., pp. 44–45.

24. Bernard Williams, *Ethics and the Limits of Philosophy* (London and New York: Routledge, 2006) and *Truth and Truthfulness* (Princeton: Princeton University Press, 2002).

25. See, e.g., *Ethics and the Limits of Philosophy*, p. 111. See also Hilary Putnam's criticism of Williams's attempt in Putnam, *Renewing Philosophy* (Cambridge: Harvard University Press, 1992) after having previously been convinced of the value of this aspect of the agenda of analytic philosophy.

26. Richard Rorty, "Worlds or Words Apart? The Consequences of Pragmatism for Literary Studies," interview with Edward Ragg, ch. 11 of *Take Care of Freedom*, p. 126.

27. Rorty and Engel, *What's the Use of Truth?*, p. 31; the French makes a pun on *essence*, which means both "gasoline" and "essence."

28. Henri Atlan, "Les frontières revisitées" ["Boundaries Revisited"], in Henri Atlan and Frans B. M. de Waal, *Les frontières de l'humain* [*The Frontiers of the Human*] (Paris: Éditions Le Pommier, 2007); Henri Atlan and Mylène Botbol-Baum, *Des embryons et des hommes* [*Of Embryos and Human Beings*] (Paris: Presses Universitaires de France, 2007).

29. See De Roo's analysis of the transition from one to the other in his *Adieu vérité*.

30. Friedrich Nietzsche, *The Gay Science*, ed. Bernard Williams, trans. Josefine Nauckhoff (Cambridge: Cambridge University Press, 2001), §110, p. 110.

31. Ibid., p. 111.

32. Ibid., §344, p. 201.

33. Ibid., pp. 200–201.

34. Ibid., §114, p. 114.

35. Ibid., §344, p. 201.

36. Ibid., §1, pp. 27–28.

37. See *EE*, ch. 9, "Naked Truth," on the necessity of lies told out of modesty or reserve that, according to the Midrash and the talmudic sayings, can be correctly evaluated only by those—the *talmidei hakhamim*, or students of the Sages—whose vocation and foremost occupation consists in establishing and constructing the truth, making it "sprout from earth." Let us also mention the short treatise that presents the sefirotic structure of the worlds of the Kabbalah and the Zohar in condensed form, a treatise whose evocative name *Book of Modesty [or Decency]* (*Sifra ditsni'uta*) recalls a principle of esoteric teaching: "unveil one cubit and hide two."

38. Nietzsche, *Gay Science*, Preface, §4, p. 8 [modified].

39. Putnam, *Renewing Philosophy*, p. xi.

40. Ibid., p. 72.

41. Ludwig Wittgenstein, *On Certainty*, eds. G. E. M. Anscombe and G. H. von Wright, trans. Denis Paul and G. E. M. Anscombe (Oxford: Blackwell, 1969), §§357–359, pp. 46e–47e [modified].

42. *TNP*.

43. Spinoza, Letter 76 to Alfred Burgh of December 1675, *The Letters*, trans. Samuel Shirley (Indianapolis: Hackett Publishing Company, 1995), p. 342.

44. "Wenn das Wahre das Begründete ist, dann ist der Grund nicht wahr, noch falsch," Wittgenstein, *On Certainty*, §205, p. 28e.

45. "Der vernünftige Mensch hat gewisse Zweifel *nicht*," ibid., §220, p. 29e.

46. "Braucht man zum Zweifel nicht Gründe?" Ibid., §122, p. 18e.

47. *SR1*, ch. 4, §2, pp. 200–207.

CHAPTER 2

1. The Gospel in fact distorts the quotation from Leviticus: it leaves out the "as yourself" from Leviticus but adds "you shall hate your enemy," which does not appear anywhere in Leviticus but is presented here as a contrast to introduce the prescription that follows: "Love your enemies!"

2. BT, Shabbat, 31a.

3. The *'alilot devarim*, "pretexts and intrigues in words," that Deuteronomy puts into the mouth of a husband unfaithful to his wife are used by the Midrash as a metaphor for divine intrigues in the conduct of human affairs (see *SR1*, pp. 96–101).

4. Michel Steiner, *Kol Nidré: Étude psychanalytique d'une prière juive* [*Kol Nidre: A Psychoanalytic Study of a Jewish Prayer*] (Paris: Hors Commerce, 2007).

5. See below, ch. 3.

6. Let us recall that talmudic interpretation generally belongs to the category of the *drash* (on this point, cf. *SR2*, ch. 12: "Levels of Signification and the Atheism of Scripture"): *midrash halakha* for the establishment of the law and *midrash aggada* for parables and for more or less mythical narratives. In other words, it does not, as is often believed, aim to provide the "true" sense of the biblical text, at what its author or authors "wanted to say." Rather, it aims at a new construction with a legal or edifying impetus, adapted, on the one hand, to the new anthropological reality of the experience of a world without prophecy and, on the other, to the [Jewish] people's loss of its national sovereignty and its dispersal among other peoples. Despite the recurrent appearance of the slightly modified formula "Rabbi X said . . . as it is written . . . ," which seems to *found* the sayings of the masters on the verses of Scripture, it often happens that talmudic interpretation makes the text say many other things than what it says explicitly. The relation between commentary and text is thus inverted: the text, far from being the basis for the commentary, instead receives one or more new illuminations from it.

7. BT, Baba Mezi'a, 58b [modified].

8. Elsewhere, I analyze other examples of such alliances linked to ancient Hebrew usage: *tree* and *counsel*, *serpent* and *divination*, *nakedness* and *cunning*, *knowledge* and *sexual union* (*SR1*, ch. 1, esp. pp. 47–48).

9. Mireille Delmas-Marty, "Certitude et incertitudes du droit [Certainty and Uncertainties of the Law]," *Le clonage humain* [*Human Cloning*], eds. Henri Atlan, Marc Augé, Mireille Delmas-Marty, Roger-Pol Droit, and Nadine Fresco (Paris: Éditions du Seuil, 1991), p. 74.

10. Ibid., p. 81; see also the debate that follows on "'Humanity' and 'Dignity,'" pp. 99–116.

11. Ibid., p. 75.

12. Giovanni Pico della Mirandola, *On the Dignity of Man*, trans. Charles Glenn Wallis (Indianapolis: The Bobbs-Merrill Company, 1965 [reprinted, with a new bibliography, Indianapolis: Hackett Publishing Company, 1998]).

13. Spinoza, *Ethics* III, prop. 29 scholium; the "Definition of the Affects/Emotions" V and XXX; and prop. 36 scholium.

14. Henri Atlan, "'Knowledge, Glory, and 'On Human Dignity,'" pp. 246–250.

15. BT, Baba Mezi'a, 59a.

16. *Perush Rashi: Torah with Rashi's Commentary*, vol. 3: Vayikra = Leviticus, ed. Yisrael Isser Zvi Herczeg, Yaakov Petroff, and Yoseph Kamenetzky, 2nd ed. (Brooklyn: Mesorah Publications, 1998), pp. 327–328.

17. Hayyim ben Joseph Vital, *The Tree of Life: Chayyim Vital's Introduction to the Kabbalah of Isaac Luria*, trans. Donald Wilder Menzi and Zwe Padeh (Northvale: Jason Aronson, 1999).

18. See below, ch. 5.

19. BT, Baba Mezi'a, 49b.

CHAPTER 3

1. Maurice Olender, "Mot, monnaie et démocratie: Lieux communs de l'intime" ["Word, Money, and Democracy: Commonplaces of the Intimate"], *Origines du langage: Une encyclopédie poétique* [*Origins of Language: A Poetic Encyclopedia*], ed. Olivier Pot (Paris: Éditions du Seuil, 2007), pp. 523–549.

2. Isidore of Seville, *Etymologiae*, quoted in Olender, ibid.

3. Plato, *The Republic*, II, 371 [modified] [on this translation, cf. D. C. Schindler, "Why Socrates Didn't Charge: Plato and the Metaphysics of Money," *Communio* 36 (Fall 2009), p. 379—*trans.*].

4. Lorenzo da Brindisi, quoted in Olender, "Mot."

5. Jean Starobinski, "Quand la parole promet de la monnaie: Échange avec Maurice Olender" ["When Speech Promises Money: An Exchange with Maurice Olender"], in Pot, ed., *Origines du langage*.

6. Michel Bréal, quoted by Starobinski, ibid.

7. Olender, "Mot."

8. See Janine Trotereau's excellent article "Le banquier" ["The Banker"], *Historia*, Sep–Oct 2007, pp. 96–98.

9. Exodus 22:24; Leviticus 25:35–38; Deuteronomy 23:20; Luke 6:35; Qur'an 2:275–281 and 3:310.

10. Aristotle, *Politics*, trans. Benjamin Jowett, *The Basic Works of Aristotle*, ed. Richard McKeon, 1941 (New York: Modern Library, 2001), bk. I, ch. 10, 1258b, p. 1137.

11. Deuteronomy 15:1–11.

12. *SR1*, ch. 5: "The Desacralization of Chance."

13. John Maynard Keynes, *A Treatise on Money*, 1930, *Collected Writings* (London: Macmillan, 1971), ch. 1, p. 3.

14. "Hillel the Elder also instituted the *prosbul* for the repair of the world [*tikkum olam*]" (BT, Giṭṭin, 34b and 36a–b, trans. Maurice Simon, pt. 3 vol. 2; see also *Mishnah, Shvi'it* 10). This is the same Hillel the Elder who, having been asked to sum up all of Torah while standing on one leg, answered with the golden rule converted to its negative form (see ch. 2). *Prosbul* is the name of a document that transfers the deed to the court, charging the latter to collect the debt in the place of the creditor. The origins, probably Greek, of the word *prosbul* are rather obscure, as is its literal meaning. A number of hypotheses exist about how the word was formed, notably several related to a Greek institution in first-century Palestine, a kind of local authority called a *boule*, and to expressions derived from this such as *pras boule*, "decision of the council," and *pros boule*, "before the council" (see BT, Giṭṭin, 36b–37a).

15. BT, Baba Mezi'a, 60b–73b.

16. *The Qur'an*, trans. M. A. S. Abdel Haleem (Oxford: Oxford University Press, 2004), sura 2, verses 278–279.

17. Ibid., sura 2, verse 275.

18. Later, I will discuss the current nature of loans and credit, which have become completely dematerialized along with money itself.

19. In his book *Your Money or Your Life: Economy and Religion in the Middle Ages*, trans. Patricia Ranum (New York: Zone Books, 1988), the historian Jacques Le Goff describes the major aspects of the evolution of the medieval Church's ambivalent relation to usury.

20. Ibid., 27, 33 and 40 [modified, emphasis HA; the last is a quotation from Thomas of Chobham].

21. Ibid., p. 41 [this is a quotation from Bernard of Clairvaux].

22. One of the Hebrew words used in the Bible to characterize loaning at interest is *neshekh*, which evokes the serpent's bite (Leviticus 25:36).

23. See André Biéler, *Calvin's Economic and Social Thought*, ed. Edward Dommen, trans. James Greig (Geneva: World Alliance of Reformed Churches/World Council of Churches, 2005).

24. François Rachline, *Que l'argent soit: Capitalisme et alchimie de l'avenir* [*Let

there be Money: Capitalism and Alchemy of the Future] (Paris: Éditions Calmann-Lévy, 1993), pp. 52–53.

25. Ibid., p. 54.

26. Ibid., pp. 54–55.

27. Henri Atlan, *L'Organisation biologique et la théorie de l'information* [*Biological Organization and Information Theory*] (Paris, Éditions Hermann, 1972; Éditions du Seuil, 2006); cf. C. E. Shannon and W. Weaver, *The Mathematical Theory of Communication* (Urbana: University of Illinois Press, 1949).

28. There is already an abundant literature on the application of models of self-organization to economic theory. One of the implications of these models that is often ignored is the necessary incompleteness of theory: theory will inevitably be unable to predict accurately how the market will develop if the market has the properties of a self-organizing system; more precisely, theory will be able to predict that it will not be able to predict the observations it will be able to make after the fact. In the context of the current financial and economic crisis, it is worthwhile to read or reread Jean-Pierre Dupuy's fundamental work, *Le Sacrifice et l'Envie: Le libéralisme aux prises avec la justice sociale* [*Sacrifice and Desire: Liberalism Versus Social Justice*] (Paris: Calmann-Lévy, 1992), especially ch. 8, in which Dupuy analyzes the determining role played by mechanisms of self-organization or by self-generating representations in the constitution of a spontaneous social order that is produced by the conjoined effects of agents but largely independent of their plans. André Orléan's work (including "Money and Mimetic Speculation," in *Violence and Truth: On the Work of René Girard*, ed. Paul Dumouchel [Stanford: Stanford University Press, 1988], pp. 101–112; "Mimétisme et anticipations rationnelles: une perspective keynésienne [Mimetism and Rational Expectations: A Keynesian Perspective]," *Recherches économiques de Louvain* [*Louvain Economic Studies*], vol. 52 no. 1 [1986]; and *Le Pouvoir de la Finance* [*The Power of Finance*] [Paris: Éditions Odile Jacob, 1999]), which is extensively cited by Dupuy, shows how the dynamics of these mechanisms can often lead to multiple balances or attractors. What then actually happens cannot be predicted but appears after the fact to have been the necessary result of thoughtful, rational collective perceptions, when in fact it is something like the amplification of an initial disarray thanks to a feedback loop of reciprocal imitations.

29. See note 4, above.

30. André Gorz, *The Immaterial: Knowledge, Value and Capital*, trans. Chris Turner (London and New York: Seagull Books, 2010).

31. Jacques Robin, *Changer d'ère* [*Changing Epochs*] (Paris: Éditions du Seuil, 1989).

32. François Rachline, *Que l'argent soit*; see also *D'où vient l'argent?* [*Where Does Money Come From?*] (Paris: Panama, 2006).

33. Ralph George Hawtrey, "Credit," *Encyclopedia of the Social Sciences*, ed. Edwin Robert Anderson Seligman (New York: Macmillan, 1930), vol. 4, pp. 545–550.

34. Ibid., p. 545.

35. See Jérôme Blanc, *Les monnaies parallèles: Unité et diversité du fait monétaire* [*Parallel Currencies: Unity and Diversity of the Monetary Phenomenon*] (Paris: L'Harmattan, 2000), as well as the dossier "Monnaies plurielles" ["Plural Currencies"] of *Transversales: sciences et culture* [*Transversals: Sciences and Culture*], 22 Dec 2007, http://grit-transversales.org/article.php3?id_article=233.

36. "[A]lmost the greater part of mankind get their knowledge of God from dreams." Tertullian, *De Anima, Ante-Nicene Christian Library: Translations of the Writings of the Fathers Down to A.D. 325*, vol. 15, eds. Alexander Roberts and James Donaldson (Edinburgh: T. and T. Clark, 1870), ch. XLVII, p. 518, quoted in Guy G. Stroumsa, *Barbarian Philosophy: The Religious Revolution of Early Christianity* (Tübingen: Mohr Siebeck Verlag, 1999), p. 207.

37. *EE*, ch. 8, "An Ethics That Falls from Heaven," and *SR2*, ch. 2.

38. The Hebrew *kesef* ("money") has the same root as one of the words for "desire," *kisuf*.

39. Benny Shanon, "Biblical Entheogens: A Speculative Hypothesis," *Time & Mind*, vol. 1 no. 1 (March 2008), pp.51–74, and *The Antipodes of the Mind: Charting the Phenomenology of the Ayahuasca Experience* (Oxford: Oxford University Press, 2002).

40. See ch. 7.

41. Winston Churchill, Speech in the House of Commons, 11 Nov 1947, *The Official Report, House of Commons* (5th Series), 11 November 1947 (London: His Majesty's Stationery Office, 1948), vol. 444, cols. 206–7.

42. Thomas Gustafson, *Representative Words: Politics, Literature, and the American Language, 1776–1865* (Cambridge: Cambridge University Press, 1992).

43. The *nature* of this verbal fraud that is described and denounced by Thucydides, the *sense* in which the meaning of words has been twisted and diverted from their natural or usual meaning to make them artificially designate actions that are the opposite of what the words signify, has been the object of numerous interpretations by Thucydides's readers and translators. Cf. Gustafson, *Representative Words*, pp. 77–81 and 415–16.

44. See ch. 8.

45. Following Gorgias, "Encomium on Helen," *Ancilla to the Pre-Socratic Philosophers*, trans. Kathleen Freeman (Oxford: Clarendon Press, 1948), p. 133, quoted in Gustafson, *Representative Words*, p. 94, following Jerome Frank, *Courts on Trial: Myth and Reality in American Justice*, 1949 (New York: Atheneum, 1969).

46. Gustafson, *Representative Words*, p. 70. For a different reading of Orpheus, see Marcel Detienne, *Les Dieux d'Orphée* [*The Gods of Orpheus*] (Paris: Éditions Gallimard, 2007).

47. Shigehisa Kuriyama, "The Life of Money and the Afflictions of the Body," *Concepts of Life* conference, Johns Hopkins University, November 2006.

48. Ibid.

49. Ibid.

50. Yamashita Kōnai, *Jōho*, Nihon Keizai Sōsho (Tokyo: Shūeisha, 1941), vol. 5, p. 6, quoted in Kuriyama, "The Life of Money."

51. For other investigations into the nature of debt, see Charles Malamoud, "Theology of the Debt," ch. 5 of *Cooking the World: Ritual and Thought in Ancient India*, trans. David White (Delhi: Oxford University Press, 1996); and based on Malamoud, Jacques Derrida has articulated a different approach to the question of debt in his "Reste—le maître, ou le supplément d'infini" in *Le disciple et ses maîtres: Pour Charles Malamoud*, ed. Lyne Bansat-Boudon and John Scheid (Paris: Éditions du Seuil, 2002).

52. Kuriyama, "The Life of Money."

53. Olender, "Mot."

54. Starobinski in Pot, ed., *Origines du langage*.

CHAPTER 4

1. Gilbert Simondon, *Du mode d'existence des objets techniques*, 1958 (Paris: Éditions Aubier-Montaigne, 1989). [There is a partial translation of this book by Ninian Mellamphy, *On the Mode of Existence of Technical Objects* (London, Ontario: University of Western Ontario, 1980), to which references are made in square brackets, following the page numbers of the French original, where applicable.—*trans.*]

2. See *SR1*, pp. 39–40.

3. Ibid., chs. 1 and 2.

4. On this point, see also the Fludd–Kepler controversy in *EE*, pp. 169–176 and 223–224.

5. Martin Heidegger, "The Question Concerning Technology," *The Question Concerning Technology, and Other Essays*, trans. William Lovitt (New York: Harper and Row, 1977), pp. 3–35, esp. p. 19 and following. [Lovitt leaves the term in German.—*trans.*]

6. Ibid., p. 16.

7. Simondon, *Du mode d'existence*, p. 168.

8. Ibid., p. 169.

9. Ibid., p. 256.

10. "l'artificiel est du naturel suscité, non du faux ou de l'humain pris pour du naturel," ibid.

11. Ibid., p. 15 [16].

12. Ibid., pp. 15–16 [16].

13. See Atlan, *L'organisation biologique et la théorie de l'information* [*Biological Organization and Information Theory*] (Paris: Hermann, 1972; Éditions du Seuil, 2006).

14. Simondon, pp. 11–12 [13].

15. Deuteronomy 5:14–15.
16. BT, Shabbat, 18a.
17. Aristotle, *Politics*, bk. I, ch. 4, 1253b–1254a, p. 1989.
18. Many examples come to mind. Let us cite just one: disposable diapers, whose obvious usefulness goes to the very heart of relations among women, men, and babies.
19. For possible interpretations of the biblical warning "See, I have placed before you today the life and the good, and the death and the evil . . ." (Deuteronomy 30:15), see *ECF*, ch. 13.

CHAPTER 5

1. BT, Baba Mezi'a, 59a–b.
2. BT, Baba Mezi'a, 59b [modified].
3. BT, Baba Mezi'a, 59b [modified]; the last phrase follows Deuteronomy 30:12.
4. BT, Baba Mezi'a, 59b [modified]; the last phrase quotes Exodus 23:2.
5. BT, Baba Mezi'a, 59b [modified].
6. BT, Rosh Hashanach, 24b.
7. BT, Baba Batra, 12a.
8. BT, 'Erubin, 13b; cf. *SR2*, ch. 12, §6, pp. 348–351. [*Elohim*, usually translated as "God," is a plural that is most often but not always conjugated with verbs in the singular. Since capital letters do not exist in Hebrew, Atlan renders it as "god(s)."—*trans*.]
9. Judah Loew ben Bezalel, *Perushe Maharal mi-Prag: le-agadot ha-Shas 'al Nedarim, Nazir, Soṭah, Ḳidushin u-Bava Metsi'a*, ed. Moshe Shlomo Kasher and Ya'akov Yehoshu'a Blacherowicz (Jerusalem: Ginze rishonim, 718 [1958]), p. 130.
10. See in particular other anecdotes reported in the Talmud, to which we will return; the first pages of the *Pirke De-Rabbi Eliezer*, the *Midrash* treatise attributed to him; and the *Prince of the Torah*, an ancient cabalistic text linked to the *Hekhalot* (see Joseph Dan, *The Ancient Jewish Mysticism*, trans. Shmuel Himelstein [Tel Aviv: MOD Books, 1993]).
11. *The Pirkei Avos Treasury: Ethics of the Fathers: the Sages' Guide to Living*, with an anthologized commentary and anecdotes by Moshe Lieber; edited, with an overview by Nosson Scherman (Brooklyn, NY: Mesorah Publications, 1995), 1:1.
12. See the commentary on ch. 4 of *Baba Mezi'a* (59b) by Yosef Hayyim ben Eliyah al-Hakham ("the Sage"), a cabalistic commentator in nineteenth-century Baghdad, in his *Ben Yehoyada* (Jerusalem: 1965), p. 73b.
13. This expression is used, precisely, to describe the words expressing the contradictory teachings of the two opposing schools of Hillel and Shammai, of which a heavenly voice (another *bat kol*!) says that "these and those are words of the living god[s]," *divrei elohim hayyim* (BT, 'Erubin, 13b). In the same way, the expression *halakha le Moshe mi-Sinai* ("it is a *halakha* [that goes back to] Moses at Sinai")

is applied to talmudic decisions whose biblical source is far from obvious. See, in *SR2*, ch. 12, the story of the new teachings created by Rabbi Akiba, who justifies them by attributing them to "Moses at Sinai" even though, according to legend, Moses himself, who is present when Rabbi Akiba expounds them, does not understand them (BT, Menahot, 29b).

14. Deuteronomy 30.
15. Deuteronomy 30:10–14.
16. Exodus 23:2; see above, note 4.
17. Deceitful speech is often denounced by the biblical text, which opposes it to the purity of the divinity's words of truth. The expression "seed of falsehood" attributes a fearsome efficacy to such speech, thanks to the "seminal" character of its self-amplifying creation of disturbances (Isaiah 57:3–4). See above, ch. 1, and *SR1*, pp. 85–86, note 52.
18. *SR2*, ch. 12.
19. BT, Menahot, 29b.
20. BT, Baba Mezi'a, 59b, [quotes modified].
21. BT, Baba Mezi'a, 59a [modified].
22. The expression "to fall on one's face" is taken from a passage in the Bible in which Moses and Aaron "fall on their faces" while invoking a "god, gods of the spirits of all flesh" capable of individually judging the actors involved in a collective behavior, according to the state of mind of each one, to which, in truth, no one has access (Numbers 16:22). The stakes of the judgment, in this context, are life and death, and this attitude of internal self-reflection is transposed into the ritual where the confrontation with one's own death is at stake. This is what the author of the book *Nefesh Hahayim*, inspired by the Zohar, explains when he discusses this ritual, which lets the spirit rise to the source of its life (called *hayia*, "living," to designate the upper part of the "soul") (Hayim of Volozhin, *Nefesh hahayim*, in *The Way of the Faithful: An Anthology of Jewish Mysticism*, ed. and trans. Raphael Ben Zion [Los Angeles: Haynes Corporation, 1945]). But this is not without danger, to the extent that one leaves behind the daily occupations that make up the world of ordinary existence. Leaving this world is thus a kind of exposure to one's own death. We can see why it is accompanied by a particular kind of anguish, in which other fears that had been more or less forgotten are reawakened.
23. BT, Baba Mezi'a, 59b.
24. BT, Baba Mezi'a, 59a.
25. Amos 7:7.
26. BT, Baba Mezi'a, 59a. Cf. the last section of ch. 6, below, on "Measures and values."
27. BT, Baba Mezi'a, 59b.
28. Exodus 22:20.
29. Literally, the proverb is actually inverted here: "If there is a case of hang-

222 Notes to Chapters 5 and 6

ing in a man's family record, say not to him, 'Hang this fish up for me'"—for, as Rashi says, the very mention of a hanging is humiliating (BT, Baba Mezi'a, 59b).

CHAPTER 6

1. BT, Baba Mezi'a, 49bff.
2. Ch. 2, end of the first section, "On evil and its banality."
3. Geneviève Guitel, *Histoire comparée des numérations écrites* [*A Comparative History of Written Numbering Systems*] (Paris: Éditions Flammarion, 1975).
4. BT, Berakot, 57b.
5. Psalm 90:4.
6. See the classic exposition of the Lurianic Kabbalah by the sixteenth-century master Hayyim ben Joseph Vital, portal 17 on *ona'ah* in his *Etz Hayyim*.
7. By another path, we also learn that the influence of the father can short-circuit this trajectory and exercise itself directly on the daughter.
8. We will return to this later in this book.
9. One-sixth of eight and two-thirds is, in fact, one plus one-third plus one-ninth. The whole portion that is furthest from eight and two-thirds in these apportionments is ten, which is greater by one and one-third, that is to say, by a divergence that is less than one-sixth of the equitable portion. The divergence of the other values, nine and eight, from the equitable portion is even smaller: one-third more and two-thirds less, respectively.
10. Or more precisely, the *sod* of the three component parts of the circumcision ritual: cutting off the foreskin, rolling back and tearing the mucosal lining, and blessing the wine (cf. Vital, *Etz Hayyim*, chs. 3 and 4 of the portal of *ona'ah*).
11. *SR2*, ch. 12.
12. *SR1*, pp. 74–79.
13. *SR1*, pp. 82–83 and 170; *EE*, ch. 9.
14. This is another example of the multiple meanings, both concrete and abstract, of a biblical term. The Hebrew *'orla*, translated as "uncircumcision," literally means "foreskin." The adjective derived from it, *'arel*, for "uncircumcised," said of the flesh (Genesis 17:11, Ezekiel 44:7), of the heart (Jeremiah 9:25), of the lips (Exodus 6:30), of the ear (Jeremiah 6:10), and of fruit trees in the first three years after being planted (Leviticus 19:23) ought to be translated (as André Chouraqui does in this last instance) by "foreskin" or "considered as if surrounded by a foreskin" or again "treated as a foreskin" (as Edourd Dhorme has it). We may also wonder about the primary meaning, for the Talmud at least, of the one that concerns circumcision proper as a sign of the alliance with Abraham in Genesis or of the foreskin of trees in the prescription, in Leviticus, not to consume their fruits during their first three years. In fact, one entire treatise of the Mishnah, *'Orla* ("Foreskin"), is dedicated to nothing but questions relating to this "foreskin" of fruit trees.
15. Ezekiel 11:19.

16. Maimonides, *Mishneh Torah*, trans. Eliyahu Touger, Sefer Shoftim, Melachim uMilchamot 6:10, http://www.chabad.org/library/article_cdo/aid/1188350/jewish/Chapter-6.htm.

17. *SR1*, pp. 47–49.

18. Genesis 17.

19. Genesis 15.

20. Vital, *Etz Hayyim*, portal of *ona'ah*, ch. 2.

21. From 20 to 60 years, 50 shekels for a man and 30 shekels for a woman; from 5 to 20 years, 20 shekels for a boy and 10 shekels for a girl; from 1 month to 5 years, 5 for a boy and 2 for a girl; over 60 years, 15 shekels for a man and 10 for a woman (Leviticus 27:2–7).

22. BT, 'Arakhin, 2a and 4b.

23. Ibid., 15b.

24. BT, Baba Mezi'a, 59a.

25. Ibid. [modified].

26. Amos 7:8 [interpolation Atlan].

27. BT, Baba Mezi'a, 44a Mishnah [modified]. For one nineteenth-century cabalistic commentator, Joseph Hayyim Ben Elijah al-Hakham ("the Wise"), there is an organic connection between the evocation of these "wicked" generations and evil in speech. He bases this view on the legend of the "sparks of randomness" that follow Adam and Eve's initial sin, from which these generations issue. And he recalls a well-known interpretation of the Genesis story according to which it is a lack of rigor in the use of speech that lies at the origin of the sin. Eve indeed says to the snake that they had been prohibited from touching the Tree of Knowledge under pain of death, when in fact they were only prohibited from eating from it. When the snake shoves her, making her touch the tree, and nothing happens, it manages to persuade her that eating from the tree would have no other effect than "opening [her] eyes" (*Ben Yehoyada* on Baba Mezi'a, 42).

28. *BT*, Baba Mezi'a, 48a.

29. Vital, *Etz Hayyim*, portal of *ona'ah*, ch. 1.

30. Maurice Olender, "Mot" [interpolations Atlan].

31. Ibid.

CHAPTER 7

1. *ECF*.

2. Émile Durkheim, *The Elementary Forms of Religious Life*, trans. Carol Cosman, ed. Mark S. Cladis (Oxford: Oxford University Press, 2008).

3. René Girard, *Violence and the Sacred*, 1972, trans. Patrick Gregory, 1977 (London: Continuum, 2005) and *Things Hidden Since the Foundation of the World*, 1978, trans. Stephen Bann and Michael Metteer (Stanford: Stanford University Press, 1987).

Notes to Chapter 7

4. Jean-Pierre Dupuy, *La Marque du Sacré* (Paris: Carnet Nord, 2008).

5. Cornelius Castoriadis, *The Imaginary Institution of Society*, 1975, trans. Kathleen Blamey (Cambridge: MIT Press, 1987).

6. Maurice Godelier, *Au fondement des sociétés humaines: Ce que nous apprend l'anthropologie* [*At the Foundation of Human Societies: What Anthropology Teaches Us*] (Paris: Éditions Albin Michel, 2007).

7. This is obvious in the case of Bergson's genealogical attempt in *The Two Sources of Morality and Religion* (trans. R. Ashley Audra and Cloudesley Brereton [Notre Dame: University of Notre Dame Press, 1977]. As it is by the way for Hegel and for many others, the consummate "religion" for Bergson is evidently Christianity, all others being but "primitive" forms that, at best, were able to "prepare" for the advent of Christianity.

8. Dupuy, *La Marque du Sacré*.

9. The rejection of the Hobbesian idea of a state of nature is the result of behavioral studies on primates (like Frans B. M. de Waal's "L'homme est-il un loup pour l'homme?" ["Are humans wolves to their fellow human beings?"] in Atlan and de Waal, *Les frontières de l'humain*) and, running parallel to those, the research of anthropologists who, ever since Michel Foucault, in 1966, underscored the recently constructed character of the notion of nature and the distinction between nature and culture (*The Order of Things* [New York: Pantheon, 1971]), have seen this distinction as a largely illusory exception produced by Western culture starting with its Greco-Roman origins (see, for example, Philippe Descola, *Par-delà nature et culture* [*Beyond Nature and Culture*] [Paris: Éditions Gallimard, 2005] and Marshall David Sahlins, *The Western Illusion of Human Nature* [Chicago: Prickly Paradigm Press, 2008]).

10. Among others: Aldous Huxley, *Doors of Perception* (Harmondsworth: Penguin, 1971) and "Visionary Experience" in *The Highest State of Consciousness*, ed. John Warren White (New York: Anchor, 1952), pp. 37–57; Holger Kalweit, *Dreamtime and Inner Space: The World of the Shaman* (Boston: Shambhala, 1988), in which the author draws especially on states of consciousness reported after experiences of imminent death; and Benny Shanon, "Biblical Entheogens: A Speculative Hypothesis," *Time & Mind*, vol. 1 no. 1 (March 2008), pp.51–74, as well as *The Antipodes of the Mind: Charting the Phenomenology of the Ayahuasca Experience* (Oxford: Oxford University Press, 2002).

11. The relatively recent rediscovery, in the West, of these "altered states of consciousness"—a phrase that is itself part of the scientific context of our contemporary culture—has given rise to periodic "shamanic" fashions that sometimes involve touristic exploitations that profit from pervasive globalization. But such degenerate and more or less infantile forms of these phenomena, easily associated with delirious research into the "paranormal," must not obscure their reality nor their anthropological importance.

12. *EE*, ch. 8, and *SR2*, ch. 2, §6.

13. "Since the Temple [in Jerusalem] was destroyed, prophecy has been taken from prophets and given to fools and children" (BT, Baba Batra, 12b).

14. We should, however, note that Tibetan Buddhism appears to have preserved practices of divination and the consultation of oracles into the present day at the same time as it opens itself to the modern world (Thubten Ngodup, with Françoise Bottereau-Gardey and Laurent Deshayes, *Nechung, l'oracle du dalaï-lama* [*Neshung, the Dalai Lama's Oracle*] [Paris: Presses de la Renaissance, 2009]). We may suppose that the encounter with science sought by the Dalai Lama will eventually modify at least the understanding of these phenomena.

15. Dupuy, *La Marque du Sacré*, p. 123.

16. This point is developed in more detail in my "Founding Violence and Divine Referent," *Violence and Truth: On the Work of René Girard*, ed. Paul Dumouchel and Jean-Pierre Dupuy (Stanford: Stanford University Press, 1988) and my forthcoming *The Role of the Sacred and the Divine in Hominization and Cultural Evolution: An Engagement with René Girard's Mimetic Theory*.

17. Arnaldo Momigliano, *Alien Wisdom: The Limits of Hellenization* (Cambridge: Cambridge University Press, 1975), p. 11.

18. Leo Strauss, *Jerusalem and Athens: Some Preliminary Reflections* (New York: City College, 1967).

19. Leo Strauss, "The Testament of Spinoza," 1932, *The Early Writings, 1921–1932*, trans. and ed. Michael Zank (Albany: SUNY Press, 2002), pp. 216–223, quotes 221.

20. Ibid., pp. 220–221.

21. Leo Strauss is a philosopher who is often misunderstood, especially in his analyses of the political, for which he is best known. Corine Pelluchon's *Leo Strauss: une autre raison, d'autres lumières: essai sur la crise de la rationalité contemporaine* [*Leo Strauss: Another Reason, Another Enlightenment. An Essay on the Crisis of Contemporary Rationality*] (Paris: Librairie Philosophique J. Vrin, 2005) is an excellent presentation of this multifaceted oeuvre, its major orientations, the exemplary honesty of its questioning, and its difficulties.

It is unfortunate that Strauss seems not to have had access to the cabalistic authors other than rather superficially by way of Gershom Scholem's historical studies. He might have found elements there of a premodern (or postmodern?) symbolic rationality unencumbered by the "foundations of religion" without however renouncing the Law and its ritual, which are at the center of its practices.

22. Plato, *Apology*, trans. Georges Maximilian Antoine Grube, *Complete Works*, pp. 17–36, here 21a–23b, pp. 21–23.

23. Heraclitus, *The Art and Thought of Heraclitus: An Edition of the Fragments with Translation and Commentary*, ed. and trans. Charles H. Kahn (Cambridge: Cambridge University Press, 1979), frag. XXXIII.

24. See, for example, Jean-Pierre Vernant, Léon Vandermeersch, Jacques Gernet, Jean Bottéro, Roland Crahay, Luc Brisson, Jeanne Carlier, Denise Grodzynski,

and Anne Retel-Laurentin, *Divination et Rationalité* [*Divination and Rationality*] (Paris: Éditions du Seuil, 1974) and Raymond Bloch, *La divination dans l'Antiquité* [*Divination in Antiquity*] (Paris: Presses Universitaires de France, 1984).

25. *SRI*, pp. 158–162 and 189–195.

26. Leo Strauss, "The Philosophical Grounding of Law," in *Philosophy and Law: Essays Toward the Understanding of Maimonides and His Predecessors*, trans. Fred Baumann (Philadelphia: Jewish Publication Society, 1987), p. 103 [emendation HA].

27. See, for example, this fragment of Heraclitus preserved by Sextus Empiricus: "Now it is this common and divine reason, by participating in which we become rational, that Heraclitus proposes as the criterion of truth" (*Against the Mathematicians*, VII.131, Appendix IIB, in Kahn, ed., *The Art and Thought of Heraclitus*, p. 294).

28. See André-Jean Festugière, *La Révélation d'Hermès Trismégiste* [*The Revelation of Hermès Trismégiste*] (Paris: Belles Lettres, 2006). On the different connotations—some laudatory, some pejorative—of the term "barbarian" in the Greek authors of late Antiquity and the first Christian authors, see Roger-Pol Droit, *Généalogie des Barbares* [*Genealogy of the Barbarians*] (Paris: Éditions Odile Jacob, 2007).

29. Diogenes Laertius, *Lives of Eminent Philosophers*, trans. R. D. Hicks (Cambridge: Harvard University Press, 1970), Prologue: vol. 1, p. 3.

30. See *EE*, pp. 339–343, and *SRI*, pp. 93–94.

31. Lucretius, *De natura*, I.731:24, III.29–30:73, II:1017–1059, II.658–660:55, III.322:81, and III.314–356:81–82.

32. Cicero, *On Divination: Book 1*, trans. David Wardle (Oxford: Clarendon Press, 2006), ¶129, p. 87 [modified].

33. Ibid., ¶117, p. 83.

34. On this question and on the supposed superiority of "barbarian philosophy" among the Greeks and the Church Fathers in the earliest centuries of the Christian era, see especially Guy G. Stroumsa, *Barbarian Philosophy: The Religious Revolution of Early Christianity* (Tübingen: Mohr Siebeck Verlag, 1999).

35. BT, Baba Batra, 12a.

36. See Droit, *Généalogie des Barbares*, pp. 93-229.

37. Flavius Josephus, *Against Apion*, *Josephus* vol. 1, Loeb Classical Library (New York: G. P. Putnam's Sons, 1926), book I, sect. 22, l. 179, p. 235.

38. Flavius Josephus, *The Jewish War*, trans. H. St. J. Thackeray, vol. 2 of *Josephus*, Loeb Classical Library (Cambridge: Harvard University Press, 1927), bk. II, ch. viii, sects. 1–2, p. 369 [modified].

39. Ibid., sect. 2, p. 369 [modified].

40. For a bibliography and a discussion of these questions, see *EE*, ch. 8, pp. 337–348, and *SRI*, pp. 93 and 192–194.

41. Jean Pierre Vernant, "La formation de la pensée positive dans la Grèce ar-

chaïque" ["The Formation of Positive Thinking in Archaic Greece"], *La Grèce ancienne* [*Ancient Greece*], vol. 1, *Du mythe à la raison* [*From Myth to Reason*], ed. Jean Pierre Vernant; Pierre Vidal-Naquet (Paris: Éditions du Seuil, 1990), pp. 226–227.

42. *SR1*, ch. 5.

43. Renée Koch, *Comment peut-on être dieu? La secte d'Epicure* [*How Can One Be God? The Sect of Epicurus*] (Paris: Éditions Belin, 2005).

44. Cicero, *On Divination*, ¶3, p. 46.

45. We know how much the question of the nature of causality has occupied philosophical reflection since antiquity, especially among the Stoics and the Scholastics. (Moreover, it continues to be raised in contemporary physics and biology.) In Spinoza we find, obviously in a quite different context, a distant echo of this double divine causality: the immanent causality of *natura naturans* in every individual's *conatus* and the efficient causality transmitted through the infinite chain of causes and effects.

46. Plato, *Timaeus*, trans. Donald J. Zeyl, *Complete Works*, pp. 1224–1291, here 71e–72b, pp. 1272–1273 [modified].

47. Plutarch, *The E at Delphi* [*De E apud Delphos*], *Moralia*, vol. 5, trans. Frank Cole Babbitt (Cambridge: Harvard University Press, 1936) 385c, p. 203.

48. Lucretius, *De natura*, I.731:24

49. Plutarch, *The Oracles at Delphi No Longer Given in Verse* [*De Pythiae oraculis*], *Moralia*, vol. 5, trans. Frank Cole Babbitt (Cambridge: Harvard University Press, 1936), section 8, p. 279.

50. Plutarch, *The Obsolescence of Oracles* [*De defectu oraculorum*], *Moralia*, vol. 5, trans. Frank Cole Babbitt (Cambridge: Harvard University Press, 1936), section 48, 436d–437a, pp. 491–493 [modified].

51. Ibid., section 20, 420f–421a, p. 409.

52. Plutarch, *De Pythiae oraculis*, ibid., sections 23–24, 405d–406f, pp. 321–329 [emphasis added].

53. Psalm 85:12; for the *Mishnah*'s interpretation of this psalm, see *EE*, ch. 9, "Naked Truth," note 9.3, p. 402.

54. BT, Sotah, 16a, trans. A. Cohen (1985), pt. 3 vol. 6.

55. BT, 'Abodah Zarah, 4a.

56. *Pirkei Avot* 2:8 and the Maharal of Prague's commentary *Derekh Hayyim*.

57. BT, Sukkah, 27b and 28a.

58. *Pirkei Avot* 2.

59. BT, 'Abodah Zarah, 16b–17a.

60. Deuteronomy 23:19.

61. Micah 1:7.

62. See, for example, BT, 'Abodah Zarah, 23a–24a, where he seeks to prohibit the purchase of animals from idolaters for sacrifice at the Temple in Jerusalem.

63. Midrash Rabba on Ecclesiastes, *Kohelet Rabba* I.8:3 and 4.

64. See chapter 5.

65. See Dan, *Ancient Jewish Mysticism*.
66. BT, Sukkah, 27b and 28a.
67. BT, Sanhedrin, 68a.
68. We know he died a martyr in Rome.
69. BT, Sanhedrin, 68a.
70. Numbers 11:4–5.
71. BT, Berakhot, 57b.
72. BT, Shabbat, 13b.
73. Ibid., 153b.
74. Exodus 22:17; Leviticus 20:27.
75. BT, Sanhedrin, 65b and 68b.
76. See also Nahmanides's commentary and the discussion between Rabbi Shimon bar Yochai (the presumed author of the Zohar) and his son Rabbi Elazar, which was reported in the *Tikunei Zohar*, about the differences between the magical manipulations of numbers and letters that are allowed within a unifying perspective and the magical manipulations of idolators, which are obviously forbidden although they appear to be identical to the former (*SR1*, pp. 57–59 and 172–173).
77. Emmanuel Lévinas, "From the Sacred to the Holy: Five New Talmudic Readings," in *Nine Talmudic Readings*, trans. Annette Aronowicz (Bloomington and Indianapolis: Indiana University Press, 1990), Preface, pp. 91–93, and ch. 3: "Desacralization and Disenchantment: Tractate *Sanhedrin* 67a–68a," pp. 136–160.
78. Ibid., p. 141.
79. Ibid., p. 159.
80. "I have always asked myself if holiness, that is, separation or purity, the essence without admixture that can be called Spirit and which animates the Jewish tradition—or to which the Jewish tradition aspires—can dwell in a world that has not been desacralized. I have asked myself—and that is the real question—whether the world is sufficiently desacralized to receive such purity" (ibid., p. 141).
81. Ibid., p. 152.
82. Ibid., p. 153.
83. Ibid., p. 141, emphasis in the original.
84. Ibid., p. 153, emphasis in the original.
85. Ibid., p. 152.
86. Ibid., p. 149.
87. See above, notes 75 and 76 in this chapter.
88. Lévinas, "From the Sacred to the Holy," pp. 147–148.
89. Cf. ibid., pp. 140–141.
90. Ibid., p. 145.
91. Ibid., p. 141.
92. Ibid., p. 149.
93. "Be removed [*prushim*, from which the word "Pharisees" is derived] from

nudities [*arayos*, "sexual immorality"] and from transgression, for wherever you find restriction of nudity mentioned in the Torah, you find a separation [*kedushah*]" (*Perush Rashi*, eds. Herczeg, Petroff, and Kamenetzky, p. 226 [modified]).

94. In this verse, the subject speaking in the first person, *ani*, "I," is not followed by the verb *to be*, "am," that is always implied in the present. It can thus be read as a third person, "is," also implied; the word *ani* will then be read as a noun: "the 'I' [is] sacred." This also applies to the conclusion of the verse, "I [am] YHVH," which is a curious expression, too, when you think about it, if it is read, as it most often is, as "I am God" or "I am the Eternal" or some other expression along those lines. What is the meaning of a god who speaks and says "I am God"? This may or may not be obvious to the person who hears it but it does not add anything, in any case. Elsewhere, I have discussed how this expression is meaningful when it, too, is read literally, as "I [is] YHVH." Just as in cabalistic typology, the "I," *ani*, refers to the *presence* of the name of the being thus associated with what I have called a "god of persons" (cf. *SR2*, ch. 5, "The God of Persons and the Form of the Human Body," pp. 125–163).

CHAPTER 8

1. *Midrash Rabba, Bereshit*, ch. 8, and Psalm 85:12. See *EE*, ch. 9.
2. BT, Sanhedrin, 97a.
3. Cf. *EE*, ch. 9.
4. Edward L. Bernays, *Propaganda* (New York: Horace Liveright, 1928). http://www.historyisaweapon.com/defcon1/bernprop.html
5. Bernays, *Propaganda*, ch. III, pp. 34–35.
6. Edward S. Herman and Noam Chomsky, *Manufacturing Consent: The Political Economy of the Mass Media* (New York: Pantheon, 1988).
7. Noam Chomsky, "On Propaganda," Interview on WBAI Radio, New York City, January 1992, http://www.chomsky.info/interviews/199201—.htm
8. Larry Tye, *The Father of Spin: Edward L. Bernays and the Birth of Public Relations* (New York: Hotland, 2002), p. 156.
9. Herbert Marcuse, *One-Dimensional Man: Studies in the Ideology of Advanced Industrial Society* (Boston: Beacon Press, 1964).
10. Tye, *The Father of Spin*, pp. 77ff.
11. Bernays, *Propaganda*, ch. II, p. 20.
12. Ibid.
13. Ibid., ch. I, p. 9.
14. Quoted in ibid., ch. II, p. 22, emphasis added.
15. Ibid.
16. Ibid., ch. II, p. 25.
17. Ibid., ch. XI, p. 150.
18. Ibid., ch. IV, p. 52, emphasis added.

19. Ibid., ch. IV, p. 54, emphasis added.
20. *SR2*, ch. 2, section 8, pp. 43–45.
21. Bernays, *Propaganda*, ch. XI, p. 159.
22. Sheldon Rampton and John Stauber, *L'Industrie du mensonge*, heavily updated and with a supplement by Roger Lenglet for the French translation, trans. Yves Coleman (Marseille: Agone, 2004).
23. In the two large volumes of his *Dictionnaire critique de la communication* (Paris: Presses Universitaires de France, 1993), Lucien Sfez and a multitude of additional authors allow us to see how a variety of different sciences and technologies have become intertwined with what Sfez, as early as 1993, analyzes as the beginnings of a new religion.
24. See Tye, *The Father of Spin*, pp. 77ff.
25. [In her segment *On ne nous dit pas tout* on the television show *Vivement Dimanche*—trans.]
26. Ronn Torossian, founder (2002) of the Los Angeles Agency 5WPR [Who, what, where, when, why? Public Relations], "Speedy Torrossian [sic]," interview with Avihu Kadosh for the EL AL in-flight magazine *Atmosphere*, November 2008, pp. 48–50, http://www.5wpr.net/?p=561.
27. Caroline Fourest, *La tentation obscurantiste* [*The Obscurantist Temptation*] (Paris: Grasset, 2005).
28. Fourest subtly analyzes how the progressive left is split into two attitudes. On the one hand, there is an attitude that prioritizes the Third World, which leads to an acceptance or willful ignorance of the risk of totalitarianism as the price of subversion and revolution—like those who used to tolerate the Stalinist "dictatorship of the proletariat." For others, who have learned from this history and the history of the pacifist left as it faced Hitler, the priority is to be sensitive to the dangers of a third totalitarianism that would repeat the freedom-quashing catastrophes, including their anti-Semitic elements, of the preceding two.
29. Gilles Kepel, *The Revenge of God: The Resurgence of Islam, Christianity, and Judaism in the Modern World*, 1991, trans. Alan Braley (University Park: Penn State University Press, 1994).
30. John Micklethwait and Adrian Wooldridge, *God is Back: How the Global Revival of Faith is Changing the World* (New York: Penguin Press, 2009).
31. The exceptions are the coercive measures and peacekeeping missions that fall under the jurisdiction of the United Nations Security Council, which is controlled by its permanent members and their veto power.
32. Guy Debord, *The Society of the Spectacle*, 1967, trans. Donald Nicholson-Smith (New York: Zone Books, 1994), p. 9 (emphasis in the original).
33. A very clear summary of these debates and their political implications can be found in Daniel Vernet, "Rétrocontroverse: 2001, le 11 Septembre et la guerre des civilisations" ["Retrocontroversy: 2001, the 11th of September and the War of Civilizations"], *Le Monde*, 24 Aug 2007.

34. Arthur Koestler, "The Fraternity of Pessimists," *The Yogi and the Commissar and Other Essays* (New York: Macmillan, 1967), p. 100; qtd. in Vernet, "Rétrocontroverse."

35. See Spinoza's response to Alfred Burgh above, at the end of ch. 1.

36. Pierre Duhem, *Aim and Structure of Physical Theory*, 1914, trans. Philip P. Wiener (Princeton: Princeton University Press, 1954).

37. See Atlan, "Underdetermination of Theories by Facts," trans. Nils F. Schott, *SW*, ch. 6, pp. 172–176.

38. Erwin Chargaff, *Heraclitean Fire: Sketches from a Life before Nature* (New York: Rockefeller University Press, 1978).

39. Ibid., p. 103.

40. Ibid., p. 191.

41. For a more detailed critique, see my preface to the French edition of Chargaff's book.

42. A detailed analysis of these malfunctions can be found as early as May 31, 1995, in the opinion issued by the French National Advisory Committee on the Ethics of the Life Sciences and of Medicine on the "Ethical Questions Arising From the Transmission of Scientific Information Concerning Research in Biology and Medicine" (http://www.ccne-ethique.fr/docs/en/avis045.pdf). Since then, and despite repeated bouts of growing awareness and attempts at correction, the developments that were criticized then have profited from the new possibilities of all-out communication offered by the Internet, among other channels.

43. See note 42 in this chapter, just above.

44. See Brian C. Martinson, Melissa S. Anderson, and Raymond de Vries, "Scientists Behaving Badly," *Nature* 435 (9 June 2005), pp. 737–738.

45. Examples include Lynn Payne, *Disease-Mongers: How Doctors, Drug Companies and Insurers Are Making You Feel Sick* (New York: Wiley, 1992); Philippe Pignarre, *Comment la dépression est devenue une épidémie* [*How Depression Became an Epidemic*] (Paris: La Découverte, 2001); David Healy, *The Anti-Depressant Era* (Cambridge: Harvard University Press, 1997); Jörg Blech, *Inventing Disease and Pushing Pills: Pharmaceutical Companies and the Medicalisation of Normal Life*, trans. Gisela Wallor Hajjar (London and New York: Routledge, 2006); and Christopher Lane, *Shyness: How Normal Behavior Became a Sickness* (New Haven: Yale University Press, 2007).

46. Vince Parry, "The Art of Branding a Condition," *Medical Marketing and Media*, May 2003, pp. 43–49, quote p. 46.

47. Cf. the section on the uses and abuses of statistics and probability in medicine and in biology in *SR2*, ch. 8.

48. See *SR2* for a review of different kinds of interpretive errors that are, nonetheless, among those most commonly encountered in the specialized scientific literature, along with critiques of them in the same literature.

49. Among other studies of the subject, see Sauveur Boukris, *Ces médicaments*

qui nous rendent malades: Sauver des vies, faire des économies [*These Drugs That Make Us Sick: Saving Lives, Saving Money*] (Paris: Le Cherche midi, 2009).

50. See, for example, François Meyer, *La Surchauffe de la croissance: Essai sur la dynamique de l'évolution* [*The Overheating of Growth: An Essay on the Dynamics of Evolution*] (Paris: Librairie Arthème Fayard, 1974), and Jacques Robin, *De la croissance économique au développement humain* [*From Economic Growth to Human Development*] (Paris: Éditions du Seuil, 1975).

51. Donella H. Meadows, Dennis L. Meadows, Jørgen Randers, and William W. Behrens, *The Limits to Growth: A Report for the Club of Rome's Project on the Predicament of Mankind* (New York: Universe Books, 1972).

52. Among other specialists who contest the IPCC conclusions, see for example David Satterthwaite (himself a former member of the IPCC), "Adaptation Options for Infrastructure in Developing Countries" (http://unfccc.int/files/cooperation_and_support/financial_mechanism/application/pdf/satterthwaite.pdf), a report of the International Institute for Environment and Development (London), which summarizes the contributions to a discussion organized by the Rockefeller Foundation on how resilience to climate change in urban areas can be built. See also Bjørn Lomborg (*Cool It: The Skeptical Environmentalist's Guide to Global Warming* [New York: Knopf, 2007]) on how the peoples of different countries that are already facing underdevelopment consider the threats connected with climate change differently. But there, too, the choice of priorities depends to a large extent on the force and the success of the public relations employed in the service of each priority.

53. Among the authors in France who rebel against eco-conformity, let us mention Christian Gerondeau, *Écologie: La grande arnarque* [*Ecology: The Great Scam*] (Paris: Éditions Albin Michel, 2007) and Jean de Kervasdoué, *Les prêcheurs de l'apocalypse: Pour en finir avec les délires écologiques et sanitaires* [*The Preachers of the Apocalypse: Putting an End to the Ecology and Public Health Madness*] (Paris: Éditions Plon, 2007). These authors do not contest the reality of current climate changes, but they bring a welcome critical spirit to bear on the politically correct consensus about the catastrophes to come, the main reasons for these catastrophes, and the remedies often suggested in the name of the all-too-well-known precautionary principle. I have already denounced this principle as one that destroys itself because it is potentially dangerous and as a principle of which prudence counsels us to be wary, and I have to approve of Jean de Kervasdoué's diagnosis: "The most profound failure of this precautionary principle, its original sin, is a sin of pride. It lets us believe that we could prepare ourselves for everything because we would always be able to detect the cause of a potential catastrophe." We may add Gil Rivière-Wekstein's *Abeilles: l'imposture écologique* [*Bees: The Ecological Fraud*] (Paris: Le Publieur, 2006), an inquiry into the matter of the "confounded" insecticides, with a preface by a former president of the French Honey Producers' Union, who recommends reading the book to "un-

derstand how, through simplifications and bad faith, the false can settle in and chase out the true."

CONCLUSION

1. See François Rachline's subtle commentary on this story, "Shylock et l'argent" ["Shylock and Money"] (*Théâtre public*, 4th trimester 1995), which shows that the stakes of the trial are not as simple as they seem. In this text, Shylock appears, among other things, as a pioneer discovering the laws of modern economics, ahead of his time and persecuted for that reason.

2. These mechanisms are the subject of a famous conjecture by the cyberneticist Heinz von Foerster, formalized in what I have called Foerster-Dupuy's Theorem; cf. Moshe Koppel, Henri Atlan, and Jean-Pierre Dupuy, "Von Foerster's Conjecture: Trivial Machines and Alienation in Systems," *International Journal of General Systems*, vol. 13 (1987), pp. 257–264, and *TNP*, ch. 1.

3. On these questions, see, in particular, Alexandre Matheron, *Individu et communauté chez Spinoza* [*The Individual and Community in Spinoza*] (Paris: Les Éditions de Minuit, 1969) and Bove, *La stratégie du conatus*.

Name Index

Aaron, 111
Abbahu, Rabbi, 145
Abraham, Karl, 31
Adam, 44, 71, 110, 114
Akiba, Rabbi, 94, 146, 148, 154
Amos, 115, 116
Antoninus Pius, Emperor, 149
Apollo, 129–30, 133, 136–37, 141–42
Aquinas, Thomas, 50
Arafat, Yasser, 176
Arendt, Hannah, 26
Aristotle, 43, 44, 46, 50, 55, 62, 81, 138, 163
Assad, Hafez al-, 176
Augustine, Saint, 43, 71, 74

Bacon, Francis, 73
Bergson, Henri, 224*n*7
Bernays, Edward, 164–75, 188, 191, 196, 198
Brandom, Robert, 16
Brindisi, Lorenzo da, 44–45
Bruno, Giordano, 71
Bush, George W., 175, 182

Cain, 9, 71
Calvin, John, 52
Castoriadis, Cornelius, 122
Chargaff, Erwin, 187, 191, 201
Chomsky, Noam, 165, 171
Cicero, 133, 138
Cohen, Hermann, 128
Confucius, 2, 27
Copernicus, 71
Curie, Marie, 188

Davidson, Donald, 16
Debord, Guy, 180
De Roo, Pierre, 212*n*18
Derrida, Jacques, 16, 43, 62

Dewey, John, 21
Diogenes Laertius, 132
Dupuy, Jean-Pierre, 122, 123, 127, 217*n*28
Durkheim, Émile, 122

Eichmann, Adolf, 26
Einstein, Albert, 188
Eisenhower, Dwight, 166, 175
Elazar, Rabbi, 115
Eleazar ben Arakh, Rabbi, 145–46
Eliezer ben Hyrcanus, Rabbi, 85–91, 94–95, 97, 136, 144–51, 155–59
Engel, Pascal, 17–18
Epicurus, 132, 138, 140
Eve, 71, 110

Foucault, Michel, 43, 62
Fourest, Caroline, 177, 227*n*28
France, Pierre Mendès, 175
Franco, Francisco, 166
Freud, Sigmund, 15, 164–65

Gamliel, Rabban, 88, 94–95
Gerondeau, Christian, 232*n*53
Girard, René, 69, 122, 127
Godelier, Maurice, 122
Goebbels, Joseph, 161, 162, 164
Gore, Al, 198
Gorz, André, 55
Gustafson, Thomas, 62–64, 126, 161

Hanina, Rabbi, 150, 153
Heidegger, Martin, 70–73, 77
Heraclitus, ix, 130, 138, 207
Hillel the Elder, 30, 48, 149, 216*n*14
Hisda, Rav, 96, 115
Hitler, Adolf, 161, 162, 163, 176
Hobbes, Thomas, 62, 63, 123

236 Name Index

Hölderlin, Friedrich, 72
Homer, 135, 143
Hosea, 29
Humboldt, Wilhelm von, 43
Hyrcanus, Eliezer ben, 40

Ildefonse, Frédérique, 138–39
Ima-Shalom, 95–96
Isaiah (prophet), 8
Ishmael, Rabbi, 144, 149

James, William, 16, 17
Jankélévitch, Vladimir, 9, 12–13, 18, 120
Jaynes, Julian, 135
Jeremiah (prophet), 112
Jeremiah, Rabbi, 87, 92
Johanan ben Zakkai, Rabbi, 145, 148
Joseph, 114
Josephus, Flavius, 127, 134–35
Joshua, Rabbi, 87–88, 90–91, 147, 148, 150

Kant, Immanuel, 8–10
Kepel, Gilles, 178
Kepler, Johannes, 71
Kervasdoué, Jean de, 232*n*53
Koch, Renée, 137
Koestler, Arthur, 185
Kripke, Saul, 16
Kuriyama, Shigehisa, 65–67

Le Goff, Jacques, 52
Lévinas, Emmanuel, 151–54
Locke, John, 62
Lucretius, 132
Luria, Isaac, 85

Machiavelli, Niccolò, 9, 129
Maharal of Prague, 89
Maimonides, Moses, 110, 129
Mao Zedong, 179
Marcuse, Herbert, 62, 166
Marty, Mireille Delmas, 36
Marx, Karl, 15, 54
McKinley, William, 167
McLuhan, Marshall, 172
Micah, 146
Micklethwait, John, 178
Mitterrand, François, 163
Momigliano, Arnaldo, 127
Montaigne, Michel de, 62

Moses, 90–92, 94, 111, 157

Nasser, Gamal Abdel, 176
Nathan, Rabbi, 88, 97
Nestor, 130
Nietzsche, Friedrich, 15, 19–21, 177

Obama, Barack, 167, 174–75
Olender, Maurice, 43–45, 68, 119
Oresme, Nicole, 43, 119
Orléan, André, 217*n*28
Orpheus, 63, 126

Paracelsus, 71
Parmenides, 19
Pascal, Blaise, 15
Pasteur, Louis, 188
Paul, Saint, 157
Peirce, Charles, 16
Pico della Mirandola, Giovanni, 31
Plato, 9, 12, 15, 16, 19, 22, 62, 129, 131–32, 137–40, 206, 207
Plutarch, 130, 136–44, 157, 159
Poe, Edgar Allan, 165
Popper, Karl, 190
Proclus, 138
Protagoras, 22
Putnam, Hilary, 16, 21
Pythagoras, 126, 130, 132, 138

Rachline, François, 53, 56, 58
Rashi, 38, 105, 155
Redfield, James, 135
Reik, Theodor, 31
Rivière-Wekstein, Gil, 232*n*53
Robin, Jacques, 55
Rocard, Michel, 175
Rorty, Richard, 16–18
Roumanoff, Anne, 173

Safra, Rav, 145
Sartre, Jean-Paul, 14
Saussure, Ferdinand de, 43
Shakespeare, William, 204
Shammai, 149
Shannon, C. E., 54
Shimon, Rabbi, 117
Simondon, Gilbert, 70, 75–78, 80
Smith, Adam, 54
Socrates, 22, 128–30

Name Index

Spinoza, Baruch, 4, 8, 10–12, 19, 23, 37, 110, 129, 131, 178, 185, 206, 207
Stalin, Joseph, 176
Starobinski, Jean, 45, 68
Steiner, Michael, 31
Strauss, Leo, 128–29, 131, 206–7, 225n21

Tarfon, Rabbi, 101
Tertullian, 60
Thucydides, 63, 126, 161
Turgot, Anne-Robert-Jacques, 43

Ulysses, 130

Vernant, Jean-Pierre, 136
Vital, Hayyim, 38

Weber, Max, 52
Williams, Bernard, 17–18
Wilson, Woodrow, 164
Winter, Jean-Pierre, 31
Wittgenstein, Ludwig, 21–23, 205
Wooldridge, Adrian, 178

Yehuda HaNasi, Rabbi, 149
Yunus, Muhammad, 59

Subject Index

Abodah Zarah, 145
Aborigines, 60, 132
Abraham, 113
Absolute truth, 16–18, 21, 42, 80, 130, 144–45, 156–59, 206. *See also* Revealed truth
Advertising, 171
Advice, quality of, 38, 42
Almost-fraud, 57
Altruism, 61
American Indians, 132
'Amit (fellow), 28, 33, 96–97
Analytic philosophy, 16–18, 21
Angels, 12, 14, 158
Animals, 3, 6
Anticolonialism, 177
Antiglobalization movement, 177
Antiracism, 177, 179
Anti-Semitism, 162, 179
Asilomar conference, 188
Assembly of Sages. *See* Great Assembly
Athens, Jerusalem vs., 126–29
Atrocities, 15, 26
Attention deficit hyperactivity disorder, 194–95

Babylonian Talmud, 48, 49, 145
Bad faith, 12–14, 38, 42, 117
Balance, of purity and impurity/rigidity and dissolution, 2, 12–14, 32, 82–83, 121, 158–59, 203–5
Banking, 52–54
Base six, 104–5
Base ten, 105
Beat Generation, 166
Being: construction of, 106–9; meanings of, 19; measurement of, 117; quantification of, 106, 114; unity and multiplicity of, 119–20

Bible, 8–9, 46, 145
Biomedicine, 191–96
Biotechnology, 73, 76, 187–88
Bipolar disorder, 194
Black Americans, 166
Bodily injuries, 39
Body, the: divisions of, 106–8, 110–11; in Japan, 65–66; knowledge and, 110–13; money and, 65–66
Book of Kings, 88
"Book of Modesty" (*Sifra ditsni'uta*), 111, 213n37
Broken vessels, 83, 85–97
Bubbles, economic, 50, 54, 56
Buddhism, 125, 178

Cabalist tradition, 104, 106–14, 117. *See also* Kabbalah
Cancellation of transactions, due to fraud, 2, 41, 100–101, 103, 113
Capitalism: development of, 50; in information age, 55–56; Protestantism and, 52
Carob trees, 87, 90
Casuistry, 13, 19
Catholic Church, 50–52
Causality and correlation, 195
Central Intelligence Agency (CIA), 166, 179
Certainty, 21–22, 193, 207–8
Christianity: anti-Semitism in, 162; development of, 127–28, 157; Eliezer and, 86, 146–47; as religion, 127–28
Circle of value, 10–12, 20, 23, 70, 130
Circumcision, 109–14
Civil Rights Movement, 166
Clash of civilizations, 183–85
Climate change, 198–200, 232n53
Clothing, 110

Club of Rome, 196, 197
Coins, 44, 46
Commercial exchanges: exchanges concerning being as model for, 114; ona'ah applicable to, 1–2, 24, 30, 33; rules governing, 116–17; as specifically human, 4, 39; truth necessary to, 10; verbal exchanges compared to, 40–41, 98–99. *See also* Money
Commercial fraud: defined, 33; intention in, 37–38; as paradigm, 41; verbal fraud compared to, 106, 203–4
Commercial injuries: defined, 33; measuring, 11, 37–38, 41; verbal injuries compared to, 41, 203–4
Commission on Human Rights (United Nations), 179
Committee on Public Information (United States), 164
Communications consultants, 167
Communism, 161–62, 176, 179
Complex systems, modeling of, 186, 193, 200
Conatus, 207
Condition branding, 194
Confucianism, 65, 125
Consciousness, and the experience of the sacred, 61, 124, 125, 131, 132, 135
Conspiracy theories, 173
Consumer society, 64
Contracts, 49, 103
Correlation and causality, 195
Counterfeit money, 5, 10, 11
Counter-propaganda, 165–66, 172
Cowrie shells, 45
Credit, 32, 53–54, 56, 58
Crimes against humanity, 6, 36, 184
Crystallized sacred, 121, 128, 159, 201
Cucumbers, 148–50
Cultural Revolution, 179
Currencies, 44–46, 105

Death: humans and, 71, 74; impurity from connection with, 83, 85; life in relation to, 71, 83, 121
Debts: cancellation of, 46, 48; social significance of, 67
Deception. *See* Commercial fraud; Fraud; Lying; Verbal fraud
Deconstruction, 16, 21

Definition, essentialist vs. gradualist, 18
Dehumanization, 162
Deliberation period, in questions of ona'ah, 100–102
Delphi, 129–30, 136–38, 142
Democracy: desacralization as factor in, 159; dictatorships vs., 163–66, 177–85, 208; and the economy, 64–65; effectiveness of, 61; and ideology, 64; and language, 62–63; and moral progress, 160; propaganda used by, 163–68, 170–75, 179–85, 208; and the sacred, 64; vulnerability of, to systemic falsehood, 163; war uncommon for, 160, 176; weakness of, 161; worm in the apple of, 63, 163–64, 166
Demonization, 162
Demons, 139
Desacralization: in biblical-to-talmudic transition, 47; democracy as outcome of, 159; of money, 46, 47; of time, 32, 47
Desire: exchange and, 4; Japanese medicine and, 66; mimetic, 69, 79; money and, 61, 64, 66; objects of, 69; and the sacred, 67
Deuteronomy, 50, 146–47, 214n3
Dialectic: interior/subjective–exterior/objective, 116–17; of sacred writing and oral interpretation, 92; of truth and lying, 13
Dictatorships and totalitarianism, 64, 160–66, 171, 176–84, 208, 230n28
Dignity, 6, 9–10, 36–37, 203
Diluted sacred, 121, 124–25, 128, 152, 201
Discourse. *See* Speech
Disease mongering, 193–94
Disenchantment, of modern societies, 125, 185
Divination, 130–33, 138–40
Divine, the. *See* God, gods, and the divine
DNA, 187–88
Doubt: grounds for, 23; truth in relation to, 15
Drash (interpretation), 93
Dreams, 60, 132, 133
Dualism, 27, 124
Durban Conference (2001), 177, 179–80

Ecology, 196–200
Economy: bubbles in, 50, 54, 56;

dematerialization of, 55; democracy and, 64–65; fraud and ordinary functioning of, 56–57; of Japan, 65–66; lending's place in, 47–53; limits in, 58; modern, 47–53, 65–66; as system, 55–59, 217n28; 2008 crisis, 50, 54, 56, 58
Eden. *See* Garden of Eden
Egypt, 176
Election campaigns, 167–68
Enchantment, 151
En-framing, 71, 72–74
Enlightenment, 129, 178
Enthronement, 175
Environmentalism, 177, 196–200
Epicureanism, 130, 132, 136, 137–38, 140–41
Epistemological relativism, 10, 15, 158
Erectile dysfunction, 194
Essence, 15, 16, 18
Essenes, 127, 135
Ethics. *See* Morality and ethics
Ethnobotany, 124, 132
Etz Hayyim, 109–10, 120
Eugenics, 9
Europe, lobbying in, 170
European Social Forum (London, 2004), 177
Evidence-based medicine, 192
Evil: absolute, 184; banality of, 26; conceptions of, 25–27; essence of, 26; in interpersonal relations, 28–29; persistence of, 25–26
Evolution, 3–4
Exchanges: human aspects of, 4; nature of, 3; of objects, 69; social bonds arising from, 2–4, 58, 66–67, 69; social significance of, 2–3; types of, 4. *See also* Commercial exchanges; Interpersonal relations; Speech
Exodus, 32–33

Fair (market) price: determination of, 11, 102; fraud dependent on, 33–34, 41–42, 57, 68, 96, 98–100; usury and, 50–51
Falling on one's face, 95, 221n22
False goods, 12
Famine, 160
Fascism, 161
Fausse monnaie (counterfeit money), 5
Fibromyalgia, 194
Fiducia, 44

Final solution, 26
Forced labor, 160
Foreigners and strangers: as fellows, 33; injuries to, 35; lending to, 51; protection of, 37, 96–97
Foreskin, 111–12, 222n14
Forgiveness, 2, 41, 57, 100
Fraud: and almost-fraud, 57; defined, 4–5; inevitability of, 106; in science, 190–91; threshold of, 57. *See also* Commercial fraud; Verbal fraud
Freedom, 8, 10
Free will, 4
French Revolution, 162, 168
Functional disorders, 193–94
Fundamentalisms, 178
Future: climate change debate and, 198–200; propaganda/promotion/advertising and, 173; vows/oaths and, 31–32

Garden of Eden, 74, 112
Gemara, 49
Gender relations, 29
Genesis, 29, 71, 110, 114
Genetically modified organisms (GMOs), 73, 76, 197
Genocide, 15, 26, 184
Globalization, 160
Global warming, 198–200, 232n53
Glory, 36–37, 110
Gnosticism, 86, 147
God, gods, and the divine: authority (Word) of, 87–89, 91–92; fear of, 34–35, 38, 46; humans' relation to, 138, 140–41; measurement by, 96, 116; nature of, 133; postbiblical Jewish conceptions of, 134; punishment wielded by, 38, 117; relationship to, 32; representations of, 60; YHVH, 107, 113, 117–18, 229n94. *See also* Sacred, the
Golden rule, 2–3, 13, 25, 27–29
Good. *See* False goods; True good
Good faith, 38, 42
Goodwill, 13
Gospel of Luke, 50
Gospel of Matthew, 27, 214n1
Great Assembly, 85, 87, 93, 117
Green economy, 196–98
Group of Eight, 179
Group of Twenty, 179

Subject Index

Halakha (practical decision), 87, 101, 144–45, 149
Half-truths, 62, 170, 185, 204, 208
Hallucinogenic plants, 60, 61, 132
Happiness, 60, 64
Harm: injunctions against, 34–35, 96–97, 99; measuring, 36; to oneself, 97; threshold of, 2. *See also* Commercial injuries; Injury; Townu; Verbal injuries
Heart, 106, 108, 110–11
Hekhalot ("palaces") literature, 147
Hillel school, 149
Hillel's prosbul, 48
Hinduism, 178
Hippies, 166
Holy, the, 151–54
Humanism, 27
Human Rights Council (United Nations), 180
Humans: commerce as peculiar to, 4, 39; crimes against humanity, 6; culture as native to, 124; and death, 71, 74; dualist conception of, 27; ethics of, 3; evil native to, 25–26; injuries peculiar to, 39; as makers, 70; price of, 115; properties and activities peculiar to, 3–4, 6, 27; and the sacred, 60; the sacred as peculiar to, 123; signification as peculiar to, 44–45; and society, 207; speech as peculiar to, 4, 39; technology as peculiar to, 4, 70, 74, 75–76; violence supposed essential to, 123–24
Humiliation, 2, 6, 35, 37, 97, 203
Hurt. *See* Harm
Husbands, 29
Hypocrisy, 12

I Ching, 125
Imaginary, the, 122
Impurity, 83, 85–86. *See also* Balance, of purity and impurity/rigidity and dissolution
India, 134
Individuals, and the social bond, 59–60, 206–7
Inflation, 56, 82
Information: machines' use of, 77–80; propaganda and, 161–75; value- and meaning-free, 54–55; vehicles of, 44–45
Information age, 55–56, 77–80
Inhumanity, 37

Injuria, 5, 24, 30
Injury: hierarchy of, 39; minimizing of, 106; ona'ah and, 32–33; scope of, 5, 30. *See also* Bodily injuries; Commercial injuries; Harm; Verbal injuries
Intention: attribution of guilt dependent on, 38; fraud occurring despite absence of, 37–38; impossibility of determining, 38–39, 41; injuries occurring despite absence of, 94–95
Interest, on loans, 32, 46–53, 57
Intergovernmental Panel on Climate Change (IPCC), 198, 199
Interior-exterior dialectic, 116
Interiority: dialectic of exteriority and, 99, 116; effects of injury on, 35; inaccessibility of, 38–39, 96, 107, 110; Talmudic Judaism and, 41
International tribunals, 184
Internet, 174
Interpersonal relations: evil in, 28–29; golden rule and, 2–3, 27–29; starting point of, 30. *See also* Exchanges; Social bond
Interpres, 45
Interpretation: contextual influences on, 92; of hidden meanings, 109; significance of, 92–93; Talmud and, 89, 214n6; violence of, 93–94
Intrinsic value, 82–83
"Invisible government," 165, 168, 171, 172
IPCC. *See* Intergovernmental Panel on Climate Change
Iraq, 176
Ish (husband), 29
Isha (wife), 29
Islam, 49–50, 128, 176–78, 182–83
Israel, 180, 181, 183

Japan, 65–66
Jerusalem, Athens vs., 126–29
Jews, and money lending, 51
Judaism: anti-Semitism and, 162, 179; Eliezer and, 144–51; major sects of, 135; postbiblical, 127, 128, 134, 144–56, 157

Kabbalah, 74, 147, 204; Lurianic, 38, 108, 118. *See also* Cabalist tradition
Kadosh (sacred, holy), 153
Kaved (honor), 37

Kavod (glory), 37
Knock (film), 193
Knowledge: and the body, 110–13; divine source of, 140; epistemological relativism, 10, 15, 158; Spinoza's method concerning, 23; truth in relation to, 19–21. *See also* Truth
Knowledge society, 55–56
Kol Nidre ritual, 31–32

Land sales, 100, 103
Language: ambivalent nature of, 30–31; democracy and, 62–63; false uses of, 30; internal and external aspects of, 61; money in relation to, 34, 43–45, 58, 68, 119–20; of oracles, 141; perversion of, 63, 126, 161–63, 179–82, 193–94; power and, 62; signification and reference in, 22–23; technical objects in relation to, 70. *See also* Speech
Latin America, 176, 179
Law: autonomy vs. heteronomy of, 205, 207; Christianity and, 157; on earth vs. in heaven, 204–5; in Judaism, 157; morality vs., 9, 10; sages as arbiters of, 88
Left, progressive, 230n28
Leviticus, 27, 28, 30, 32–34, 155, 214n1
Lex talionis, 39, 204
Liberation theology, 177
Life: death in relation to, 71, 83, 121; impurity in relation to, 85–86; right to, 36; value of, 10
Limits. *See* Thresholds
Loans: Aristotle on, 46; the Bible on, 46–47; Catholic Church on, 50–52; economic role of, 47–53; interest on, 32, 46–53, 57; Islam on, 49–50; profits linked to, 49–50; Talmud on, 48–49; and time, 32; usury, 50–52
Lobbying: in biomedicine, 191–96; in environmental field, 196–97; and propaganda, 170–71
Logos, 8, 130, 132
Lurianic Kabbalah, 38, 108, 118
Lying: absolute condemnation of, 7–10; acceptance of, 12; disproportionate significance given to, 8, 11; political use of, 9, 184–85; pragmatic conception of, 22; in service of truth, 14. See also Systemic falsehood

Machines, open, 77–80
Magic: Eliezer and, 147–52; philosophy and, 134, 137; and the sacred, 132; science and, 147, 155; technical objects and, 70–71, 75
Majority rule, 87–89, 91–93
Maoism, 162, 166, 179
Marketing consultants, 167
Market price. *See* Fair (market) price
Market research, 167
Marriage, 29
Marxism, 161
Massacres. *See* Atrocities
Mass media, 165, 170
Measure: of commercial injuries, 11, 37–38, 41; value in relation to, 114–20, 204; of verbal injuries, 36, 38, 39, 107, 116, 204. *See also* Weights and measures
Medical ethics, 13
Medicine: in Japan, 65–66; pharmaceutical industry and, 191–96
Merchant of Venice, The (Shakespeare), 204
Meta-truth, 16, 22
Microcredit, 59
Midrash, 115, 147, 158, 213n37
Military-industrial complex, 166
Mimetic desire, 69, 79
Miracles, 40, 87–89, 148
Mishnah, 80–81, 101, 145
Mishnah Baba Mezi'a, ix, 48
Mistakes, 11
Modernity, 126, 129, 178
Modesty, 21, 158
Molecular biology, 187–88
Moneta, 45
Money: and the body, 65–66; circulation of, 47, 52–58, 64–66; credit in relation to, 58; deceptions about, 103; dematerialization of, 44–45, 52–57; and desire, 61, 64, 66; inflation involving, 56; internal and external aspects of, 61; language in relation to, 34, 43–45, 58, 68, 119–20; limits on, 58; in political campaigns, 167–68; sacred character of, 45–46; shame concerning, 64–65, 67; signification and reference of, 22. *See also* Commercial exchanges
Monnaie, 44
Monotheism, 60, 125
Morality and ethics: casuistry in, 13, 19; evolutionary basis of, 3; golden rule, 2–3,

13, 25, 27–29; law vs., 9, 10; local norms and criteria of, 16; philosophical issues underlying, 18; progress in, 159–60; propaganda and, 168–69
Moral relativism, 10, 15, 158
Mount Sinai, 87–88, 90–92, 104
Muslim Brotherhood, 177
Mythology, 126, 133–34
Mythos, 130

Naming, of biomedical conditions, 193–94
Natural catastrophes, 25–26
Nature: Epicureanism on, 138; state of, 123–24; technology in relation to, 70, 72–74, 76–77
Nazism, 161–64, 184, 198
Nedarim (Vows), 31
Neighbors, 28, 96–97
Neoplatonism, 136, 137, 138
Neuropsychiatry, 193–94
Nomisma, 44
North Korea, 176
Numerology, 104–9, 118–19
Nuremberg trials, 184

Oaths, 30–32, 47
Obesity, 194
Office of Research Integrity (United States), 191
Ona'ah: commerce and speech as fields for, 1–2, 24, 30, 33–34; defined, 1–2, 30; and injury, 32–33; one-sixth rule as defining, 100–101, 103, 114; subjective and objective aspects of, 102–3; tolerance in world of, 83, 98, 117, 119, 120; world of, 5, 24, 32, 57, 68, 82–83, 116, 126, 158, 185, 203, 204–5
Ona'at dvarim (ona'ah of words), 2
One-eighteenth of being, 106–9
One-sixth rule, 100–105; considerations in applying, 102–3; methods of applying, 102; ona'ah defined by, 100–101, 103, 114; one-third rule as alternate to, 101; rationale for, 103–9; threshold set by, 41–42, 57, 68, 100, 204, 208; transactions exempt from, 100, 103
Oracles, 129–44
Oral Torah, 91, 157
Organic farming, 196–97
Organizational noise, 78

Other reality, 60–61, 124, 132
Oven of Akhnai, 40, 42, 84–97, 115, 144

Pacifism, 163
Palestine Liberation Organization, 176
Palestinian Arabs, 181
Pardon, 31
Passions, 8, 10
Perspective taking, 11
Pharisees, 135, 155
Pharmaceutical industry, 191–96
Pharmakon (poison, remedy), 63
Philosophy: analytic school of, 16–18, 21; Plutarch and, 136–44; and prophecy, 130–33, 137, 139–40; as search for wisdom, 129–30; and technology, 76; and truth, 14–22, 212n18. *See also* Reason
Plumb line, 96, 115–16
Politics: ecology and, 196–200; language use in, 62–63; lying in, 9
Postmodernity, 126
Power: language and, 62; in social relations in information age, 79–80
Powers of speech, 22
Pragmatism, 16–19, 21–24
Precautionary principle, 199, 232n53
Price: of land, 100; of persons, 115; value in relation to, 10–11. *See also* Fair (market) price
Pricelessness, 10–11, 114, 120
Progress, 159–60
Progressive left, 230n28
Promises, 30–32, 47
Propaganda, 161–75; ancient instances of, 161; connotations of, 168; counter-, 165–66, 172; democracies' use of, 163–68, 170–75, 179–85, 208; dictatorships' use of, 161–64, 179–85; international, 179–82; Internet, 174; lobbying and, 170–71; methods of, 168–69; morality of, 168–69; origins of modern, 164; psychological factors in, 169–70; and spin, 172–73; and truth, 173
Prophets and prophecy, 88, 129–36
Prostitution, 146–47
Protocols of the Elders of Zion, The, 162
Psalms, 7
Public good, 9
Public opinion: democratic uses and manipulation of, 163–68; international, 175–85

Public relations: and environmentalism, 196–98; and propaganda, 164–65, 167, 174; and science, 186–92
Purgatory, 52
Purity. *See* Balance, of purity and impurity/rigidity and dissolution
Pythia, 129, 136–42

Qaeda, al-, 182, 183
Qur'an, 46, 49

Radical Islam, 176–78, 182–83
Randomness, 78
Rashi, 155
Rea' (friend), 28, 33
Re'ah (ra'yah), 29
Realism, 17–18
Reality. *See* Other reality
Reason: and divination, 139–40; faith vs., 126–29; and mythology, 133–34; and the passions, 10; and society, 61; technology and, 70–71. *See also* Philosophy
Redress: cabalistic notion of, 74–75; nature of, 86; for verbal injuries, 38, 39–40
Reductionism, 17–18, 21
Reference, 22–23
Reformation, 52
Relative relativism, 15–16, 158
Relativism. *See* Epistemological relativism; Moral relativism
Religion: Christianity's contribution to, 127–28; modernity and, 178; political manifestations of, 178, 182–83; reason vs., 126–29; the sacred in relation to, 123, 125; science in relation to, 185; technology in relation to, 75
Revealed truth, 14, 15, 131, 138–39, 157–59, 207. *See also* Absolute truth
Rhetoric, 22, 163
Rigveda, 132
Ritalin, 194–95
Rites and ritual, 129
Robotics, 82
Roman Empire, 127, 129, 130, 134–36, 146–47

Sacred, the: degeneration of, 151; democracy and, 64; desire and, 67; experience of, 59–61, 67, 123–25; function of, 121–23, 125; the holy in relation to, 151–54; life associated with, 83; modern remainders of, 151; money as, 45–46; original experiences of, 124–25, 128; religion in relation to, 123, 125; as specifically human, 123; violence and, 121–22. *See also* Crystallized sacred; Desacralization; Diluted sacred; God, gods, and the divine
Sacrifice, 69, 122
Sadducees, 135
Salvation, 60, 64
Sanhedrin, 148, 151
Schoolhouse walls, 87, 90–91
Science: and environmentalism, 197–200; expansion of, 186–87; magic and, 147, 155; and public relations, 186–91; religion in relation to, 185; systematic falsehood in, 185–200; technology in relation to, 70–72, 76; theories and models in, 185–86, 189–90, 200; and totalitarian regimes, 198; and truth, 17–20, 126, 185
Scientific misconduct, 190–91
Sela (currency), 105
Self, and the social bond, 59–60, 206–7
Self-fulfilling prophecies, 173
Self-interest, 28
Self-organizing systems, 55–56, 77–79, 217n28
September 11, 2001 attacks, 183
Sex, 110–13
Shabbat (Sabbath), 80–81
Shamanism, 125, 130–31
Shame, 64–65, 67
Shammai school, 149
Sharia, 49–50
Shoah, 184
Sifra ditsni'uata ("Book of Modesty"), 111
Sinai. *See* Mount Sinai
Sincerity, 12–13
Skepticism, 18
Skin, 110
Slaves and slavery, 81, 103, 160, 181–82
Social bond: breaching of, 66–67; creation of, 43; exchanges as component of, 2–4, 58, 66–67, 69; and the imaginary, 122; individuals' place in, 59–60, 206–7; ona'ah and, 5, 57; reason and, 61; the sacred as stabilizer of, 61, 122–25; solidarity in, 48, 57, 59. *See also* Interpersonal relations

Subject Index

Sociobiology, 61
Sod (hidden meaning), 109–14
Soviet Union, 162, 176, 198
Speech: commercial exchanges compared to, 40–41, 98–99; exchanges concerning being as model for, 114; inflation involving, 56; ona'ah applicable to, 1–2, 24, 30, 33; powers of, 22; pragmatic conception of, 23–24; as specifically human, 4, 39. *See also* Language
Spin and spin doctors, 172–73
State of nature, 123–24
Statistics, 195
Stoicism, 8, 132, 135, 136, 141
Strangers. *See* Foreigners and strangers
Streams, 87, 90
Students of the Sages, 14, 88, 134, 213n37
Subjective-objective dialectic, 116–17
Syria, 176
Systemic falsehood, 2, 32, 63, 121, 126, 152, 159–202; and international public opinion, 175–85; propaganda, 161–75; in science, 185–200

Talmud: Babylonian, 48, 49, 145; on commercial exchanges, 57; cucumbers in, 149; interpretive character and purpose of, 89, 214n6; legends of, 14, 89; on loans, 48–49; method of, 33; ona'ah in, 1, 5, 32–33; and one-sixth rule, 104–5, 107; Oven of Akhnai, 85–97, 115, 144; philosophical characteristics of, 127; on protection of foreigners/strangers, 37; on technology, 80–81; on threshold of ona'ah, 2, 41–42, 98–99; on values, 114–15; verbal fraud in, 33–35; vows discussed in, 31–32; wise men of, 134
Teachers, 51
Technical objects, 69–83; autonomy of, 73, 78–82; biological, 73, 76; contingency and diversity of, 72, 73, 75; creation of, 23; en-framing by, 71, 72–74; errors and lies of, 70; essence of, 72–75; Heidegger on, 70–73; human context in which used, 79–80; in the information age, 77–80; language in relation to, 70; magical quality of, 70–71, 75; mythic origins of, 71, 74; nature in relation to, 70, 72–74, 76–77; ona'ah applicable to, 2; philosophy and, 76; religion and, 75; Simondon on, 70, 75–78; as specifically human, 4, 70, 74, 75–76; theory in relation to, 70–72, 74–76
Temple of Jerusalem, 37, 48, 83, 95, 144, 146, 157
Terror, the (France), 162
Terrorism, 181
Theory, 70–72, 74–76, 185–86, 189–90, 200
Thresholds, 98–105; in commercial fraud, 68; determination of, 5, 41–42, 203; on interest, 57; talmudic legislation on, 2, 41; in verbal fraud, 42, 68. *See also* One-sixth rule
Thucydidean moment, 63, 126, 161
Tibetan Buddhism, 225n14
Tikkun (redress), 74–75
Time, 32, 47. *See also* Future
Tolerance, in world of ona'ah, 83, 98, 117, 119, 120, 203, 204
Torah, 30, 87–88, 91, 94, 135, 156, 157
Torture, 160
Totalitarianism. *See* Dictatorships and totalitarianism
Townu (hurt), 32–33, 34, 36, 99. *See also* Harm
Treaty of Versailles, 163
Tree of Life and of Knowledge, 71, 74, 112
Trees, 112
True good, 11–12
True ideas, 12
Truth: absolute, 16–18, 21, 40, 82, 130, 144–45, 156–59, 206; atrocities committed in name of, 15, 26; construction of, 14; covering of, 21; dissolution of, 174; divine source of, 131–32; doubt about, 15–17; foundational quality of, 11; "from the earth," 14, 144, 158, 207; knowledge in relation to, 19–21; lethal capacities of, 121; local/empirical, 14, 16, 17; meta-truth, 16, 22; modesty concerning, 21, 158; Nietzsche on, 19–21; philosophy and, 14–22, 212n18; possession of vs. seeking, 14; post-prophetic/oracular relation to, 136; pragmatic conception of, 16–19, 21; propaganda and, 173; revealed, 14, 15, 131, 138–39, 157–59, 207; science and, 17–21, 126, 185; search for, 207–8; as supreme value, 8–11, 16; value in relation to, 10–12, 23. *See also* Knowledge

"Truthful talk" (parler vrai), 175

United Nations, 179–80
United States: and international politics, 182–83; lobbying in, 170; politics and language in, 63
United States Office of Science and Technology Policy, 191
Universal Declaration of Human Rights, 36, 179
Universal Movement for Scientific Responsibility, 188
University lecturers, 51
Use value, 82–83
Usury, 50–52, 57

Value: circle of, 10–12, 20, 23, 70, 130; defining, 10; environmentalism and, 196; intrinsic, 82–83; language and money in relation to, 43; measures in relation to, 114–20; price in relation to, 10–11; truth in relation to, 10–12, 23; use, 82–83
Verbal exchanges. *See* Speech
Verbal fraud, 33–42; commercial fraud compared to, 106, 203–4; examples from Torah of, 33–35; inevitability of, 68; intention in, 38–39, 41; in pharmaceutical lobbying, 193; in political contexts, 62–63
Verbal injuries, 33–42; commercial injuries compared to, 41, 203–4; context of, 39; effects of, 94–96; inevitability of, 68; interpretation as source of, 93–94; measuring, 36, 38, 39, 107, 116, 204; nature of, 24, 93; Oven of Akhnai and, 89–97; redress for, 38, 39–40; significance of, 39
Vessels. *See* Broken vessels
Viagra, 194
Victimhood, 181–82
Vietnam War, 166
Violence: desire and, 69; and the sacred, 121–22; social management of, 122, 127; supposedly native to humans, 123–24; totalitarian, 165–66
Vows, 30–32, 47

War, 160
War crimes, 160, 184
Wars, 183
Weights and measures, 103, 117–18, 158. *See also* Measure
Wives, 29
Women, protection of, 37
World Conference Against Racism (Durban, 2001), 177, 179–80
World Social Forum (Porto Allegre, 2002), 177
World Trade Organization, 179
World War I, 164
Worm-in-the-apple effect, 63, 160–61, 163–64, 166, 192

YHVH, 107, 113, 117–18, 229n94
Yom Kippur, 31, 88, 146

Zealots, 134–35
Zionism, 176, 179, 180, 181, 183
Zohar, 111, 112

Cultural Memory in the Present

Niklas Luhmann, *Theory of Society, Volume 2*

Ilit Ferber, *Philosophy and Melancholy: Benjamin's Early Reflections on Theater and Language*

Alexandre Lefebvre, *Human Rights as a Way of Life: On Bergson's Political Philosophy*

Theodore W. Jennings, Jr., *Outlaw Justice: The Messianic Politics of Paul*

Alexander Etkind, *Warped Mourning: Stories of the Undead in the Land of the Unburied*

Denis Guénoun, *About Europe: Philosophical Hypotheses*

Maria Boletsi, *Barbarism and Its Discontents*

Roberto Esposito, *Living Thought: The Origins and Actuality of Italian Philosophy*

Sigrid Weigel, *Walter Benjamin: Images, the Creaturely, and the Holy*

Rüdiger Campe, *The Game of Probability: Literature and Calculation from Pascal to Kleist*

Rodolphe Gasché, *Phenomenology and Phantasmatology: On the Philosophy of Georges Bataille*

Jean-Luc Marion, *In the Self's Place: The Approach of Saint Augustine*

Niklas Luhmann, *Theory of Society, Volume 1*

Henri Atlan, *The Sparks of Randomness, Volume 2: The Atheism of Scripture*

Niklas Luhmann, *A Systems Theory of Religion*

Alessia Ricciardi, *After* La Dolce Vita: *A Cultural Prehistory of Berlusconi's Italy*

Daniel Innerarity, *The Future and Its Enemies: In Defense of Political Hope*

Patricia Pisters, *The Neuro-Image: A Deleuzian Film-Philosophy of Digital Screen Culture*

François-David Sebbah, *Testing the Limit: Derrida, Henry, Levinas, and the Phenomenological Tradition*

Erik Peterson, *Theological Tractates*, edited by Michael J. Hollerich

Feisal G. Mohamed, *Milton and the Post-Secular Present: Ethics, Politics, Terrorism*

Pierre Hadot, *The Present Alone Is Our Happiness, Second Edition: Conversations with Jeannie Carlier and Arnold I. Davidson*

Yasco Horsman, *Theaters of Justice: Judging, Staging, and Working Through in Arendt, Brecht, and Delbo*

Jacques Derrida, *Parages*, edited by John P. Leavey

Henri Atlan, *The Sparks of Randomness, Volume 1: Spermatic Knowledge*

Rebecca Comay, *Mourning Sickness: Hegel and the French Revolution*

Djelal Kadir, *Memos from the Besieged City: Lifelines for Cultural Sustainability*

Stanley Cavell, *Little Did I Know: Excerpts from Memory*

Jeffrey Mehlman, *Adventures in the French Trade: Fragments Toward a Life*

Jacob Rogozinski, *The Ego and the Flesh: An Introduction to Egoanalysis*

Marcel Hénaff, *The Price of Truth: Gift, Money, and Philosophy*

Paul Patton, *Deleuzian Concepts: Philosophy, Colonialization, Politics*

Michael Fagenblat, *A Covenant of Creatures: Levinas's Philosophy of Judaism*

Stefanos Geroulanos, *An Atheism that Is Not Humanist Emerges in French Thought*

Andrew Herscher, *Violence Taking Place: The Architecture of the Kosovo Conflict*

Hans-Jörg Rheinberger, *On Historicizing Epistemology: An Essay*

Jacob Taubes, *From Cult to Culture*, edited by Charlotte Fonrobert and Amir Engel

Peter Hitchcock, *The Long Space: Transnationalism and Postcolonial Form*

Lambert Wiesing, *Artificial Presence: Philosophical Studies in Image Theory*

Jacob Taubes, *Occidental Eschatology*

Freddie Rokem, *Philosophers and Thespians: Thinking Performance*

Roberto Esposito, *Communitas: The Origin and Destiny of Community*

Vilashini Cooppan, *Worlds Within: National Narratives and Global Connections in Postcolonial Writing*

Josef Früchtl, *The Impertinent Self: A Heroic History of Modernity*

Frank Ankersmit, Ewa Domanska, and Hans Kellner, eds., *Re-Figuring Hayden White*

Michael Rothberg, *Multidirectional Memory: Remembering the Holocaust in the Age of Decolonization*

Jean-François Lyotard, *Enthusiasm: The Kantian Critique of History*

Ernst van Alphen, Mieke Bal, and Carel Smith, eds., *The Rhetoric of Sincerity*

Stéphane Mosès, *The Angel of History: Rosenzweig, Benjamin, Scholem*

Pierre Hadot, *The Present Alone Is Our Happiness: Conversations with Jeannie Carlier and Arnold I. Davidson*

Alexandre Lefebvre, *The Image of the Law: Deleuze, Bergson, Spinoza*

Samira Haj, *Reconfiguring Islamic Tradition: Reform, Rationality, and Modernity*

Diane Perpich, *The Ethics of Emmanuel Levinas*

Marcel Detienne, *Comparing the Incomparable*

François Delaporte, *Anatomy of the Passions*

René Girard, *Mimesis and Theory: Essays on Literature and Criticism, 1959-2005*

Richard Baxstrom, *Houses in Motion: The Experience of Place and the Problem of Belief in Urban Malaysia*

Jennifer L. Culbert, *Dead Certainty: The Death Penalty and the Problem of Judgment*

Samantha Frost, *Lessons from a Materialist Thinker: Hobbesian Reflections on Ethics and Politics*

Regina Mara Schwartz, *Sacramental Poetics at the Dawn of Secularism: When God Left the World*

Gil Anidjar, *Semites: Race, Religion, Literature*

Ranjana Khanna, *Algeria Cuts: Women and Representation, 1830 to the Present*

Esther Peeren, *Intersubjectivities and Popular Culture: Bakhtin and Beyond*

Eyal Peretz, *Becoming Visionary: Brian De Palma's Cinematic Education of the Senses*

Diana Sorensen, *A Turbulent Decade Remembered: Scenes from the Latin American Sixties*

Hubert Damisch, *A Childhood Memory by Piero della Francesca*

José van Dijck, *Mediated Memories in the Digital Age*

Dana Hollander, *Exemplarity and Chosenness: Rosenzweig and Derrida on the Nation of Philosophy*

Asja Szafraniec, *Beckett, Derrida, and the Event of Literature*

Sara Guyer, *Romanticism After Auschwitz*

Alison Ross, *The Aesthetic Paths of Philosophy: Presentation in Kant, Heidegger, Lacoue-Labarthe, and Nancy*

Gerhard Richter, *Thought-Images: Frankfurt School Writers' Reflections from Damaged Life*

Bella Brodzki, *Can These Bones Live? Translation, Survival, and Cultural Memory*

Rodolphe Gasché, *The Honor of Thinking: Critique, Theory, Philosophy*

Brigitte Peucker, *The Material Image: Art and the Real in Film*

Natalie Melas, *All the Difference in the World: Postcoloniality and the Ends of Comparison*

Jonathan Culler, *The Literary in Theory*

Michael G. Levine, *The Belated Witness: Literature, Testimony, and the Question of Holocaust Survival*

Jennifer A. Jordan, *Structures of Memory: Understanding German Change in Berlin and Beyond*

Christoph Menke, *Reflections of Equality*

Marlène Zarader, *The Unthought Debt: Heidegger and the Hebraic Heritage*

Jan Assmann, *Religion and Cultural Memory: Ten Studies*

David Scott and Charles Hirschkind, *Powers of the Secular Modern: Talal Asad and His Interlocutors*

Gyanendra Pandey, *Routine Violence: Nations, Fragments, Histories*

James Siegel, *Naming the Witch*

J. M. Bernstein, *Against Voluptuous Bodies: Late Modernism and the Meaning of Painting*

Theodore W. Jennings, Jr., *Reading Derrida / Thinking Paul: On Justice*

Richard Rorty and Eduardo Mendieta, *Take Care of Freedom and Truth Will Take Care of Itself: Interviews with Richard Rorty*

Jacques Derrida, *Paper Machine*

Renaud Barbaras, *Desire and Distance: Introduction to a Phenomenology of Perception*

Jill Bennett, *Empathic Vision: Affect, Trauma, and Contemporary Art*

Ban Wang, *Illuminations from the Past: Trauma, Memory, and History in Modern China*

James Phillips, *Heidegger's* Volk: *Between National Socialism and Poetry*

Frank Ankersmit, *Sublime Historical Experience*

István Rév, *Retroactive Justice: Prehistory of Post-Communism*

Paola Marrati, *Genesis and Trace: Derrida Reading Husserl and Heidegger*

Krzysztof Ziarek, *The Force of Art*

Marie-José Mondzain, *Image, Icon, Economy: The Byzantine Origins of the Contemporary Imaginary*

Cecilia Sjöholm, *The Antigone Complex: Ethics and the Invention of Feminine Desire*

Jacques Derrida and Elisabeth Roudinesco, *For What Tomorrow . . . : A Dialogue*

Elisabeth Weber, *Questioning Judaism: Interviews by Elisabeth Weber*

Jacques Derrida and Catherine Malabou, *Counterpath: Traveling with Jacques Derrida*

Martin Seel, *Aesthetics of Appearing*

Nanette Salomon, *Shifting Priorities: Gender and Genre in Seventeenth-Century Dutch Painting*

Jacob Taubes, *The Political Theology of Paul*

Jean-Luc Marion, *The Crossing of the Visible*

Eric Michaud, *The Cult of Art in Nazi Germany*

Anne Freadman, *The Machinery of Talk: Charles Peirce and the Sign Hypothesis*

Stanley Cavell, *Emerson's Transcendental Etudes*

Stuart McLean, *The Event and Its Terrors: Ireland, Famine, Modernity*

Beate Rössler, ed., *Privacies: Philosophical Evaluations*

Bernard Faure, *Double Exposure: Cutting Across Buddhist and Western Discourses*

Alessia Ricciardi, *The Ends of Mourning: Psychoanalysis, Literature, Film*

Alain Badiou, *Saint Paul: The Foundation of Universalism*

Gil Anidjar, *The Jew, the Arab: A History of the Enemy*

Jonathan Culler and Kevin Lamb, eds., *Just Being Difficult? Academic Writing in the Public Arena*

Jean-Luc Nancy, *A Finite Thinking*, edited by Simon Sparks

Theodor W. Adorno, *Can One Live after Auschwitz? A Philosophical Reader*, edited by Rolf Tiedemann

Patricia Pisters, *The Matrix of Visual Culture: Working with Deleuze in Film Theory*

Andreas Huyssen, *Present Pasts: Urban Palimpsests and the Politics of Memory*

Talal Asad, *Formations of the Secular: Christianity, Islam, Modernity*

Dorothea von Mücke, *The Rise of the Fantastic Tale*

Marc Redfield, *The Politics of Aesthetics: Nationalism, Gender, Romanticism*

Emmanuel Levinas, *On Escape*

Dan Zahavi, *Husserl's Phenomenology*

Rodolphe Gasché, *The Idea of Form: Rethinking Kant's Aesthetics*

Michael Naas, *Taking on the Tradition: Jacques Derrida and the Legacies of Deconstruction*

Herlinde Pauer-Studer, ed., *Constructions of Practical Reason: Interviews on Moral and Political Philosophy*

Jean-Luc Marion, *Being Given That: Toward a Phenomenology of Givenness*

Theodor W. Adorno and Max Horkheimer, *Dialectic of Enlightenment*

Ian Balfour, *The Rhetoric of Romantic Prophecy*

Martin Stokhof, *World and Life as One: Ethics and Ontology in Wittgenstein's Early Thought*

Gianni Vattimo, *Nietzsche: An Introduction*

Jacques Derrida, *Negotiations: Interventions and Interviews, 1971-1998*, ed. Elizabeth Rottenberg

Brett Levinson, *The Ends of Literature: The Latin American "Boom" in the Neoliberal Marketplace*

Timothy J. Reiss, *Against Autonomy: Cultural Instruments, Mutualities, and the Fictive Imagination*

Hent de Vries and Samuel Weber, eds., *Religion and Media*

Niklas Luhmann, *Theories of Distinction: Re-Describing the Descriptions of Modernity*, ed. and introd. William Rasch

Johannes Fabian, *Anthropology with an Attitude: Critical Essays*

Michel Henry, *I Am the Truth: Toward a Philosophy of Christianity*

Gil Anidjar, *"Our Place in Al-Andalus": Kabbalah, Philosophy, Literature in Arab-Jewish Letters*

Hélène Cixous and Jacques Derrida, *Veils*

F. R. Ankersmit, *Historical Representation*

F. R. Ankersmit, *Political Representation*

Elissa Marder, *Dead Time: Temporal Disorders in the Wake of Modernity (Baudelaire and Flaubert)*

Reinhart Koselleck, *The Practice of Conceptual History: Timing History, Spacing Concepts*

Niklas Luhmann, *The Reality of the Mass Media*

Hubert Damisch, *A Theory of /Cloud/: Toward a History of Painting*

Jean-Luc Nancy, *The Speculative Remark: (One of Hegel's bon mots)*

Jean-François Lyotard, *Soundproof Room: Malraux's Anti-Aesthetics*

Jan Patočka, *Plato and Europe*

Hubert Damisch, *Skyline: The Narcissistic City*

Isabel Hoving, *In Praise of New Travelers: Reading Caribbean Migrant Women Writers*

Richard Rand, ed., *Futures: Of Jacques Derrida*

William Rasch, *Niklas Luhmann's Modernity: The Paradoxes of Differentiation*

Jacques Derrida and Anne Dufourmantelle, *Of Hospitality*

Jean-François Lyotard, *The Confession of Augustine*

Kaja Silverman, *World Spectators*

Samuel Weber, *Institution and Interpretation: Expanded Edition*

Jeffrey S. Librett, *The Rhetoric of Cultural Dialogue: Jews and Germans in the Epoch of Emancipation*

Ulrich Baer, *Remnants of Song: Trauma and the Experience of Modernity in Charles Baudelaire and Paul Celan*

Samuel C. Wheeler III, *Deconstruction as Analytic Philosophy*

David S. Ferris, *Silent Urns: Romanticism, Hellenism, Modernity*

Rodolphe Gasché, *Of Minimal Things: Studies on the Notion of Relation*

Sarah Winter, *Freud and the Institution of Psychoanalytic Knowledge*

Samuel Weber, *The Legend of Freud: Expanded Edition*

Aris Fioretos, ed., *The Solid Letter: Readings of Friedrich Hölderlin*

J. Hillis Miller / Manuel Asensi, *Black Holes / J. Hillis Miller; or, Boustrophedonic Reading*

Miryam Sas, *Fault Lines: Cultural Memory and Japanese Surrealism*

Peter Schwenger, *Fantasm and Fiction: On Textual Envisioning*

Didier Maleuvre, *Museum Memories: History, Technology, Art*

Jacques Derrida, *Monolingualism of the Other; or, The Prosthesis of Origin*

Andrew Baruch Wachtel, *Making a Nation, Breaking a Nation: Literature and Cultural Politics in Yugoslavia*

Niklas Luhmann, *Love as Passion: The Codification of Intimacy*

Mieke Bal, ed., *The Practice of Cultural Analysis: Exposing Interdisciplinary Interpretation*

Jacques Derrida and Gianni Vattimo, eds., *Religion*